The Online Tutor's Toolkit

This book contains everything you need to know to get started as an online tutor. It covers the essentials of tutoring, choosing your tech and software, managing homework, and getting set up alongside detailed guidance focusing on each level of tuition. With techniques developed through research and first-hand experience, the author explains exactly how to turn existing subject knowledge into effective tutoring for students of all ages in a variety of subjects.

Divided into two parts, the first answers the logistical questions facing every new tutor such as: what equipment do I need? Where can I apply? How much should I charge? The second half focuses on how to tutor different age groups effectively and subject-specific areas including English, Maths, and Science, as well as the author's tried-and-tested '5 step' process for choosing a subject, assessing a student, and planning their first lessons. There is also information on how to support students writing personal statements and applying to university, as well as teaching English as a Second Language.

Alongside tailored, up-to-date information on available software, hardware, exam specifications, and the online tutoring marketplace, the book contains a 10-week timetable of adaptable lesson plans so new tutors can get started immediately. Finally, there are two additional downloadable chapters which expand on less common subjects and another which includes a digital download of every resource from the book.

With suggestions for resources, homework, and timings to support you at every stage, this is an essential read for anyone wanting to succeed as an online tutor.

Molly Bolding has extensive experience of individual and group tutoring in the UK and overseas. She is a regular contributor to Tes Magazine and contributed to chapters in the bestselling books by Mark Roberts *You Can't Revise for GCSE English!* and *You Can't Revise for A Level English Literature!*

"*The Online Tutor's Toolkit* is essential reading for both novice and experienced tutors. Detailed, pragmatic and eminently practical, this book offers a comprehensive approach to each stage of the online tutoring process. A warm and accessible guide, Bolding channels her personal experiences and hard-won wisdom to ensure that readers of the Toolkit will acquire the satisfaction and financial rewards of online tutoring. So, whether you're planning to become a KS2 literacy tutor, or you're already mentoring an A Level maths student who's aiming for Oxbridge, this is the book for you."

Mark Roberts, *English Teacher and Author of* You Can't Revise for GCSE English! *and* You Can't Revise for A Level English Literature!

The Online Tutor's Toolkit

Everything You Need to Know to Succeed as an Online Tutor

Molly Bolding

Routledge
Taylor & Francis Group

LONDON AND NEW YORK

Cover image: Sarah Hoyle

First published 2023
by Routledge
4 Park Square, Milton Park, Abingdon, Oxon OX14 4RN

and by Routledge
605 Third Avenue, New York, NY 10158

Routledge is an imprint of the Taylor & Francis Group, an informa business

British Library Cataloguing-in-Publication Data
A catalogue record for this book is available from the British Library

Library of Congress Cataloging-in-Publication Data
Names: Bolding, Molly, author.
Title: The online tutor's toolkit : everything you need to know to succeed as an online tutor / Molly Bolding.
Description: Abingdon, Oxon ; New York, NY : Routledge, 2023. | Includes bibliographical references and index.
Identifiers: LCCN 2022014952 | ISBN 9781032078083 (hardcover) | ISBN 9781032078113 (paperback) | ISBN 9781003211648 (ebook)
Subjects: LCSH: Tutors and tutoring—Handbooks, manuals, etc. | Tutors and tutoring—Technological innovations—Handbooks, manuals, etc. | Web-based instruction—Handbooks, manuals, etc.
Classification: LCC LC41 .B65 2023 | DDC 371.39/4—dc23/eng/20220701
LC record available at https://lccn.loc.gov/2022014952

ISBN: 978-1-032-07808-3 (hbk)
ISBN: 978-1-032-07811-3 (pbk)
ISBN: 978-1-003-21164-8 (ebk)

DOI: 10.4324/9781003211648

Typeset in Melior
by Apex CoVantage, LLC

Access the Support Material: www.routledge.com/9781032078113

To my younger self – for surviving.

Contents

Foreword   ix
Acknowledgements   xiii
Glossary   xv

Section 1: Becoming a tutor   **1**

  1   **Introduction**   3

  2   **Online tutoring basics**   7

  3   **Tutoring tech**   27

  4   **Homework and paid marking time**   33

Section 2: How to tutor   **39**

  5   **What am I tutoring?**   41

  6   **What does the student need?**   62

  7   **How do I plan and deliver a lesson?**   79

  8   **KS2**   102

8.1   **Other KS2 subjects** ☎   Online

  9   **11+**   123

10   **KS3**   132

Contents

10.1 Other KS3 subjects ☏   Online

11   GCSE English   155

12   GCSE Maths   175

13   Other GCSEs   186

14   A-level English Literature   208

15   A-level Maths   226

16   Other A-levels   236

17   Personal statement mentoring   259

18   Higher education applications   274

19   English as a Foreign Language   284

20   Lesson plans   301

21   Resources ☏   324

Index   353

Foreword

Public education systems, much like public transport systems, have gaps. When you walk to a bus station, you don't expect the driver to take you to your exact destination. Instead, the bus driver will collect you near where you start and take you near where you want to go. If you miss the bus, you're left behind. If you're ahead of the bus, you have to wait until it gets to you.

If you want to be taken on a bespoke journey, you have to book a taxi.

Just as adept taxi drivers help to fill gaps in the routes and schedules of public transport systems, so can skilled tutors help to fill gaps in a student's educational journey. Tutors can meet students where they are, when they want, and take them where they need to go. The power of tutoring is supported by more robust evidence than almost any other form of academic intervention, and great tutors can have a profound impact that goes far beyond a student's academic outcomes to their lifelong confidence and approach to learning.

Yet isn't it disconcerting that, while taxi drivers have a choice of navigation systems to help them get their passengers where they need to go as efficiently as possible, many independent tutors are forced to plot their own routes, miss helpful shortcuts, and discover dead ends that more experienced and better supported tutors now know to avoid?

The need for a more systematic approach to tutoring has never been clearer, and I've witnessed this growing need first hand. School closures at the start of the COVID-19 pandemic in 2020 shone a light on students' existing learning gaps, as well as opening up new ones. Expectations and pressure on teachers reached unsustainable levels, and online tutoring became mainstream.

The UK government's flagship National Tutoring Programme sought to help over 500,000 students in 2021 alone, with MyTutor, the company I co-founded and run as CEO, as the largest provider. When we founded MyTutor over 8 years ago, online tutoring was still nascent, and there were no widespread government initiatives to promote its use. Just 5 years ago, fewer than 10% of our customers had prior experience of online tutoring, and we were helping fewer than 10,000 students each year, with only around 1,000 tutors on the platform. Now, over 50% of families we survey have prior experience with online tutoring, we work with almost a quarter of all secondary schools, and over 100,000 families come to us each year with over 10,000 tutors to choose from.

Excitingly, this dramatic growth in online tutoring feels like just the start. I both hope and expect that one-to-one and small group tutoring will only become more deeply embedded within education systems, so that any child can access personalised help as and when they need it rather than being held back or left behind. While families will continue to fund tutoring privately, governments will play a more prominent role in promoting, regulating, and widening access to tutoring. Matt Kraft of Brown University compares these long-term expectations for systemic change to the historic expansion of public kindergarten over a 30-year period in the United States – where instead of remaining as an 'ancillary, compartmentalized, and temporary intervention' he sees tutoring becoming 'a core feature of public schools over time'.

As tutoring becomes an increasingly core ingredient of the wider education system, it's essential to set and maintain high standards. Today, best practice exists in the tutoring industry; it's just unevenly distributed. In an age where information can move freely, we do a disservice to students where this best practice in tutoring remains poorly documented. The life-changing impact Molly alone has made on hundreds of students' lives since she first started as a tutor is a remarkable testament to tutoring's potential when done well.

This book is a thoughtful, engaging, and pragmatic gift to the tutoring industry. I'm excited for everyone engaged in this high-stakes and high-impact profession to have it as a guide. I also hope it inspires many more publications like it. The practical advice includes planning lessons, setting homework, and even managing parent–tutor and student–tutor relationships. It will serve as a lifeline for first-time online tutors, as well as lowering barriers to entry and encouraging more high-performing individuals into the industry. It will also serve as a reminder of best practice to the more experienced practitioners to help them reach a higher standard. And finally, this book is a source of insight into the process of effective tutoring for the growing number of parents, teachers, and students who choose to work with online tutors.

I'm proud to promote Molly's work. The impact it will have on our sector aligns closely to MyTutor's founding purpose – to inspire, motivate, and support every student to a better future. At a time when tutoring plays an increasingly pivotal role in students' education across the world, Molly's publication provides a comprehensive map for anyone looking to build on best practice; dodge dead ends; and inspire, motivate, and support students to a better future.

Bertie Hubbard,
co-founder and CEO of MyTutor

Acknowledgements

For a book that I wrote largely on my own in my living room, I have so many people to thank.

Firstly, my editor, Annamarie Kino, and editorial assistant and namesake, Molly Selby, for bearing with my regular, nervous emails and providing useful feedback.

Next, Bertie Hubbard, for taking the time out of his very busy schedule to write a brilliant foreword.

And Mark Roberts, for his endless patience as my English teacher; for pointing me to my first national by-line; and for encouraging me to run with my idea for 'something about online tutoring'. This book would not exist without you.

A huge thank you must also go to Adi Jacobson, Annabel Hunt, Ashika Vijay, Bukky Oluseye, Callum Cockburn, Emma Barber, Tom Coleman, and all the tutors I have met online over the last few years who have given me their time and stories. I hope you enjoy reading this book as much as I enjoyed writing it.

I would also like to formally thank Cleo and Paul Bolding – my Mum and Dad – who have provided so much love, support and encouragement, in the form of emojis, calls, and promises to wear a t-shirt with the cover of this book on it. My sister Erin didn't really do much for this book, but I love her so she gets an honourable mention too.

Also, to Hannah – thank you for being a wonderful friend (and doing so much to help me write this even though you had no idea!).

Finally, to my partner Ralph, who has been there for me every step of this process and more. For your kind words, calming presence, and seemingly telepathic ability to sense when coffee was needed – I can't thank you enough.

Glossary

A-level

A-level is an abbreviation of General Certificate of Education Advanced Level. Each A-level is offered in a particular subject and graded on a scale of E (low) to A* (high). A-levels form a core part of university applications in the UK. There are also international versions of A-levels offered by Edexcel or CIE, which are mostly used by international schools and UK private schools.

Until 2017, A-levels were assessed in two parts: AS exams at the end of Year 12 and A-level exams at the end of Year 13. This system has since been reformed so all exams are taken at the end of Year 13 and individual exams cannot be re-sat. Some tutors and students may be more familiar with this system and so should be careful to ensure they are following the correct specification.

Exam board

An examining and certifying body, which produces and marks exams and issues certificates. The four major exam boards in England and Wales are AQA, OCR, Edexcel, and Eduqas (WJEC).

GCSE

GCSE is an acronym for General Certificate of Secondary Education. Each GCSE is offered in a particular subject and graded on a scale of 1 (low) to 9 (high). There are also international versions of GCSEs (colloquially called iGCSEs) offered by Edexcel or CIE, which are mostly used by international schools and UK private schools.

Until 2017, grades were issued using letters, with G (equivalent to 1) to A* (equivalent to 9), and some tutors and students may be more familiar with this system.

Humanities

This general term refers to all essay-based/writing-based or arts subjects, such as English, History, Geography, Languages, Drama, Media Studies, and so on. It is generally used an umbrella term for any non-STEM subject.

Key Stage 2

Key Stage 2, also written as KS2, is the name for the curriculum which covers 8–10-year-olds in the UK. Lower Key Stage 2 covers Years 3 and 4, while Upper Key Stage 2 covers Years 5 and 6.

Key Stage 3

Key Stage 3, also written as KS3, is the name for the curriculum which covers 11–14-year-olds in the UK. Key Stage 3 covers Years 7, 8, and 9 – in other words, pre-GCSE.

Key Stage 4

Key Stage 4, also written as KS4, is the name for the curriculum which covers 14–16-year-olds in the UK. Key Stage 4 officially covers Years 10 and 11, although some schools start this content in Year 9, and ends with GCSE exams.

Key Stage 5

Key Stage 5, also written as KS5, is a name used for the final stage of formal education, also called Sixth Form or Year 12 and 13. Because students choose their own qualifications from a range of subjects, including A-levels and BTECs, there isn't a set curriculum as for the previous Key Stages. However, for consistency, some schools still call this Key Stage 5.

Private

The word 'private' denotes a student who is either themselves paying for their tuition or whose parent is doing so. Private tutoring lessons are not government funded and are generally sought for a wider range of subjects than those offered to Pupil Premium students.

Pupil Premium

Sometimes abbreviated to PP, Pupil Premium is the name of a government scheme which provides additional funding for students to access tutoring, among other services.

Since 2011, the UK government has run this scheme, sometimes shortened to PP, which provides money that is set aside in the education budget specifically to support disadvantaged students. This includes the Free School Meals program, allowances for care leavers, breakfast clubs, and funding for trips and visits. However, during the COVID-19 pandemic, which led to mass online schooling and cancelled exams, it became clear that many students would need something in the form of catch-up measures. Pupil Premium is now being used to fund 1:1 and group tutoring for students to ensure that they are confident to take exams, and this tutoring is being delivered by a range of online tutoring organisations.

Many agencies and student marketplaces offer the opportunity to support PP students at a reduced fee – usually around £10 an hour.

RAG

This acronym stands for Red/Amber/Green, in reference to the colours used on traffic lights. Students can use this to self-evaluate and report their confidence on a particular topic: Red means they don't understand it all, Amber means they understand somewhat but need more help, and Green means they are happy with the topic and ready to be assessed on it if needed.

SPAG

This acronym stands for Spelling, Punctuation and Grammar. This term refers to the core writing skills that are assessed, along with the student's knowledge of the subject content, in most exams.

STEM

This acronym stands for Science, Technology, Engineering, and Maths. It is generally used as an umbrella term for any non-Humanities subject, so it may also include subjects like computing, construction, and so on.

Student marketplace

This term refers to the websites and organisations that give tutors and students the opportunity to register on a searchable database, which they can then use to find each other and arrange lessons.

Marketplaces are not agencies – they won't do any of the administrative work to bring tutors and students together – but they help put tutors and those seeking tutors in the same place to make it easier to find each other. They may also offer other support or protections, such as generic codes of conduct or terms and conditions, technical help, or opportunities for full-time work.

The 11+ (also the 13+, 16+)

The 11+ is an optional assessment test offered to Year 6 students, usually taken by those who perform well academically and are looking to get into selective education institutions.

There also exist 13+ and 16+ assessments, which are less uniform and are usually unique to each school. The number before the plus sign indicates the age at which the assessment is taken.

Becoming a tutor

Chapter 1

Introduction

Welcome to the Online Tutor's Toolkit!

Whether you're starting out as an undergraduate or have been tutoring for years, this book should have something useful for you.

As you hold this book in your hands, it might seem like a lot of reading before you start doing something that, let's be honest here, you could probably already do fairly well. But the point of this book isn't just to give you some practical information about what websites are good or which specification to use: this book is designed to help you become the best tutor you can possibly be, as quickly as possible. Every person you ever tutor, from your first student to your one hundredth student, deserves the opportunity to succeed.

It's important to note, right at the start, that becoming an online tutor is a steep learning curve. The only real way to become a better tutor is through experience, which can only be gained by tutoring students. This might sound nerve-wracking, like diving straight into the deep end, but this book will equip you with the knowledge and skills you will need to feel confident even in your very first lesson.

Think of this book more as a springboard rather than a script. Once you've taught a few lessons, you can begin to refine the suggested techniques and test out your own methods of teaching, assessing and supporting your students. Every tutor works slightly differently, and that diversity of styles is hugely beneficial for students, but it can help to have some tried-and-tested methods to get started with.

And when I say 'tried and tested', I mean it, because this book is the culmination of more than 700 hours of experience as both an online and in-person tutor and many more of writing this book.

Looking back over all those lessons, I can see how much improvement I have made in my tutoring practice. The best example of this is two of my earliest

DOI: 10.4324/9781003211648-2

students, who were a twin brother and sister. I taught them both for GCSE English from the beginning of Year 10 through to their final exams in Year 11. They were my first consistent students: I saw them both separately every week for almost 18 months and had the privilege of watching them achieve 8s in their Language and Literature exams.

Reading back over my plans from their early lessons showed me how much the sheer quantity of experience I had in that time improved my delivery, choice of activities, and time management. The more I taught, the more opportunities I had to see what worked and what didn't, what students appreciated and what they wanted less of, and what I could reasonably fit into an hour with different students.

And you will undoubtedly have the same experience. The difference is that you have this book, so you don't need 18 months to figure that out. Instead, you'll be able to deliver high-quality lessons from your very first student.

Why you should start tutoring at university

The vast majority of online tutors are students and recent graduates, just like me! It makes a lot of sense: tutoring online builds on knowledge and skills you already have, doesn't require a huge time commitment, and can be easily fitted in around classes and extracurriculars. Plus, you just took the exams that your students are about to take, so you have recent, first-hand experience of the content and skills they will be tested on.

Moreover, tutoring is an accessible way to work while studying, compared to something like a part-time job. While some universities discourage their students from working, it was an undeniable necessity for me and is for thousands of students every year. Especially during the COVID-19 pandemic, tutoring online has become an increasingly popular, safe, and reliable way to earn money during termtime and holidays.

One of the less obvious reasons to become an online tutor while at university is the benefits that it can bring you – the tutor. Besides being a reliable source of income, the most useful thing I got out of tutoring as an undergraduate was the constant revision of the foundation of my subject. I was an English undergraduate teaching KS2, KS3, GCSE, and A-level English, constantly adding new areas of expertise to my repertoire and returning to texts I hadn't studied for a few years with a new eye for detail. This is especially true for Maths and Science tutors: the opportunity to refresh your memory of basic topics while studying their complex counterparts is repeatedly cited as one of the most useful benefits of becoming a tutor.

I vividly remember the first time I was asked about the Robert Browning poem 'My Last Duchess' during one of my university supervisions, which is currently on the GCSE English Literature syllabus, only to be able to reply that I had been working on it with a student the previous day!

And even once you've graduated, that doesn't mean you have to stop tutoring – many graduates, and those going into post-graduate courses, continue tutoring for the same reasons they started.

Where do I start?

If everything I've said so far sounds good to you, then you may be keen to get going – and that's where the rest of the book comes in.

Section 1 is all about the logistics of being a tutor: what to tutor, where to tutor, and how to manage the necessary tech and practicalities. I'll discuss the different types of tutoring, how to set your hourly rate, how to keep yourself and your students safe, and good practice for tutors.

Once you're ready, Section 2 will walk you through how to tutor: assessing new students, figuring out what you'll be teaching, and then a detailed list of lesson techniques for each age group and subject. Chapter 7, 'How Do I Plan and Deliver a Lesson?', contains all of the 'basic lesson techniques': the straightforward strategies you can use with any student. Once you've mastered those, you can find more specific tasks and ideas for resources in each of the individual chapters.

The most common subjects in each age group are available in this book, but there are also two downloadable chapters on additional subjects at KS2 and KS3 – namely History, Geography, and Science – which may come in handy.

Chapter 21 is also available as a downloadable chapter, which contains a digital copy of all of the resources and diagrams in this book as well as some helpful extras. You can photocopy the images in the physical book to use with in-person students or download them to use in your online classroom.

And finally . . .

I wrote this book during the pandemic, at a time when technology and education are becoming even more enmeshed, with online schooling and virtual classrooms quickly becoming the 'new norm'. Given the impact of COVID-19 on

Becoming a tutor

GCSE and A-level exam courses and the UK government's investment in Pupil Premium tutoring, it is likely that there will be a need for confident, competent online tutors for a long time to come.

It is my hope that this book will help you to get comfortable tutoring online and able to deliver the best possible lessons for your students. Good luck, and enjoy!

Chapter 2

Online tutoring basics

In this chapter, you will find information about the different types of tutoring – what they are and what that means for you – as well as all the basic information you will need: where to tutor, how to set your hourly rate, how to protect children while you work, and what best practice for tutors looks like. In each section, I will recommend good ideas for getting started based on my experiences, which will help you to get tutoring as soon as you are ready.

DIFFERENT TYPES OF TUTORING

In-person vs online

This book is focused on online tutoring, but much the same principles apply to in-person tutoring.

Tutoring is much like conventional classroom teaching – easier done in person than online. So, it would be irresponsible to ignore the fact that it has some disadvantages compared to in-person tutoring.

Traditionally, in-person tutors visit schools/homes, so the most significant problem with online tutoring is that not everyone has access to a computer and/ or the internet to connect them to a tutor: technology poverty prevents many students from participating.

The broader issues are often more apparent with younger students. Older students (ages 16+) generally have longer attention spans and are confidently computer literate, while also being more engaged either because they enjoy it, want to achieve, or recognise the benefits of having tutoring. Younger students often struggle to sit at the computer for an hour, either because they are tired or because the technology feels less accessible. In-person tutors can use games and speaking exercises more easily while being close at hand to help with any misunderstandings, whereas online tutors are physically distant and must rely on speech and visual cues.

DOI: 10.4324/9781003211648-3

In addition, online tutoring creates a fundamental barrier between the tutor and the student: the screen. This is especially true when students don't have access to webcams or an internet connection that supports video. Students can feel disengaged by the distance, take the lesson less seriously, or think that they can get away with playing on their phone under the desk. This requires tutors to be more vigilant about poor behaviour while also understanding its causes and taking appropriate steps to adapt their lessons. For example, students who are very young, very busy, or very tired may benefit from having shorter lessons more often.

However, the advantages of online tutoring far outweigh the disadvantages. The first and most obvious advantage is that, with online tutoring, *you and your student can be anywhere in the world with an internet connection.* Meeting with a student in-person can be expensive and time-consuming and, in a pandemic, unsafe. Online tutoring means that you can deliver lessons all over the world without any travel time. Students can have tutoring immediately after school or early in the morning, and undergraduate tutors can easily fit lessons in between lectures, classes, and social activities.

1:1 vs groups

Most online tutoring is done 1:1, although group tutoring is becoming more popular and more available as the number of Pupil Premium students has increased. 1:1 tutoring, whether private or PP, gives tutors the opportunity to focus on exactly what the student needs: slow progress doesn't impact other students, there's no audience for mistakes, and you can develop personal relationships to help foster engagement.

Online tutoring for groups was already happening before the pandemic, as part of online summer schools and crash courses, but it is becoming an increasingly popular option for tuition providers.

Group tutoring is a very different experience to 1:1 tutoring. First, 'group tutoring' is a variable term but is usually taken to mean a single tutor working with 2 to 6 students. This variation in group size between providers can result in a sliding scale of experiences: tutoring smaller groups is generally easier, but an experienced tutor should be able to deliver tailored tutoring even in a larger group. Bigger groups also give tutors the opportunity to use games, speaking exercises, and discussions.

You may be tutoring a group for a short, intense period – most 'crash course'–style tutoring is a group lesson every day of a week – or you may seem the same group each week over a long period of time, usually a school term. There are lots of issues to account for either way: the students that turn up may vary each time, different students may prefer different exercises, the students may all be in the same room or may be spread out over the country/world, and you may have a mixed-ability group. This can make group tutoring a very unpredictable experience compared to 1:1 tutoring, so I would generally recommend not tutoring groups until you have plenty of experience and are entirely confident that you can handle whatever might come up.

Young people vs adults

The majority of those seeking tutoring are children or the parents of children. That said, there are also many adult learners looking for tutors to help them learn English or a foreign language for pleasure or for work, as well as adults looking to return to school qualifications. The COVID-19 pandemic has seen an increase in adults looking to get their GCSEs in English/Maths who have been able to access online tutoring while working from home.

Tutoring adults, especially those of a similar age to you, can be uncomfortable to start with, but it simply requires open communication and a recognition of what each of your roles are.

Adults are generally more proactive students than young people, since they're spending their own money and using their limited free time. I usually find that adult students will want more homework, work through content more quickly, and are able to articulate their concerns specifically. This can be helpful, since it reduces the work needed to assess them. However, some adults may struggle with taking feedback and can be more demanding. Being confident in your own expertise, understanding what the student wants to learn, and trying to accommodate all reasonable requests while respecting your own boundaries around time and work are all skills that you will need to develop to work comfortably with adult students.

Academic vs non-academic

Academic tutoring, in this context, means tutoring that is specifically aimed at students who are going to be taking an exam in that subject or who are following an exam curriculum. This can include KS2, KS3, GCSE, A-level, and English as a Foreign Language (EFL) students and adult learners retaking exams. These students will often know what they need to focus on, have some idea of their working level, and at a minimum will need to follow a government curriculum or exam board specification during both their in-school lessons and their tutoring. Therefore, writing these lesson plans can be easier, as the student will either be able to point you to exactly what they need to know or you can use that curriculum as a guide.

Academic tutoring should always be viewed as a supplement, as the main bulk of the student's learning will come through their school teaching. You should always try to focus on what the student wants to look at or the areas where you think they are struggling most, even if that means going over the same topic a few times, rather than trying to teach other, potentially new, content that may be irrelevant or confusing.

Non-academic tutoring here means students who are not studying for an exam. Most non-academic tutoring, in my experience, is either with younger children or adult learners, outside the compulsory school age, and is usually EFL tutoring. You can find more information about this in the 'EFL tutoring' chapter. These students will likely have some idea of what they want to look at during lessons, but it will mostly be down to you to figure what the best course of study will be.

UK exams vs TEFL

Most tutors based in the UK will deal with students who are also based in the UK and are taking compulsory exams like GCSEs and A-levels and some overseas students who are also studying for UK-based exam boards or international versions like the iGCSE. This means that most tutors only need to accommodate exam board variation at a national level, like the difference between AQA, OCR, Edexcel, and Eduqas (WJEC), for example.

However, many students from around the world study the same subjects in English for international exam boards – notably, international school entrance exams or standardised English exams like those in Singapore and Hong Kong. You may also come across students who are studying English for work or pleasure, or an English proficiency test for a university or job.

If the student is studying for an exam board or proficiency test, it is important to be as familiar as possible with its specification and the style of examination so you can help them tailor their knowledge to the demands of the exam.

Private vs Pupil Premium

Some tutors only see private students and others only PP, while most will tutor a mix of students from these categories.

Private students are the most common. With these students, you'll be able to set your own rates, teach whatever subjects they're looking for, and arrange lessons whenever is convenient for you both. Tutors usually make more money from their private students, as PP only pays a set amount per hour, and private students seek a greater range of subjects than PP students, who usually only receive lessons on core subjects.

However, from a tutor's point of view, there are many incentives to tutor Pupil Premium lessons: they are generally booked in blocks, as many as 10 or 20 weeks; there are many students who need support in the most common subjects (GCSE English and Maths); and you get to support the students who need the help most. You may also be able to find work as a 'cover tutor', where regular PP tutors are unavailable for one or two lessons and you can step in at the last minute and earn some additional money.

However, the downsides are that, first, Pupil Premium funding is limited, so your hourly rate will be set and much lower than that for a private student. There are even some sites or schemes that ask you to volunteer some of your time to offer free tutoring to disadvantaged students, which can be rewarding but isn't accessible for tutors who are reliant on tutoring as their main income. In addition, with PP students, you are likely to be dealing with students who are not choosing to have tutoring and may be reluctant to engage. There are also lots of reports of issues around technology with PP students, who are often using school computers during school hours and are rarely provided with a webcam, microphone, and other necessary equipment.

Personally, I would recommend that new tutors who have the option to teach PP students as well as private ones and can afford to do so try teaching students of both kinds. It allows you to access the greatest number of students, which means more money and experience, as well as garnering the most experience from the greatest range of students, subjects, and behaviours.

Setting your hourly rate

Setting a reasonable hourly rate is an important process for two main reasons: your rate needs to appropriately reward your time and effort, but it also needs to be affordable for the majority of parents and students. Tutoring can quickly become a costly process, so you need to ensure a balance of these factors to attract students.

You will need to consider:

- **How much preparatory work is required for the lesson**. The amount you are paid for the hour in which you are face to face with the student shouldn't just cover the time required by the session – you should also factor in how much time you needed to prepare your lesson plan and resources and mark home-work. If you are tutoring through an agency which provides the lessons plans and resources for you, then you may need to compromise for a slightly lower rate, as that work is done for you.

- **Your expenditure on resources, software, fees, and so on**. If you need to pay for software subscriptions or hardware costs to provide your tuition, then you should consider how much you need to make per lesson to cover those costs. If you are tutoring on a student marketplace or as part of an agency that allows you to set your own rates, you should also factor in any fees you have to pay in order to work on their site. Some sites, like MyTutor, deduct fees from the parents' hourly payment automatically before the rest is sent to you, while others may require a monthly or weekly flat payment.

- **What the level the lesson is aimed at**. Some tutors prefer to have a flat hourly rate so that regardless of whether the lesson is for a KS2 lesson or an A-level lesson, parents and students pay the same amount. Other tutors feel that the higher the level of the lesson, the more it should cost – higher-level teaching requires a higher qualification level from the tutor, as well as potentially more time and effort to prepare for.

- **How many hours of tuition the student needs**. For most tutors, their income is made up of one or two 60-minute lessons a week with each of several students. As a result, these tutors often prefer a high hourly rate, as the work is not guaranteed. However, if a student books a block of lessons, say, 10 hours, in advance, or wants daily tuition, then you may wish to consider a slightly discounted rate to reflect the fact that that income is reliable.

- **Whether you are providing tuition live or through a different medium**. Most of the time, online tutoring is provided through video calls/digital classrooms, and your hourly rate is determined by the amount of time you are engaging with the student directly. However, many tutors also offer paid marking time (covered in more detail in 'Homework and Paid Marking Time', pages 33–38) for coursework drafts or even opportunities for students to 'chat' with them through message forums about homework or to practise the foreign language they are learning. In these instances, you will need to decide how much time and effort is taken up by these services and therefore how much to charge per hour.

- **Your qualifications in your subject area**. If you are tutoring as part of an agency or student marketplace, then there will likely be minimum requirements for tutors – some agencies require an A or above at A-level in the subject you want to tutor, or similar. If you are an independent tutor, then you will need to decide for yourself how qualified you are to teach certain subjects. Holding the qualification one level above the level you wish to tutor is a good rule. This is especially relevant if you begin tutoring as an undergraduate and your degree is in the subject area which you teach, as you may wish to increase your rate once you have graduated to reflect your relative expertise in that area.

- **Your own experience level**. Gaining experience as a tutor can ultimately only be done by tutoring students, but some parents and students may be reluctant to pay for a relatively new and inexperienced tutor. Keeping your prices low as you start out, and building a bank of reviews and experiences, is the best way to establish yourself as a tutor. Once you have a few lessons and lots of positive reviews/feedback under your belt, then you can decide whether to increase your rate.

So far, this guidance has largely addressed 1:1 tuition. When it comes to teaching groups, there are other factors to consider.

There will likely be a slightly greater amount of preparation needed for these classes compared to a 1:1 lesson, as you will need to prepare work and activities which are appropriate for groups. Groups may also take up more time outside of lesson time, as you will be creating or marking a few pieces of homework or class work rather than one. Alternatively, groups can require longer lesson times to ensure that all students have equal opportunity to ask questions and access resources.

In addition, it is important to remember that the tutoring experience is more demanding in a group setting. Tutoring groups should usually be taken on once you have a reasonable amount of 1:1 tutoring experience. Regardless of whether the students are together in the same room or each at their own computer, there is a class-control element required to ensure that students can focus and engage with the work. I have taught group lessons in a variety of contexts – most commonly tutoring sessions with groups of students who are each at their own individual computer at home. This is generally more straightforward than teaching students who are all attending the online lesson through the same computer or from the same room, where the likelihood of typical behaviours like chatting and phone use usually requires the presence of supervising staff. However, lessons where students are each using their own computer separately can result in new difficulties, such as muting themselves, misusing any chat function, or Googling answers during the lesson.

Becoming a tutor

As outlined previously, tutoring groups requires a slightly more complex skillset than 1:1 tutoring, and this only increases with group size. You may want to set a 'small group' (2–4 students) rate and a 'large group' (5+ students) rate, or something similar, to reflect this.

In all situations, tutors should bear in mind a 'sliding scale' approach, taking the range of factors explored here into consideration. You may wish to decide on an absolute maximum and minimum hourly rate and then adjust the actual rate you charge according the requirements of each student or situation.

It is also worth noting that you should be prepared to negotiate with agencies, clients, and parents to reach an appropriate rate. Some agencies and student marketplaces have 'bands' or 'scales' of set prices, but you can pick your own rates from them, while others set the rate themselves. Whatever the case, be confident in your assessment of your time's worth – it is important to accumulate experience and good reviews at the beginning, but not at the expense of the value of your time.

As a guide, tutors at the beginning of their career should expect to make £10–£15 an hour teaching GCSE level, rising incrementally to £30–£55 an hour for tutors with several years of experience and at least one degree who teach a broad range of levels and abilities.

Increasing your rate

As you become established as a tutor, gaining both experience and qualifications, there may come a point at which you will want to increase your rates.

The easiest way to do this is simply to offer a higher rate to any new students you pick up after you decide on the increase. Many tutors keep their rates consistent for their existing students as a gesture of goodwill for their early support and just charge more for new ones until such time as older students take their exams/graduate/head to university and no longer need tuition.

However, this is not always possible – you may have students you have been tutoring for a long time, during which your level of experience has significantly increased, or students who want you to continue tutoring them as they transition from GCSE to A-level. In this case, you will need to have a conversation with the parent or student about this and discuss an affordable increase. Ideally you will be able to point to specific qualifications or good reviews to justify the increase.

Try to avoid increasing your prices during termtime, as parents are not likely to appreciate the sudden price hike. The best time to increase your rate is usually at the beginning of the academic year or, if increasing it at another time is unavoidable, with at least 3 months' notice.

Where to tutor

There are lots of options as to where and how you tutor. In this section, I will take you through the different places you can tutor, what the pros and cons of each are, and some examples of each.

Online tutoring

Agency

Tutoring through an agency can be an option for new tutors, but they usually want experienced tutors who are looking for full-time work. Many agencies work on the basis that you are employed by them and then assign you as many hours of tutoring as you request from their database of students seeking tutors, so you can quickly build up to full-time hours. Some agencies offer both online and in-person tuition, while others specialise in one or the other.

Some agencies specialise in a particular subject or a particular age group, and some require additional languages to English to support students overseas.

Agency tutoring usually follows a fairly rigid framework: they decide what you get paid, which students you work with, and when your sessions with those students are based on your qualifications, experience, and availability.

Pros:

- **Everything is decided for you and assigned to you, so you don't have to 'shop around' for students or do any advertising or admin**. The agency will advertise itself to parents, manage its roster of tutors and students, and pay you centrally, so you just have to make yourself available at convenient times, turn up, and tutor.

- **You can expect reasonable rates of pay**. Agencies usually advertise themselves to parents at international, private, or grammar schools, so they can afford to pay higher prices for quality tutoring on a customised schedule.

- **You can get a lot of work if you want it**. Agencies will generally have a lot of students looking for tutoring, so if they hire you, then there will be plenty of work available. Some agencies like to book in blocks of lessons, while others will have rolling bookings – either way, it creates reliable work.

Cons:

- **Agencies can have high entry requirements for tutor applicants, so you may need to wait until you have more experience**. Agencies usually have a requirement for at least one degree, sometimes at certain institutions, and potentially will seek tutors with additional languages. They usually have some form of interview and assessed lesson as part of the application process.

- **You have much less control over your working conditions**. You can always request time off or not to work on certain days, but you're going to have a lot less control overall about when you work, how much you get paid, and which students you work with.

Examples of agencies: Titanium Tutors, Fleet Tutors, Owl Tutors, Keystone Tutors, Minerva Tutors . . .

Freelance

Freelance tutoring is the alternative to agency tutoring, and I would recommend that all new tutors start here. There are two main ways to find students as a freelance tutor: the first is to advertise yourself as a tutor and find students through word of mouth or on the internet, and the second is to use 'student marketplaces'.

Student marketplaces are the halfway point between agency tutoring and freelance tutoring. You create a profile, advertise your specialisms and your availability, and students can then search for tutors they think will be a good fit for them. Student marketplaces make finding students much easier, especially for new tutors. However, there are some important limitations to student marketplaces which you may eventually outgrow once you have more experience.

Freelancing tutoring without using student marketplaces

Pros:

- **You will have complete control over your schedule**. You get to decide when you teach, so you can decide when you want to be available for lessons, marking, and so on.

- **You will have complete control over your hourly rate**. You get to decide how much you charge, how long your lessons will be, and so on.

- **You'll be able to keep the entirety of your pay**. You won't have to pay anyone fees, because you're doing all of your own customer service, advertising, software selection, and so on. The only expenses you will have will be the software and resources you choose to use, which can be done cheaply if you use free or open-source resources, but you'll have to find them and learn how to use them yourself.

- **You can decide which subjects you are qualified to teach and what level you want to teach them at.** You will be able to decide what subjects you want to teach, based on the qualifications you have. A good rule of thumb is to always be qualified at least one level above the level you want to teach and to make sure you have a strong understanding of the subject and are confident enough in it to tutor it. However, as long as parents and students understand exactly what level you are qualified to, it is up to them to decide whether they are happy for you to tutor them.

- **You may already have personal relationships with students' families, so the arrangement can be personalised.** If the people you're tutoring are family friends, children of colleagues, or relatives of yours, then you can have much greater flexibility as a freelance tutor to decide exactly how you want the lessons to be. You can choose how to communicate with parents/students and accommodate specific requests more easily.

Cons:

- **Especially when you're a new tutor, it can be hard to find students.** Advertising yourself as a tutor, especially when you have limited experience, can be really hard. A lot of parents prefer to use tutoring sites because of their vetting procedures, so they may not be willing to try a freelance tutor if they don't already know them, and it can be hard to reach students outside of your immediate circle of friends and family.

- **You will have to do all of your own customer service, scheduling, planning, and advertising.** You are the whole business, so you'll need to deal with parents and students, plan your schedule, find resources, advertise yourself, and more, all within your chosen working hours and hourly rate.

- **You will need to pay for all of your own software and resources.** You will need to do research about the best websites and classroom software to use. This gives you a lot of flexibility, but conversely it requires at least some initial investment of time.

Freelance tutoring using student marketplaces

Pros:

- **You have access to their online classroom and teaching and scheduling software.** One of the many advantages of using a student marketplace is that they usually provide this software as part of using their site. These sites often put a lot of research into their online classroom software, with some providing an interactive whiteboard, annotation and drawing tools, virtual Maths equipment and graph paper, a chat function, video players, and more. You will need to do your research when signing up for a site to find out what they provide, but this should start you off with all the tools you need without having to pay for them upfront. It also means that someone else is responsible for monitoring and maintaining the software side of the site.

- **You have access to customer service and tech support**. These sites usually have some full-time staff who manage their websites and offer various customer services, like a tech support team, helpline, or safeguarding reporting service, so you won't be responsible for following up on any technological issues or issues with parents/students.

- **You and your students are kept safe by site conduct rules**. Many sites have specific codes of conduct for students, parents, and tutors, such as not allowing the exchange of personal data. While this can have its limitations, it is also very valuable, especially for new tutors who might be unsure about appropriate boundaries with students. If you have any issues with overzealous parents, safeguarding concerns, or inappropriate behaviour from students, you will have a support team to turn to or report to, which keeps you and your students safe.

- **You can set your own schedule, within reasonable limits**. Even on the sites that do set limits on when you can teach, you will still have a lot of control over your scheduling. They usually have a booking system so you can indicate when you are available to tutor, what times you prefer, and so on. However, you will usually have to teach lessons of a prescribed length, such as 50 minutes to an hour.

- **You can set your own hourly rate, again within reasonable limits**. A few sites let you set the rate, but most sites offer a band or tier system so parents can get an idea of what they're paying for at different hourly rates and tutors can feel a sense of progression as they gain experience. You won't have full control over your rate, but you can choose which band or tier you want to work at. This can also be useful as a guide to how much you should be earning at different experience levels. See 'Setting Your Hourly Rate', pages 11–13, for more information on this.

- **Students will be able to find you very easily**. Tutoring sites are designed to make the match between students and tutors as easy as possible, so there will be hundreds, if not thousands, of students looking for tutors on the site, with tools to help them find the right tutor for them.

- **You don't need to worry about advertising your services or finding the right audience**. These sites do their own advertising, to the extent that the more popular ones have TV ads and social media campaigns, so you will not have to spend any money advertising yourself and your services.

- **You may be able to find other work or opportunities through the sites**. There may be other opportunities available through these companies, which often advertise for roles such as video production, surveys, and salaried positions to their tutor database. It can be an advantage for them to hire people who are already familiar with their site, and this can be a great way to find interesting graduate positions or additional freelance work.

Cons:

- **You pay for all of the 'pros' as a percentage of your hourly rate**. These sites usually take a cut of your hourly rate to pay for the services they provide, which can vary anywhere between 10% and 30%. You will need to decide whether the services you receive are sufficient for the amount you will have to pay for them – they usually are, but it can be worth investigating the different sites' offerings and percentage cuts to find the one that suits you best.

- **You may be limited in the software and resources you can use in lessons**. You will usually have to use the provided classroom software to teach, which may have some software limitations. You may not be able to share your screen or play videos, for example.

- **You may be limited by what the site will allow you to teach, according to your qualifications**. Some sites set limits on what subjects you can teach and what level you can teach them at. MyTutor, for example, requires tutors to have at least an A or A* in the A-level of a subject to tutor that same subject at GCSE level. This means you may be familiar with a particular subject or exam but won't be considered qualified to teach it. The limits are usually reasonable, in that tutors should be very familiar and competent in their subject to best help their students, but it is worth considering whether this will affect the subjects you want to tutor.

Examples of student marketplaces: MyTutor, Revision Centre, Tutorful, Tutor Class, Tutor Choice, Preply . . .

In-person tutoring

I won't spend too much time discussing in-person tutoring, as the topic merits a whole book of its own, but it is worth highlighting the opportunities available to confident online tutors looking to transfer towards higher-paying, higher-commitment work. There are lots of different kinds of in-person tutoring, including freelance, agency, and residential tutoring. Freelance and agency tutoring are much the same as their online counterparts, with the additional logistics of either travelling to students' houses or schools or having them travel to you. Residential tutoring is a greater commitment: it usually requires you to live in a school or alternative educational provision, with accommodation provided as part of a contract for tutoring work. These roles vary from short, part-time contracts over the summer to long-term partnerships, with some offering work abroad, so it is worth investigating once you have plenty of experience.

Safeguarding

While your main role as a tutor is to support your students' learning, it is also expected that you will recognise the duty of care that you have for the children you may interact with.

In schools, there is a legal framework that requires that teachers be trained to safeguard children and have systems for reporting issues. While tutors, whether freelance or agency, don't have the same requirements and frameworks, the duty of care expected of all education professionals does extend to you – you need to think of yourself as your own 'safeguarding lead'. It is vitally important that tutors recognise their responsibility for recognising and reporting abuse or neglect.

That's why many student marketplaces, agencies, and organisations will require you to get a DBS check before you have your first lesson with a student. A DBS check, originally called a CRB check, is a survey of any criminal charges or arrests you may have. In an education context, this is used to ensure that you do not have any previous charges that may indicate that it is not appropriate or safe for you to work with children. In the UK this is run by the Disclosure and Barring Service. They offer a Basic check (£23), which only looks at unspent criminal convictions; a Standard check (£23), which checks both current and previous convictions; and an Enhanced check (£40), which is the usual minimum requirement in education settings. In addition to the Enhanced DBS check, educational employers often request 'barred list' checks, which ensure that any previous or current convictions are not on the list of offences which would prevent you from working with children or vulnerable adults. Enhanced DBS checks can only be requested by organisations, like agencies or student marketplaces, so it can be difficult to get one as a freelance tutor unless you are also a member of one of those.

Some agencies and student marketplaces will require you to obtain a DBS check as part of their application process, while others will only require one if you will be working with school-age children or if you will be working with PP students. Regardless of whether one is required, I would recommend that all tutors get, at minimum, a Basic DBS check, and ideally an Enhanced DBS check if you are able to. Not only will this be reassuring for parents and students, but it is also good professional practice for any future education-related roles you may be interested in. You should also sign up to the DBS Update Service within the time window to keep your check up to date.

In addition, there are several documents that it is recommended that online tutors use. A useful note here: almost all agencies and student marketplaces will have their own version of the documents that I am about to explore, which you will have to sign to become a member of their site. This is really helpful for new tutors – it means you're protected if you, a child, or a parent becomes unhappy about part of the service, and it gives clear guidance on what is expected from both sides. It's still good to read the following sections and understand exactly what is included and why, because it's important information with potentially serious legal consequences, but you don't need to worry about writing or conducting any of your own before you start tutoring.

However, if you are interested in becoming a fully freelance tutor, then I would recommend getting some child protection training through a reputable organisation like the National Society for the Prevention of Cruelty to Children (NSPCC).

'Child protection' is the legal term for the safeguarding and protection of children from harm, abuse, or neglect, used by police and education and health. organisations like schools, Childline, and the NHS. It is not a legal requirement for tutors to have child protection training, but it is highly recommended so you can help to report any issues you witness or that a child discloses to you.

There are lots of online resources available, but I would always recommend that you start with the NSPCC website. They have information on how to keep your lesson space (both online and in person) safe, how to spot signs of neglect or abuse, and what to do if you suspect a child is not safe. In addition, the Department of Education has a voluntary code of safeguarding practice for what they call 'out-of-school settings', or OOSSs, which includes both in-person and online tutoring, which you can find on their website here: (https://assets.publishing.service.gov.uk/government/uploads/system/uploads/attachment_data/file/940872/Keeping_children_safe_code_of_practice.pdf).

Most usefully, the NSPCC offers a range of paid online courses designed to support anyone who works will children to understand how to better protect young people from harm. They even have a specific 'Child Protection Training for Tutors' course, which is aimed at both in-person and online tutors (which can be found here https://learning.nspcc.org.uk/safeguarding-child-protection/tutors#heading-top). I would recommend that all tutors, especially those who are not protected by the terms of an online tutoring site or student marketplace, take this short, accessible course – it's about £25, explains everything you need to know, and can be done at your own pace, totalling about 4 hours. Like the DBS check, it is also good practice for any future education-related roles.

Whether you decide to get that training or not, it is worth exploring the details of each of the following documents and drawing up your own versions to agree with parents and students before you begin tutoring with them. These are:

Codes of conduct

A code of conduct is a document which codifies the behaviour and procedures that parents and students can expect from you, as well as those that you expect from them. When you were younger, you may have had to sign one at school or at an extracurricular club as a condition of participating.

While it is not required that freelance tutors have codes of conduct, they can be extremely useful in establishing boundaries with both parents and students. They set out clearly what you expect from the student/parent and what they can expect from you.

It is up to you what you include in your code of conduct, but there are lots of templates online if you are struggling to come up with things. The NSPCC website has one you use.

Some examples of items in a code of conduct might be:

- Expecting the student to be on time to the lesson and ready to learn

- Expecting the parent to provide the necessary equipment and a quiet space for the student to use

- Expecting the parent to pay the lesson fee 24 hours in advance of the lesson

- Letting the student know that it is okay for them to ask to go to the bathroom or get a drink during the lesson

- Setting a time limit for when homework needs to be handed in and a time frame for when it will be marked and returned

If you are going to be tutoring freelance, it may be worth drawing up a code of conduct for students and parents that is discussed and signed by you both before lessons begin. That way, you have a point of reference if there are any issues further down the line. However, if you are tutoring through an agency or student marketplace, parents and tutors should both have already had to sign a similar document, so you shouldn't need one in those instances. You can always discuss any additional requirements you have with parents before lessons begin.

Safeguarding policy

A safeguarding policy is a document which sets out your stance on child safeguarding and the procedure you would follow if you had a concern about a child's safety. This policy should be reviewed and updated regularly, as well as being shared with parents at the start of lessons with a new student.

Again, a document like this can be extremely useful in letting parents know what they can expect from you, as well as reassuring them that you are actively engaging with your responsibility for children's safety in your online classroom.

Some examples of items in a tutor's safeguarding policy might be:

- Your commitment to keeping children safe in your online classroom

- Whom the policy applies to – which should be all students you work with who are under the age of 18

- Your understanding of any relevant child protection legislation – reiterate your personal and professional responsibility and refer to the NSPCC for more details

- Practical details of what you would do if you had a concern, such as what you would make a note of, who you would speak to, what organisations you would report it to – again, refer to the NSPCC for more details

- A confidentiality statement, outlining your understanding that you may have to share your concerns about a child, even if they ask you not to

- A date and your signature, with a commitment to review it at a future time

Good practice for tutors

An important question that every tutor should ask themselves before they start tutoring is: what makes a good tutor? If I were a student, what would I want my tutor to say/do/ask/understand? Every tutor will give you a slightly different answer, but it can be useful to start with some lessons from experience while you figure out what kind of tutor you want to be.

In my opinion, being a good tutor is:

- **Knowing your subject really, really well**. While you may want to teach a dozen subjects, it is important to only offer subjects that you know inside out and back to front.

- **Being punctual, prepared, and ready to tutor every lesson**. This is not to say that tutors aren't allowed to have a difficult day – we all have them! – but, as a rule, tutors should be in their online classroom before the student arrives, with all of the materials they need for the lesson ready, having revised any topics they haven't taught in a while.

- **Being honest with parents and students**. If you're not feeling well and don't think you'll be able to teach today, tell the students and parents. If you don't know how to teach that exam board, tell them. The last thing you want is to be stuck in an awkward situation with a parent or student, so it is always best to be honest – and the vast majority of the time, both parents and students are really understanding.

- **Being patient, even if it means explaining the same topic over and over again**. Sometimes students just don't get it, even after they've studied it in class, done their homework, and discussed it with you. Sometimes you might need to go over what a simile looks like, or how to rearrange an equation, two or three lessons in a row before it sticks. As boring as that might sound to you, this is what tutoring is ultimately all about: giving your students the best chance at getting good at the basics of their subjects before moving onto more complex material in school.

- **Being confident in yourself and your skills and recognising your own expertise**. Something you might come across in your time as a tutor is people who say, 'but you don't have a PGCE!' They're probably right; you most likely are not a qualified teacher, but you don't need to be to be an excellent tutor. The reason many tutoring organisations recruit undergraduates or recent graduates is because they don't want teachers – they want students who did really well in their GCSEs and A-levels and, more importantly, remember exactly what it's like to take those exams!

- **Being flexible with lesson planning to accommodate students varying needs and wants**. Some students like playing games, others want 45-minute lessons, and some just want to get their heads down. Whatever your student wants and needs, you need to be able to tailor your lessons to them. Learning to distinguish between what a student wants and what they need – which aren't always the same thing – will help you to strike a good balance of enjoyment and learning.

- **Being understanding and kind if students are tired, overworked, or unproductive**. Just like you, sometimes students don't have enough energy to get through everything they need to do. Some students might be going through tough life circumstances, and others might have a dozen other tutoring lessons that week. I've known students who were having two or three hours of tutoring every evening on top of school or summer crash courses! If it becomes a repeat issue, be prepared to have a chat with their parents to discuss cutting back on lessons or managing their other commitments.

- **Being calm and resilient when students misbehave and having a comprehensive plan for what to do next**. Children misbehave – it happens. It's not your job as a tutor to parent or punish; you just need to have a plan for what to do if it happens. Most tutoring sites offer a helpline or reporting system, or, if you're tutoring freelance, you can discuss any major issues with their parents.

- **Being positive and effusive, helping to build students' confidence**. Tutoring is the perfect opportunity to give students the extra attention they may not get in class, and for many this means that a boost in confidence is what they take away most from their tutoring lessons. This is especially important for young female students: I have noticed a consistent pattern of young women being less confident to give answers or feeling like they have to caveat their responses with phrases like 'I'm not sure if this is right . . .' or 'I don't think this is the right answer, but . . .'. As their tutor, you are perfectly positioned to offer praise and remind them that they are capable.

- **Being a good role model for students, offering advice and support**. During your time as their tutor, you will undoubtedly develop a rapport with your students, and they might ask you about things outside of the subject you're helping with. I've had young students ask about secondary school and older students ask about university. Being open and honest, as far as you feel comfortable, and offering advice about school and learning is all part of modelling positive engagement with education.

- **Having appropriate boundaries with students and parents**. The best time to discuss boundaries with parents and students is right at the start. I like to be clear with parents about what they can expect from me and what I expect from them. It means that your interactions always have a positive framework, and you have options in case you feel uncomfortable or want to stop working with them. Codes of conduct, safeguarding policies, and other initial documents become really important, as they give you a point of reference for your expectations for parents to follow.

- **Being inclusive and welcoming of all identities in your space.** As a tutor, you might be the only person students talk to who isn't their parents, teachers, or friends, so you might bring a very different social and cultural background to theirs. As such, you must always ensure that your online space is inclusive and that you welcome all gender identities, expressions, sexualities, races, religions, socioeconomic backgrounds, and so on. Finding opportunities to have positive conversations about diversity and difference as part of your tutoring is crucial.

TOP TIP

When starting out, try to get as broad a range of experiences as possible – and make sure to keep track of how many hours you've taught, what ages/qualifications you've taught, and the names of the different sites and agencies you're tutoring with. You may also want to ask parents/students to provide reviews or comments at regular intervals or before you finish tutoring them. You can use these details on your CV or as testimonies for future parents/students/sites.

QUESTION

What are the most important qualities that you think a tutor should have?

Tutoring tech

In this chapter, I will discuss the 'online' part of 'online tutoring': the technology! Here you will find my recommendations about the basic physical and digital tech, as well as guidance about choosing video conferencing software and some suggestions for upgrades once you've got started.

In the following, I have broken down all of the essential digital and physical tools you will need to get started, as well as providing some suggestions for equipment that you don't necessarily need but might consider investing in at a later date.

Digital tools

The only digital tools you absolutely must have to become an online tutor are a reliable internet connection and some form of video call or online classroom software.

When it comes to internet connections, the majority of online tutoring companies will have their own minimum requirements, but as a general rule, minimum download and upload speeds of 4 Mbps with a ping of less than 100 ms (milliseconds) is a good start. You can test your internet speed by searching for 'speed test' in your browser. This means both camera feeds and microphones will work without lagging and any online classroom software will update in real time. It is possible to teach with less-than-ideal internet conditions – with adaptations like turning off your cameras or using a text chat function rather than a mic – but you run the risk of the student disengaging or losing the lesson connection altogether. One solution I have found, especially since moving to an urban area, is that if your router stops working or there's a power issue right before a lesson, then the connection provided by your phone's internet hotspot function is usually more than strong enough to host a lesson without eating up all of your data. I have never found online classroom software to use more data than a video call typically uses, which is around 3 MB of data per minute.

DOI: 10.4324/9781003211648-4

Becoming a tutor

There are several ways to approach the question of virtual classrooms. If you're going to be working through an agency or site which has its own online classroom software, like MyTutor or Tutorful, then you don't need to worry about this – everything you need, including video and audio and digital tools, will be provided for you. That is the main reason I recommend new tutors start on a site like these: they take all of the stress and fuss out of familiarising yourself with online tutoring tech, for a small percentage of your earnings. If you're starting to move towards a private tutoring style, where you'll keep 100% of your earnings and provide all the online tools yourself, then you'll need software like Zoom or Skype, which will allow you to schedule lessons and interact with students.

In the following, I've outlined the most popular software for creating online classrooms and scheduling lessons, with pros and cons for each. My personal recommendation would be to use Zoom, for the reasons outlined subsequently, but I would encourage you to do some research before you choose. They all have different tools, requirements, and advantages, so it is important to find the one that suits your tutoring style and needs.

Zoom (preferred)

- **pros:** free for 1:1 lessons indefinitely and 4+ people for under 40 mins, inbuilt whiteboard and annotation tools, easy customisable layout, screensharing, chat function, students can use the same link to access multiple lessons

- **cons:** limited lesson length on free plan, expensive upgrades, occasional safety issues, easier for students to use when software is downloaded

BigBlueButton

- **pros:** free for any size group; inbuilt whiteboard and annotation tools; lots of additional features, including video play, polls, and shared notes; screensharing; chat function

- **cons:** complicated set-up; minimal customer service support for independent users; increased popularity during high use leads to limited lesson length

Microsoft Teams

- **pros:** host unlimited video calls and phone calls, can send messages and store files in message threads, easy to schedule using inbuilt calendar function, chat function

- **cons:** no whiteboard or annotation function, expensive if you aren't already paying for Microsoft Office, requires download

Skype

- **pros:** free for any size group, can send messages and store files in message threads, screensharing

- **cons:** no whiteboard or annotation function, easier for students to use when software is downloaded

Google Meet

- **pros:** free for any size group; easy to schedule using inbuilt calendar function; easily connected to other Google features, like Google Drive or Google Classroom

- **cons:** limited lesson tools; some safety concerns, though new moderation tools have been added

Other digital tools

1. Digital whiteboards

Several of the online classrooms listed previously have in-built whiteboards and annotation tools as part of their offering, such as Zoom and BigBlueButton, but some don't, and you may prefer to use a different whiteboard software anyway.

SMART Whiteboard is an excellent tool, but a full subscription can be very expensive, and the free tool only has a limited trial version.

2. Slideshows

Later in the book, I will explore where slideshows can be most effective with online tutees, but regardless of whether you use them with students, they can be a brilliant lesson planning tool and are invaluable for creating customisable files that can be easily turned into worksheets or PDFs. You can use paid software, like Microsoft PowerPoint and Adobe PDF, or free software, like basic image files or sites like Prezi.

3. Maths tools

There are dozens of sites, like GeoGebra, FluidMath, or Brilliant, that offer animated or interactive Maths whiteboards free or for a small subscription fee. This includes tools to draw graphs; use protractors, rulers, or compasses; or interact with more complex diagrams. If you're a Maths tutor who will be needing tools like this regularly, and they aren't provided through the online classroom software you're using, it can be worth looking at reviews to find a reliable set of virtual Maths tools.

Physical tools

Online tutoring is a very accessible way to earn money for most university students and graduates because it only requires you to have something you probably already own: a laptop! Almost all laptops have built-in microphones, webcams, and speakers, so you already have everything you need to teach anyone, anywhere in the world, over the internet. If you have a desktop PC rather than a laptop, you will need to invest in an external webcam and microphone – many of which can be bought combined – so that students can see and hear you.

The only other piece of equipment I would say is essential for tutors – and students – is headphones or earphones. They don't need to be high-tech or expensive, but they exponentially improve the quality of the lesson. First, it brings the microphone closer to your mouth, which improves the sound quality and means the student can hear you more easily, and second, it prevents any feedback or sound looping which may occur if your laptop tries to listen to its own speakers. Finally, it also ensures that the lesson space is more private – no one else in your room or house can hear the student, and background noise is less likely to interfere with your teaching.

Once you've been tutoring for a while, you may decide to invest in some new equipment to make the process slightly easier and more convenient. I would like to say that none of the following suggestions are necessary at all – I simply used my laptop and some earphones for the first two and half years – but they can come in handy if you have a bit of experience and want to streamline your lessons.

1. Wireless headphones (or earphones)

As I mention previously, any kind of headphones or earphones will infinitely improve the quality of the tutoring experience. If you do decide to invest in some headphones specifically for tutoring, I would recommend you investigate wireless headphones. Being able to teach while standing at a table or standing desk and not be physically tethered to your laptop can be really helpful if you start tutoring many hours a week and don't want to be sat down all day.

2. A computer mouse

To anyone using a desktop PC, this is obvious, but for laptop users, a plugin or wireless mouse can alleviate some of the frustrations of trying to draw spider diagrams or navigate online classrooms with a touchpad. You can get cheap wireless mice online for less than £10.

3. A tablet

Almost all the software you will need, from video calls to online classrooms, works on a mobile format, so a tablet with a built-in camera and microphone can be the perfect tool for teaching on the go. If you're going to be tutoring while travelling, moving house, or in an office space outside of your home, a tablet can be the perfect way to have the functionality you need without lugging a laptop around.

I use my iPad Air, which has great hardware and is a reasonable size, but any other tablets with front-facing cameras and good-sized screens would also work fine.

4. A graphics tablet

This is perhaps the least necessary piece of equipment and can be one of the most expensive, so only consider this if you have the need and the funds. That said, it can be very useful if you want to be able to draw accurately on an online whiteboard.

I would personally recommend Wacom's graphics tablets, as they are affordable and come in a range of sizes – from taking up half your desk to fitting into your backpack or handbag. I use the Wacom One in the smallest size, which is only around £30, and it's brilliant for handwriting on an online whiteboard or writing equations and drawing diagrams in Maths and Science lessons. It also comes with stylus pens included.

5. A visualiser

Finally, visualisers are an increasingly popular bit of kit both in classrooms and for online tutors. They consist of a small webcam on the end of a flexible metal or plastic stem, designed to face down onto your desk to focus on pages of a textbook, a drawing or whiteboard, or your hands. They can also be used for other generic webcam needs, like video calls or recording lessons.

If you incorporate any practical elements into your lessons – textbooks, experiments, demonstrations, or handwritten working – then this is a cheap and easy way to optimise those techniques. I like to use mine to look at passages or images in books or hand-drawn diagrams, which saves me having to scan and upload them.

Again, this is something you should only consider buying if you need an external webcam or are keen to use elements like those listed previously. A good visualiser with lighting and manual focus will cost around £60, though there are cheaper ones available.

TOP TIP

Only invest in additional software, resources, or equipment if you need it. You can teach any subject, at any age, on almost any site, with the standard offering of a laptop or tablet and a pair of cheap earphones. There are thousands of sites with free resources and dozens more cheap textbooks and workbooks. If you do decide to invest in a book or piece of equipment, check second-hand sites like eBay first to keep costs down.

QUESTION

Which virtual classroom tools are most important to you?

Chapter 4

Homework and paid marking time

This chapter is all about homework: when to set it, what to set, and how to incorporate it into your tutoring. Used right, homework can be a brilliant tool for learning, so you can use the recommendations in this chapter to figure out how to start setting effective tasks for your students.

Setting homework

Homework can be a contentious topic among tutors, with some arguing that tutoring is already an additional pressure for students and others noting the advantages it can bring, especially for older students and those who are revising. In fact, the Education Endowment Foundation have collated studies which suggest that setting short, frequent, high-quality homework for secondary school students can increase their attainment, equivalent to an additional 6 months of learning.

As you become a more experienced tutor, it will be up to you to decide whether to use it. However, I think homework can be a positive and practical tool for helping your tutees to excel, and one that I would recommend that you use when starting out.

Some students and parents ask tutors to set homework; others ask them not to – some will leave it up to you. It is always worth discussing homework in your initial meeting or discussion with parents or in your first lesson with a new student. PP students or students you're only taking for a cover lesson won't need homework, but any student you'll be teaching for a length of time will benefit from it.

Identifying where homework is helpful

Homework can be really useful, but it is more effective with certain subjects and students than others. You will need to identify where homework will be most helpful and which students will benefit the most from the additional work.

DOI: 10.4324/9781003211648-5

Homework, in a tutoring context, is most effective for *long response tasks*. Whether it's paragraph practice in English, written answers in Science, or multi-step Maths questions, the limitations of an hour's lesson mean that you can rarely afford students the full amount of time to answer long response questions in full.

Long response questions usually garner the most marks, so their practice is important, but the actual writing time is often better left outside of the lesson where students can take as much time as they need. This is especially true for younger students or students who struggle with typing, as handwriting is a relatively inaccessible medium in online lessons.

The other useful homework is *memorisation tasks* – any whole pieces of information that a student needs to be able to recall quickly to use in other situations. Using tutoring to help students learn information by rote is an inefficient use of lesson time, unless they are very young or really struggling with memory techniques.

Setting memorisation homework can help maximise the time spent in lesson on *how* to use that knowledge rather than on the knowledge itself. This is especially helpful with cumulative knowledge like times tables, spelling tests, or vocabulary in foreign languages, where students can return to their memorisation practise whenever is convenient throughout the week. There's never a guarantee that students will do this type of homework – after all, it's not the most exciting task – but those who do, or are supported to do so, benefit massively.

Whenever I start work with a new student who clearly has a limited vocabulary, whether English is their first or second language, I set up a weekly spelling test with age-appropriate words to ensure that they are getting some practice for free between lessons. You can also use this with older students for learning key words for exams, like the definitions of technical terms in English, Science, or Psychology or learning places and statistics in Geography. Alternatively, you can do times tables tests or mental Maths starters to ensure that they are practising those skills regularly.

Deciding what to set as homework and how to use it

Once you know where homework will be most effective, it's then a question of what to set. Any task you set needs to be, at minimum, *relevant*, *useful*, and *in line with their learning goals*.

One of the most common ways homework is set is simply as an extension of the lesson: if there was a key piece of work that needed to have been completed in the lesson, but the student turned up late or struggled with earlier tasks, then it can be set as homework. You can then use their answers to form a starter exercise in the next lesson. However, you may sometimes want to set specific homework tasks. You can find suggestions for these tasks in each Section 2 chapter.

Modelling good homework practice

As well as setting homework, tutors can discuss the best strategies for independent learning.

Tutors need to encourage students to use *active revision/learning strategies* rather than passive ones. Passive revision/learning strategies are things like reading notes, highlighting, copying out notes, and so on. Instead, students need to be grouping the information effectively and incorporating recall exercises.

To help your students to learn how to revise properly, you can demonstrate active revision/learning strategies with them. Here are some top tips for modelling the most common strategies:

- **Mind maps** – best used for overviews of whole topics or 'question-guessing' exercises; use paper or an online tool like Mindmup or Mindmeister; use images/doodles/shapes and other visual clues; identify key words/acronyms clearly; use colour-coding at the end to group key information

- **Lists** – break them down into short sections and group relevant elements together; create and update lists regularly; use them as a recall exercise or to make other resources, like flash cards

- **Flash cards** – use paper or an app like Quizlet or Anki; first, create flash cards that summarise the key information for a question/topic; second, create flash cards that ask questions or prompt recall to use as regular tests; keep the details short; only colour-code if it will help; give yourself time to recall the answer before you turn the card over

- **Self-evaluation** – get comfortable receiving feedback and evaluating your own work; get familiar with the relevant marking criteria; read model answers so you know what a 'good' answer looks like; ask to focus on your weaknesses or elements you feel less confident on

For students who are in the latter stages of a course or who have been working on memorisation tasks regularly, you can introduce regular quizzes to ensure they are practising their recall. I usually use summary questions or quick exam question starters to do this. This ensures that your students spread their revision out over time, which improves their performance and gives them a chance to revisit any information or strategies they aren't sure about later.

Including marking time in your hourly rate

One key thing you will need to consider is the fact that homework will need marking – either in the lesson or before it. You will need to factor that time into your lesson plan and hourly rate.

If you've never marked someone else's work before, you may be surprised at the amount of time it takes. Reading a student's handwriting or understanding their grammar can slow you down a lot, and you will want to spend time on their strengths, weaknesses, and incorporating your findings into future lesson plans. This quickly adds up, especially if you have several students or see a student very frequently. As a rule, you shouldn't be setting homework that will take more than 30 minutes to mark. If a student wants to write a full essay, complete an entire past paper, or do multiple practice questions, beyond that 30 minutes of marking, then I would suggest speaking to whomever pays for the lesson about booking a session of paid marking time instead. This ensures that you can spend as much time as you need on the marking while still earning an appropriate amount for the service provided.

For more information about how to factor weekly marking time into your hourly rate, you can refer to the 'Online tutoring basics' section (pages 7–26).

Anticipating homework not being finished

You undoubtedly remember it from your school days – there was always the occasional time where you lost, forgot, or simply didn't have time for a piece of homework, and your students are no different.

If your students are repeatedly not doing homework, and you're confident that their parents want them to be doing homework and that you're setting homework which they are capable of doing, then there's probably an issue you don't know about. This may simply be that they have too much on their plate and didn't get to your homework or that they are finding the homework you set particularly difficult for some reason. If you suspect that they are just not doing it because they don't want to, then you may need to speak to their parent or teacher about this issue.

Some key things to remember about missed homework:

- **Don't make homework a central part of lessons, so there won't be significant consequences for you if it doesn't get finished**. Homework is a useful tool, but the student's take-home tasks shouldn't ever be the backbone of your lesson planning. That way, you can decide whether to make time for the homework in the lesson time without it derailing your lesson.

- **Be understanding, and don't punish or upset students if they haven't completed their homework**. Lots of students want to do the best they can, but there may be other factors at play that mean they simply don't have time. Always assume the best intentions for students unless you have good reason to believe otherwise, and offer them opportunities to try the homework again or finish it with you in that day's lesson.

- **Help students to see the value of their homework, and reward them with positivity and encouragement when they do it and do it well**. Especially when they are young, students respond positively to seeing ticks and smiley faces, so make sure to praise students who get answers right and frame any mistakes as learning opportunities rather than failures.

- **Anticipate unfinished homework and make sure to include those topics in other areas of the lessons**. If you've done a lesson about fractions and set some follow-up homework about fractions which doesn't get finished, then look at using some fractions questions as a starter or quick exercise in the following lesson to give them a chance to practise again. If it becomes clear that a student has forgotten important information on the topic or doesn't feel confident about it, then you can plan another lesson about it in the future.

- **Talk to the student about their workload**. It's good to check in with your student about how they're finding your tutoring, even if they're quite young, to give them the opportunity to tell you how they're finding your lessons and homework. If you ever have concerns, you can ask them if they need more time or less work, or you can speak to their parent or teacher.

Paid marking time

If you set homework, then it is reasonable for students and parents to expect some marking time included in the rate for an hour's lesson, but sometimes they might want more marking or feedback than usual. Paid marking time, sometimes called a written work review (WWR) or additional marking, is when a student or parent pays an hourly rate for dedicated marking time. This can be used to mark additional practice papers or essays, provide feedback on coursework drafts or interview preparation, review a personal statement draft, and so on.

Paid marking time is usually charged at the same rate as lessons, but you can decide how much time you think the marking will take and charge accordingly.

I would recommend that you bear in mind how time marking takes, the amount of effort you will want to put into providing quality feedback, and the amount of reading required, and take care not to undervalue your time. It is up to parents and students whether they want to pay for your lessons and marking time, so you shouldn't lower your rates to an unreasonable level just because you won't be working directly with a student.

My recommendation is that, in writing subjects, properly marking any piece of work up to 2,000 words merits an hour of paid marking time. An equivalent in a Maths or Science subject might be two complete past papers. Feel free to use these numbers as a guide for your own rates.

You may occasionally come across students who try to abuse the paid marking time system, so make sure to familiarise yourself with any relevant restrictions on marking in your subject. For A-level English coursework, for example, there are usually restrictions on the number of times a coursework draft can be marked before submission. Students may sometimes try to use a PMT arrangement to pay you to write a piece of work or complete a paper for them, which you should always politely refuse.

TOP TIP

Don't be afraid to ask parents to pay for your marking time if it goes longer than you expected or if they ask you to mark additional work, and be firm if they are difficult about it. Your insight is just as valuable when written down as it is given directly to the student in lesson.

QUESTION

What homework do you think your students will find most useful?

How to tutor

Chapter 5

What am I tutoring?

In this chapter, I will summarise everything you need to know about tutoring each age group, key stage, and subject, from the content and skills you'll need to cover to parent and student expectations.

Working out what you will be tutoring

Some parents will want you to work with their child on the reading and skills in line with their school's schedule to help them with their in-class assessments, while others will be fine with you choosing your own lesson content to cover the key skills.

Whichever is this case, you should always discuss with the parent and student exactly what they want help with and how they would like you to cover the content and skills.

Tutors should draw directly on the National Curriculum where relevant, as I have done in later chapters, to ensure that they are covering all required skills, as well as on any Key Stage–specific textbooks.

Familiarising yourself with the different topics listed in the subjects you want to tutor will help you to understand your student's descriptions of their work in lessons, as well as making it easier to find appropriate and relevant worksheets and resources online. Using the key words outlined in each subject in the following will make it easier to find practice papers and worksheets for each unit.

Tutoring at KS2

The end of KS2 is when students take the SATs: external exams in English and Maths and teacher assessments in Science. Schools may also assess students informally in History, Geography, Religious Education, and others. The syllabi for these exams provide a framework of expectations of this age group for all subjects.

DOI: 10.4324/9781003211648-7   **41**

Parents generally seek tutoring for their KS2 children for two reasons: with Year 5s and 6s it's usually for academic reasons, looking for them to do well in their SATs, 11+, or other end of Key Stage assessments, and with Year 3s and 4s it's usually for extracurricular enrichment. The former group often have a syllabus from their child's school or some other specific guidance, while the latter tend to give you freer rein. Regardless of whether the parent specifically says to follow it, the SATs curriculum provides a useful guide for all tutors of this age group.

In the following, I have outlined the key information you need to know about what to tutor in each KS2 subject. You will find the details for English and Maths here, and information for subjects such as History, Geography, and Science can be found in the online chapters.

English

The focus in English at KS2 is on skills rather than specific knowledge: the SATs do not have set texts, unlike GCSE English and A-level, and schools typically use a wide range of texts and encourage students to pursue reading that interests them in their own time.

For the youngest students (Years 3–4), these skills include:

- **Essential reading** – reading confidently out loud; able to answer simple comprehension questions and decoding the meaning and pronunciation of words they don't know

- **Essential writing** – writing fluently, in full sentences with readable grammar and punctuation

- **Essential literacy skills** – developing an age-appropriate level of vocabulary, spelling, and grammar with fluency and confidence

For older students (Years 5–6), you should cover all of the previous, in addition to:

- **Extended reading** – reading confidently both out loud and internally; able to discuss the content of their reading; inferring the meaning of words they don't know

- **Extended writing** – writing fluently, in full sentences with few mistakes

- **Basic analytical skills** – articulating the effect of language on the reader, with some grasp of technical language

- **Creative writing skills** – writing with an understanding of the effect of language on the reader; experimenting with new concepts they have learned from their reading

Tutors should focus on building students' skills by introducing a range of fiction and non-fiction that they have either chosen themselves from primary texts or found in textbooks and online resources. Some parents may ask for reading recommendations that they can borrow at the library or use when book buying, and others may want you to incorporate reading practice into lessons.

Maths

For KS2 Maths, students are expected to learn a number of basic skills to support their numeracy.

For the youngest students (Years 3 and 4), these skills include:

- **Essential arithmetic** – working with whole numbers, fractions, and decimals; all four operations; understand and work with basic measurements; identify basic shapes; times tables up to the 12s

- **Essential Maths knowledge** – ability to spell Maths terminology correctly; use both written and mental calculation methods

- **Basic problem solving** – solve single-step and word-based problems

For older students (Years 5 and 6), you should cover all of the previous, in addition to:

- **Confident arithmetic** – using times table knowledge to solve basic number problems; fluent use of addition, subtraction, and both written and mental multiplication and division and understanding of conversion between fractions, decimals, and percentages

- **Extended problem solving** – solving simple problems with multiple steps or stages

In addition to key skills, there is also a range of basic subject content that students are expected to know for their SATs. For Years 3 and 4, this includes:

- **Number** – counting in multiples; understanding of place value; estimation and inverse operations; ordering and writing numbers in numerals and words; basic number problems; written and mental Maths with 3- and 4-digit numbers; written and mental multiplication and division; factor pairs; recognising, writing, adding, and subtracting simple fractions and decimals; understanding of negative numbers; correspondence problems

- **Measurement** – measuring, adding, and subtracting units of length, mass, volume, and money; telling time with 12- and 24-hour clocks, both analogue and digital; estimating measuring time of all durations; conversions between types of measurement and unit; basic area via counting

- **Geometry** – drawing, making, and identifying 2D and 3D shapes; identify angles in units of 90 degrees; acute and obtuse angles; recognise various arrangements of lines, including horizontal, vertical, perpendicular, and parallel lines; basic symmetry; co-ordinates and translation

- **Statistics** – reading and drawing bar charts, pictograms, and tables; simple data interpretation; understanding discrete and continuous data

For Years 5 and 6, this includes all of the previous, in addition to:

- **Number** – read, write, order, and count up to 1 million; rounding; Roman numerals; linear sequences; addition and subtraction of 4+ digit numbers both written and mental; long and short multiplication and division; order of operations; factors and factorisation; short division and remainders; multiples, squares, and cubes; fractions, decimals, and percentages, including simplification, mixed numbers, improper fractions, conversions, and ordering; negative numbers; estimation

- **Ratio and proportion** – proportionality and ratio; problem solving using calculation and comparison of quantities and percentages; scale factor; solving sharing and grouping problems, such as in recipes

- **Algebra** – simple formulae; linear number sequences; missing number problems; solving for variables and unknowns

- **Measurement** – conversion between metric and imperial units; use of large and small units and cubic units; perimeter and area; estimation of volume and capacity; use of all major operations with all types of units, including length, mass, time, money, and so on; basic formulae

- **Geometry** – all common shapes and their properties; angles in units of 90 degrees and relationships between angles and lines; commonalities between 2D and 3D shapes (i.e. square and cube); angle properties; missing length and angle problems; acute, obtuse, and reflex angles; reflections and other translations on co-ordinate grids; nets and surface area; properties of circles; shape relations

- **Statistics** – line graphs and pie charts; timetables; mean as average

Tutoring the 11+

Many parents want 11+ tutoring, as the assessment tests for several skills that are not specifically taught in school. It is also one of the few exams where simply completing a lot of practice papers and practising specific questions styles repeatedly is a guarantee that students will perform better in the real thing. Thus, 11+ tutors are in high demand.

One of the challenges of tutoring the 11+ is that there is no official curriculum, although there are official examining bodies. The format of the 11+, including the number of papers, the topics, and the timings, all vary from year to year and from school to school. This means that schools rarely publish past papers and the exam boards rarely publicly share the changes they have made, ostensibly as a means of making the examination more accurate to the students' performance on the day. Thus, you will need to know what school each of their students is applying to and stay up to date with any changes that are made to the exams each year.

The two most common examining bodies for the 11+ are GL Assessment, or GL, and the Centre for Evaluation & Monitoring at Cambridge Assessment, or CEM. There are some generalisations that can be made about the differences between these two boards – like the fact that GL uses question banks to make papers while CEM doesn't or that CEM doesn't separate the questions into topic papers – which do need to be taken into consideration, but essentially both cover the same skills and material. In addition, some of the most prestigious schools write their own papers, which you can find details of online, and there are several smaller exam boards in use. The main variations are in the style of the paper – computer test or paper, multiple choice or long answer – but the content remains very similar between all of them.

One important variation is that not all schools assess English in their 11+ exam. Generally, the more competitive the applications are at that school, the more likely it is to have an English paper.

Many schools publish information about their 11+ exam on their website, including parent guides and sample papers, which will help you to see which exam board they use and whether they have any school-specific requirements for the exam.

There are four main areas that are typically covered by the 11+:

- English (only offered by GL and often only included for the most competitive schools)

- Maths (offered by both, but CEM calls this 'numerical reasoning')

- Verbal reasoning (VR)

- Non-verbal reasoning (NVR)

The English section is usually split in two, with the first half covering reading comprehension, inference, and language analysis and the second half covering creative writing, both fiction and non-fiction. This format is only a guide, as it can vary a lot between schools and will depend heavily on which exam board and school the student is applying to.

The Maths section typically covers a range of topics from the standard Year 5 and 6 National Curriculum guidance, but in recent years more and more advanced questions have made their way into papers. Tutors should focus on helping students to be confident on all of the content from their age group before introducing questions as high as GCSE standard with very strong students.

The verbal reasoning and non-verbal reasoning sections are the main reason parents look for 11+ tutors, because these kinds of questions are not part of the National Curriculum. Both are skills-based assessments that test the way that students understand and solve puzzles, using words, letters, and spelling with verbal reasoning and using letters, images, and shapes with non-verbal reasoning.

If you offer 11+ tutoring, you may also be asked to help with other entrance exams for selective schools. These can include the 13+ and 16+, which test many of the same skills but at an appropriate level for older students. The 13+ can be tutored in much the same way as the 11+, but the 16+ tends to be even more school specific. In fact, some 16+ assessments are more similar to university entrance exams, like the TSAs, so you can use the material in the 'HE Applications' chapter for them.

Tutoring at KS3

I have taught students from all three year groups of KS3 for different reasons: they missed a chunk of primary school, they aren't confident in their new classes, they've recently moved to a new school, they need some subject-specific support as non-native English speakers. . . . The common factor is that they aren't doing GCSE courses yet and may not know which GCSE courses they want to take.

Typically, there are two kinds of KS3 tutoring students: those who want their tutoring to line up with what they're studying at school and those looking for more generalised support in the subject. Each comes with its own challenges, since the former students are not always able to communicate what they're studying at school clearly enough to follow, and the latter students may require you to build a bit of a curriculum of your own. This section will cover the basic skills and content required in the two most common subjects, English and Maths, as well as History, Geography, and Sciences.

English

If the student is asking you to follow their curriculum at school, you'll need to get more details about which texts they are using. You may also find it helpful to ask which exam board their school uses at GCSE, so you can use relevant resources and exam-style questions.

If the student wants more general guidance, you will need to think about which texts, resources, and worksheets you would like to use with your student and how you are going to structure your lessons.

Either way, the core skills you will need to cover in their lessons are:

● **Essential literacy** – reading, writing, vocabulary, spelling and grammar, building on their KS2 learning

● **Extended reading** – exploring a range of forms, genres, and styles of texts, including prose, poetry, drama, and non-fiction texts

● **Extended writing** – learning to write fluently and confidently for a range of purposes, including essays, speeches, and arguments

● **Analytical skills** – selecting relevant quotations; identifying devices/techniques; explaining authorial intent and effect on the reader

● **Creative writing skills** – learning to write fluently and confidently with a range of literary devices and an imaginative grasp of syntax, grammar, formatting, and paragraphing

With GCSE tutoring, there should be a much heavier focus on specific content from the key texts of a student's exam board, as they need to know them in close detail. However, KS3 students often study practice texts that they won't be tested on later, so they can focus on the necessary skills instead.

Tutors should try, where possible, to support the student's knowledge and understanding of specific texts they are being taught in school, as many schools choose a selection of texts to teach at KS3 that support their GCSE learning. However, this is not always possible: the student may not want help with the texts as much as the skills, or it may be a non-exam board text which the tutor is unfamiliar with.

Whatever the case, I would recommend that tutors select a range of extracts from age-appropriate texts to use for practice in lessons, so that students are exposed to a wide range of text forms and styles which will build their confidence when it comes to preparing for assessments and, later, their GCSEs. There are some reading list suggestions in the Resources chapter at the end of the book (pages 324–351).

Something to bear in mind is that, particularly at KS3, there seems to be a fairly even divide between students who are confident creative writers in their own time who simply need their spelling, grammar, and structuring refined for the demands of the exam and students who not at all keen on creative writing and prefer the analytical questions. Figuring out exactly what your student needs to work on, and adapting your lesson plans to them, is a great way to get started.

Maths

Since there is little variation between GCSE Maths exam boards and there are lots of generic KS3 Maths resources available online and in print, you don't need to worry about using exam-board–specific resources at this stage.

The core skills you will need to cover in their lessons are:

- **Fluent arithmetic** – confidence in all areas of basic Maths; understanding and precise use of mathematical terminology; able to work with a variety of expressions, equations, and representations

- **Mathematical reasoning** – interpreting the demands of a question in relation to their own skills and understanding; extend their understanding of patterns and relationships using algebra and other tools

- **Problem solving** – begin making connections between different areas of Maths; working through increasingly complex questions, including some multi-step questions

In addition to these skills, KS3 Maths students are also expected to cover a set of basic subject content. This includes:

- **Number** – fractions, decimals, and percentages; place value for decimals, measures, and integers of any size; ordering positive and negative integers, decimals and fractions; number lines; prime numbers, HCF, LCM, prime factorisation; all four operations, both written and mental, with integers, decimals, proper and improper fractions, and mixed numbers, all both positive and negative; order of operations; powers and roots; standard form; standard units of measures; rounding, estimation, and degrees of accuracy

- **Algebra** – basic algebraic notation, including coefficients and brackets; basic formulae and expressions; vocabulary of expressions, equations, inequalities, terms, and factors; simplifying and rearranging; modelling linear and quadratic equations using graphs and co-ordinates; solving equations; $y = mx + c$; simultaneous linear equations; problem-solving using linear, exponential, and reciprocal graphs; arithmetic and geometric sequences

- **Ratio, proportion and rates of change** – standard units; scale factors, scale diagrams, and maps; ratio notation and simplest form; basic ratios; ratios, fractions and linear functions; percentage change; direct and inverse proportion; problem-solving using compound units

- **Geometry and measures** – perimeter and area of triangles, parallelograms, trapezia, cubes, other prisms, and 2D shapes; areas of circles and composite shapes; line segments and angles; drawing perpendiculars and bisectors; sketching parallel lines, perpendicular lines, right angles, regular polygons; symmetry; congruence and enlargement; translations, rotations, and reflections; properties of angles, at a point, on a straight line, and vertically opposite; parallel lines and alternate and corresponding angles; sum of angles inside triangles and polygons; Pythagoras' theorem and simple proofs; problem-solving with right-angled triangles; problem-solving with 3D shapes

- **Probability** – simple probability experiments involving randomness, fairness, and equally and unequally likely outcomes; 0–1 probability scale; express sets as tables, grids, and Venn diagrams; single and combined events; mutually exclusive outcomes

- **Statistics** – discrete, continuous, and grouped data; averages, including mean, mode, median; spread, including range and consideration of outliers; tables, charts, and diagrams, including frequency tables, bar charts, pie charts, pictograms, and scatter graphs

Tutoring at KS4 (GCSE)

GCSE English and Maths are by far the most common GCSE tutoring requests, because they are compulsory for all students, but some students who are struggling with other subjects or are aiming for selective schools or sixth-form colleges may inquire about tutoring for other GCSEs. In this chapter, you will find guidance on GCSE English and Maths, as well as History, Geography, and core/triple Science.

These are by no means the only other GCSEs that people want tutors for – that list includes computing, languages, astronomy, child development, and more – but this chapter should cover enough subjects to give you a good idea of how to adapt the assessments, lesson techniques, and planning to suit any student in a subject you are able to tutor.

GCSE English

GCSE English is split into two qualifications, English Literature and English Language. Each GCSE is composed of two papers, Paper 1 and Paper 2, each of which tests a different set of skills with a variety of questions. As a tutor, you will need to be familiar with the exam board the student is studying for so that you know which papers and questions they will need to answer.

All UK students have to take GCSE English Literature and GCSE English Language and are expected to get at least a level 4 (equivalent to a C grade) or above in order to pass the courses. Most Pupil Premium tutoring is looking to help students achieve a passing grade, while many private students are seeking tutoring to help them to get a level 8 or 9 to get onto sixth-form courses or into selective schools.

Regardless of exam board, all students will need to practise these skills:

- **Reading comprehension** – reading for key information; inferring additional details; having a confident grasp of themes, plot, and language devices

- **Extended writing** – learning to write fluently and confidently, for a range of purposes including essays, speeches, and arguments

- **Analytical skills** – selecting relevant quotations; identifying devices/techniques; explaining authorial intent and effect on the reader

- **Creative writing skills** – learning to write fluently and confidently with a range of literary devices and an imaginative grasp of syntax, grammar, formatting, and paragraphing

A more detailed breakdown of each can be found in the Assessment Objectives (AOs) that exam boards use to mark the papers – these are the same for all exam boards, and you can find all of the details you'll need on their websites. These

AOs, numbered 1–5, divide these generic skills into specific expectations for each answer in each exam paper. As a rule, it's best not to rely on AOs in lessons, as you are not receiving the same training on them as a teacher or examiner would and some students won't be familiar with them, but they can be a helpful resource when marking students' work to give feedback.

Once you know which exam board a student is studying for, it is best to start by familiarising yourself with the specification for their exams on the websites of the exam boards, as well as with the past papers and sample answers that they provide. You should always find this information first, as well as refreshing your memory of it whenever they announce changes, as it is crucial that your student receive accurate information from you that doesn't clash with what they're being taught in school.

The exam board specification will give you an up-to-date list of the papers and types of questions that the student will have to answer, as well as the list of texts they will be using in their GCSE English Literature preparation.

If you're only tutoring English Language, you won't need to work on any set texts, but in English Literature, the set texts are a core part of the course. Because there are several different set texts within each exam board and schools can pick any combination of them, you may not be familiar with some of the texts that students ask you to cover with them. You may only be familiar with the texts you studied in school yourself, in which case you'll need to be clear with students and parents which texts you feel qualified to tutor. If you've done further English study, you may feel confident tutoring a whole range of texts, but it is always worth looking at GCSE-level resources for whichever texts you're asked to tutor to make sure that you keep your lessons at an appropriate academic level.

The advantage of tutoring English at GCSE level is that most students will know which texts they are going to be relying on in the exam, so you can make your lessons specific to their school's exam board and text selection. All exam boards require at least a Shakespeare play, two prose texts, and a poetry anthology, and more details of the most common exam boards and their requirements can be found in the 'GCSE English' chapter (pages 155–174).

GCSE Maths

All UK students have to take GCSE Maths and are expected to get at least a level 4 (equivalent to a C grade) or above in order to pass the course. Some students may also be taking GCSE Further Maths, and, while I won't be covering that course in this chapter, many of these techniques can also be used to support them with that advanced material.

All GCSE Maths courses are composed of three papers, each of which tests a different set of skills with a variety of questions. Each paper may be calculator or non-calculator, with the usual format of the early questions of each paper being easier and the final questions more difficult. Exam boards also offer a Foundation and Higher tier, with additional topics for Higher students – the topics are distributed between the tiers by Ofqual and are the same for all exam boards. Foundation students can achieve a maximum of a level 5, and Higher students can achieve levels 3–9. As a tutor, you will need to be familiar with the exam board the student is studying for so that you know which papers and questions they will need to answer and therefore which topics to cover.

In addition to these skills, GCSE Maths students are also expected to cover a set of basic subject content. This content is fairly prescriptive depending on which exam board the student is studying for, with some more similar than others. Also, students studying for Higher papers will have additional topics to the Foundation papers, and there is some variation between the topics included in the papers of different exam boards. Finally, these exams have undergone several specification changes in the last few years, so I would go directly to the websites of the exam board to establish the core content that your student will need to cover.

Moreover, their exam board specification will give you an up-to-date list of the papers and types of questions for their particular GCSE Maths course, as well as links to their official resources.

GCSE History and Geography

Each exam board specification contains a list of the topics that schools can choose from, but each school will have chosen a slightly different combination and teach them on their own schedule.

The first step to working with a GCSE History or Geography student is to find out which exam board they're studying for and which topics their school has chosen.

Because of all of the potential variations in topic and content, I can't offer the same consolidation of key skills and topics as I do in other subjects in this book. Instead, I would suggest tutors do the following to establish what they are able to tutor and what the student will need from them:

- **Only tutor students who are doing the same exam board and topics as you did or are doing an exam board and topics you know well.** Even if you have studied or are studying History or Geography at university, the range of topics is huge and the format changes from board to board, so you shouldn't run the risk of offering incorrect or limited information in your lessons. Only agree to tutor students whose exam paper formats you know well and whose topics you have previously studied.

- **Find out which exam board, topics, and exact specification they are studying for before you begin tutoring them**. Some students may not know all of this information off the top of their head, so you can ask them to show you their textbooks or to ask their teacher for the answers to these questions before you start. This ensures that you know exactly what is expected of you and where to find the resources you need and that you are familiar with the style of paper and marking they will need help with. Their exam board specification will give you an up-to-date list of the papers and types of questions, as well as information on each of the topics the student will need to study for GCSE History or Geography.

- **All subjects have their AOs set by Ofqual, which are the same for every exam board, so you can check those as well**. Every student will need to know the basic skills set out by Ofqual for each of their qualifications, and they can be found in the Assessment Objectives which exam boards use to mark the papers – in all of their specifications as well as on the Ofqual section of the UK government's website. While these can be unhelpfully vague, they are a point of consistency across the subjects and can be helpful when marking, though you should not rely on them in lesson, as you will not receive the same training on them as a teacher would.

Once you know which exam board a student is studying for, it is best to start by familiarising yourself with the specification for their exams on the websites of the exam boards, as well as with the past papers and sample answers that they provide.

Their exam board specification will give you an up-to-date list of the papers and types of questions, as well as the list of case studies they will need to learn.

GCSE Sciences

GCSE Science, in this book, is used as an umbrella term for the many ways that Science is assessed at GCSE. It can be delivered either as a single subject, as in one of the three Science qualifications individually, or as a 'Core' subject which combines all three into one; as a double or combined Science qualification, which covers some of each; or as three subjects, in the Triple or Separate Science GCSEs of Biology, Chemistry, and Physics.

Once you know their exam board, you use their website to find the specification for their exams, which will contain a detailed list of the topics they will need to cover for their Science qualifications. You must make sure that you know exactly which qualification(s) the student is studying for, so if they are not sure, you can ask them to ask their parent or teacher or to show you their textbooks. Once you have the correct specification, you can use the headings on their lists to find resources for each topic that you will need to tutor.

Tutoring at KS5 (A-level)

A-level tutoring is much less common but may be sought by students aiming for exclusive universities. In this chapter, you will find guidance on GCSE English and Maths, as well as History, Geography, and Core/Triple Science.

English

I will not be covering A-level English Language, which is largely a linguistics-based course and not offered by as many schools, or the combined A-level English Literature and Language. However, you can still use much of this chapter as a template to tutor those qualifications when combined with the abundance of resources available for them online.

A-level English is a desirable A-level subject and one which many pursue as part of a university application. It is also a significant step up from the demands of the English GCSEs in terms of the format of the exam papers and the style of writing, which can lead students to seek tutoring to support them in both the early and later stages of the course.

Now, there are a number of generic key skills which tutors should be covering with A-level English Literature students. Regardless of which exam board they are studying for, they will need to understand and have a confident grasp of each of these areas of the subject.

These include:

- **Close reading** – reading and interrogating the text through a range of lenses; recognising the significance of linguistic, contextual and structural factors; judiciously selecting quotations, themes, and other evidence to use in essays

- **Extended writing** – writing full essay answers confidently and cohesively; developing and maintaining comprehensive arguments; incorporating a range of evidence and analysis

- **Analytical skills** – confident and precise textual analysis applied to texts of all kinds; identifying structure and language features accurately and commenting on them in detail

- **SPAG and fluency** – consistently correct spelling, punctuation, and grammar; employing a variety of complex terminology precisely and with purpose

Every single student will need to know these skills, and they can be found in the Assessment Objectives which exam boards use to mark the papers – these are the same for all exam boards, and you can find all of the details you'll need on their websites. These AOs, numbered 1–5, divide these generic skills into specific expectations for each answer in each exam paper. As a rule, it's best not to rely on AOs in lessons, as you are not receiving the same training on them as a teacher or examiner would and some students won't be familiar with them, but they can be a helpful resource when marking students' work to give feedback.

Once you know which exam board a student is studying for, it is best to start by familiarising yourself with the specification for their exams on the websites of the exam boards, as well as with the past papers and sample answers that they provide.

Their exam board specification will give you an up-to-date list of the papers and types of questions, as well as the list of texts they will be using for A-level English Literature.

The advantage of tutoring A-level English Literature is that all students should know which texts they are studying, so you can make your lessons specific to their school's exam board and text selection. All exam boards require at least a Shakespeare play, a poetry anthology, a modern drama, and a modern prose text, and more details of the most common exam boards and their requirements can be found at the end of this chapter.

Maths

With the exception of WJEC, which has four units, A-level Maths is usually a 2-year course with three exams at the end. Every course covers Pure Mathematics, Statistics, and Mechanics, but each exam board splits the content over the exams slightly differently.

The key skills include:

- **Fluent arithmetic** – confidence in all areas of basic and advanced Maths; understanding and precise use of mathematical terminology; able to work with a variety of expressions, equations, and representations

- **Mathematical reasoning** – interpreting the demands of a question in relation to their own skills and understanding; able to construct mathematical arguments about patterns and relationships using algebra and other tools

- **Problem solving** – making connections between different areas of Maths; working through complex multi-step questions with confidence and accuracy

In addition to these skills, A-level Maths students are also expected to cover a set of basic subject content. This content is fairly prescriptive depending on which exam board the student is studying for, with some more similar than others. They have also undergone several specification changes in the last few years, so I would go directly to the websites of the exam board to establish the core content that your student will need to cover.

Moreover, their exam board specification will give you an up-to-date list of the papers and types of questions for their particular A-level Maths course, as links to their official resources.

A-level History and Geography

Each exam board specification contains a list of the topics that schools can choose from, but each school will have chosen a slightly different combination and teach them on their own schedule.

The first step to working with an A-level History or Geography student is to find out which exam board they're studying for and which topics their school has chosen.

Because of all of the potential variations in topic and content, I can't offer the same consolidation of key skills and topics as I do in other subjects in this book. Instead, I would suggest tutors do the following to establish what they are able to tutor and what the student will need from them:

- **Only tutor students who are doing the same exam board and topics as you did or are doing an exam board and topics you know well**. Even if you have studied or are studying History or Geography at university, the range of topics is huge and the format changes from board to board, so you shouldn't run the risk of offering incorrect or limited information in your lessons. Only agree to tutor students whose exam paper formats you know well and whose topics you have previously studied.

- **Find out which exam board, topics, and exact specification they are studying for before you begin tutoring them**. Some students may not know all of this information off the top of their head, so you can ask them to show you their textbooks or to ask their teacher for the answers to these questions before you start. This ensures that you know exactly what is expected of you and where to find the resources you need and that you are familiar with the style of paper and marking they will need help with. Their exam board specification will give you an up-to-date list of the papers and types of questions, as well as information on each of the topics the student will need to study for A-level History.

- **All subjects have their AOs set by Ofqual, which are the same for every exam board, or Geography so you can check those as well**. Every student will need to know the basic skills set out by Ofqual for each of their qualifications, and they can be found in the Assessment Objectives which exam boards use to mark the papers – in all their specifications as well as on the Ofqual section of the UK government's website. While these are unhelpfully vague in a subject like History, they are a point of consistency across the subject and can be helpful when marking, though you should not rely on them in lessons, as you will not receive the same training on them as a teacher would.

A-level Science

A-level Science is taken here to mean the three Sciences courses offered by all major exam boards, which are Biology, Chemistry, and Physics. If the student is requesting tutoring in more than one subject, it is up to you, and the preference of the student, whether you teach all three subjects in each lesson, whether you teach a different subject each week, or whether you do a chunk of lessons on one subject before moving onto the next.

Once you know their exam board, you can use their website to find the specification for their exams, which will contain a detailed list of the topics they will need to cover for their Science qualifications. You must make sure that you know exactly which qualification(s) the student is studying for, so if they are not sure, you can ask them to ask their parent or teacher or to show you their textbooks. Once you have the correct specification, you can use the headings on their lists to find resources for each topic that you will need to tutor.

Tutoring EFL

This is perhaps the most popular kind of tutoring for adults and non-UK students: English as a Foreign or Second Language (EFL/ESL).

The first thing to note is that the difference between tutoring English qualifications with native English-speaking students and with non-native speakers is slight but significant, so this chapter will cover the key skills that tutors who want to start working with EFL students will need.

The second thing to note is that people can be learning English for lots of different reasons: some are students looking to get an English qualification so they can apply to UK universities, some are adults who are looking to move to the UK or US for a job, some are young children whose parents want them to grow up bi- or tri-lingual, and some are learning English at a UK school and are struggling to keep up. What you will notice is that most EFL students fall into two categories: people learning English for a specific qualification and people learning English for more general reasons. This chapter explores techniques that will work for both categories.

The final thing that you should know if you want to become an EFL specialist tutor is that, just like all other kinds of tutoring, you don't need a qualification to get started.

However, before you start tutoring EFL, I would highly recommend investing in a Teaching English as a Foreign Language (TEFL) qualification. There are several reasons for this:

- **The way English as a subject is taught to native speakers in UK schools has a minimal focus on the technicalities of English grammar and vocabulary, because we learn them colloquially growing up, so it can be challenging to teach someone English verb tenses when you don't fully understand their names and conjugations yourself.** Students can sometimes ask difficult questions about why something is formed a particular way or why you can say something one way but not another, and saying, 'I don't know, it just does,' only leads to more confusion! All TEFL qualifications will give you a solid grounding in English grammar and supporting resources which will help you answer all of your students' questions and prevent you from accidentally teaching them something inaccurate.

- **TEFL qualifications are affordable and easy and can be completed as online or correspondence courses so they are very accessible.** You don't need to worry about travelling to a college or working with students in person if you've never done that before, and many courses now offer an 'online teaching'–specific TEFL qualification that was designed with online tutors in mind.

- **They give you options if you decide to pursue a career in teaching through a Postgraduate Certificate/Diploma in Education (PGCE/PGDE), an in-person tutoring job, or a teaching job abroad.** TEFL qualifications are valid across the world, with an international certification organisation that allows you to teach English anywhere in the world. They can be used as concrete evidence of what you have learned as a tutor and demonstrate your interest and experience in the role, which can be helpful when applying for agency tutoring or other education-based jobs.

Be aware: there isn't a standardised TEFL qualification, which can make the process of choosing one a little confusing, but there are lots of comparison websites that can show you all of the internationally certified options and prices. Once you've completed your qualification, you receive a certificate and registration number that you can use to secure an in-person TEFL job if you ever want to teach and travel. If you are interested in doing a TEFL qualification, there is more information in the Resources section at the end of this book.

I did my qualification through TEFL.org, which I would highly recommend, but there are other options such as The TEFL Academy, i-to-i, and TEFL UK.

Tutoring for EFL qualifications

The first step to working with an EFL student is to find out which exam board they're studying for and whether they're studying for an English as a First Language qualification, English as a Second Language qualification, or another type of qualification, like an English proficiency test. The most common qualifications are iGCSEs and IELTS/TOEFL, as these are often required for UK university applications, but there are many others, so this should be established as soon as possible. Ideally, you will want to find out the exam board and the qualification code so you know exactly which exam they are studying for, because many of them have the same title or name.

Across all exam boards, the key skills include:

- **Basic language skills** – reading, writing, listening, and speaking in English, with largely correct punctuation, grammar, and spelling

- **Reading comprehension** – reading for key information; inferring additional details and having a confident grasp of themes, plot, and language devices

- **Extended writing** – learning to write fluently and confidently, for a range of purposes including essays, speeches, and arguments

- **Analytical skills** – selecting relevant quotations; identifying devices/techniques; explaining authorial intent and effect on the reader

- **Creative writing skills** – learning to write fluently and confidently with a range of literary devices and an imaginative grasp of syntax, grammar, formatting, and paragraphing

Once you know which exam board a student is studying for, it is best to start by familiarising yourself with the specification for their exams on the websites of the exam boards, as well as with the past papers and sample answers that they provide. You should always find this information first, as well as refreshing your memory of it whenever they announce changes, as it is crucial that your student receive accurate information from you, and some of the recent changes to paper formats have been significant.

The exam board specification will give you an up-to-date list of the papers and types of questions that the student will have to answer.

General EFL tutoring

Tutoring English as a foreign language more generally can be both fun and challenging for tutors – there's no specification to work from, so you will need to develop a curriculum of content in conjunction with the student to ensure that you cover everything they want to learn.

There are some generally recognised categories of EFL that can be useful to use both in your discussion with your student and when you are searching for resources online. These aren't standardised terms but are useful descriptors of the kinds of learners you might come across as an EFL tutor.

These include:

- **General English** – this describes the general English ability that most students are seeking: confidence in reading, writing, speaking, and listening to English, with an understanding of grammar and punctuation and a wide vocabulary. What this looks like in specific cases will vary, with some tutors working off their own experience of learning English, some making their own curriculum and some working from the many courses or texts that have been published on this subject. Whatever you use, you will need to discuss with the student what they want to learn, what they already know, what their strengths and weaknesses are, and what their goals are for the lessons. Once you know what they want out of your sessions together, you can create some goals and aims for the future and use these to check their progress over time.

- **Business English** – this descriptor refers to a specific set of skills, grammar, and vocabulary that is typically sought by young professionals. Depending on the industry they work in or want to work in, you may need adapt your curriculum. For example, if they want to work in marketing or sales, they will need to be confident speaking on the telephone and using formal English in letter and email formats and learn a set of vocabulary related to office environments, sales calls, and so on. You can discuss with the student what they want to be confident speaking and writing about and what they think their priorities as an English learner are, on top of the general English tutoring you will give them.

- **Young learners** – this term refers to English tutoring with children and teenagers which isn't part of a qualification. This more casual support is sometimes sought by schools to help children of non-native English speakers or by parents who want to give their young children some support outside of school hours. You will need to discuss with the parents what their expectations are of the sessions, what they think their child needs to learn, and any areas of focus (reading, speaking, fluency, etc.). Several of the young learners I have worked with were being given tutoring because they usually spoke their native language at home and their parents didn't want their English to become rusty during school holidays.

TOP TIP

Make sure you understand as much as possible about what you will be expected to tutor before you start with a new student. That way, you can be sure that you are able to tutor it properly, and you can prepare your lessons in advance. Don't be afraid to discuss new aims or goals once you have been tutoring that student for a while, as they may change over time.

QUESTION

Which ages/subjects/qualifications are you going to specialise in?

Chapter 6

What does the student need?

This chapter will cover all of the basic principles of starting with a new student, from gathering the important information to checking their progress.

Congratulations – a new student! Once you've got all the logistics of when and how you'll tutor them out of the way, there are 5 steps you will need to follow. In this chapter, you'll find Steps 1 and 2:

1. Gather the important information

2. Assess their current level

1: Gather the important information

In the previous chapter, you can find all the information about your student's age group, school year or qualification, and subject.

Remember, the first questions you will need ask are:

- What subject do they want help with?

- What year and Key Stage are they in (if relevant)?

- What qualification are they taking (if relevant)?

Once you know these answers, you can work out what other details you will need. In the following flow chart, you can find the additional questions you will need to ask. Some of the questions, immediately underneath the Key Stage or qualification heading, apply to any student in that category, while the rest are subject specific.

    DOI: 10.4324/9781003211648-8

ADDITIONAL QUESTIONS

KS2

- Are they studying for the SATs yet?
- Will they be taking the 11+ as well?
  - English
    - Is English their first language?
  - Maths
    - Do they know all of their times tables?
    - Do they struggle more with mental or written Maths?

11+

- Which school are they applying for?
- Does that school have an English section in its 11+?
- Which exam board does that school use? Do they make their own examination?
- Have they studied VR/NVR yet?

KS3

- What are the key issues?
- What exam board does the school use for that subject?
  - English
    - What texts are they studying?
  - Maths
    - Will they want to take GCSE Further Maths?
  - History
    - What topics are they studying?

How to tutor

- ○ Geography

    - ■ What topics are they studying?

- ○ Sciences

GCSE

- Which exam board does the school use for that subject?

- What year are they in?

    - ○ English

        - ■ Do they need help with English Literature, English Language, both, or the combined course?

    - ○ Maths

        - ■ Are they taking Foundation or Higher tier papers?
        - ■ Are they also studying Further Maths? Do you want their tutoring to incorporate those topics as well?

    - ○ History

        - ■ What topics are they studying?

    - ○ Geography

        - ■ What topics are they studying?

    - ○ Sciences

        - ■ Are they doing Core ('Single') Science, Additional ('Double') Science, or Triple Science?
        - ■ Are they taking Foundation or Higher tier papers?

A-level

- Which exam board does the school use for that subject?

- What year are they in?

    - ○ English

        - ■ Do they need help with English Literature, English Language, both, or the combined course?

- Maths
  - Are they also studying Further Maths?
- History
  - What topics are they studying?
- Geography
  - What topics are they studying?
- Sciences
  - Which of the three Sciences are they studying?

EFL

- Are you studying generally or for a qualification?
  - Qualification
    - Is it an EFL qualification (i.e. iGCSE) or an English proficiency test (i.e. IELTS)?
    - Which qualification is it? Please give the qualification code if known.
  - General English
    - Do you want to learn a specific topic in English?
      - Business English?
      - Young learners?
    - What level are you currently at (i.e. beginner, intermediate, etc.)? Self-assessment is fine.

Once you have all of the specific information you need, you can also have a conversation about what the student (or parent/teacher) feels they need to focus on. You can structure this conversation as:

- What are your strengths and weaknesses in this subject?
- What are your goals for this tutoring? What would you like to achieve?
- Which topics do you find the easiest/most difficult?
- Which papers/topics are your most and least favourite?
- Using a RAG sheet or specification summary

Regardless of their age and subject, you should always ensure that the student you'll be working with has an opportunity to discuss their tutoring goals: even if they aren't able to tell you much beyond what they like and dislike about certain lesson activities, it helps the student to feel heard and engaged.

2: Assess their current level

The first few lessons with a new student should be used to assess their current working level.

The methods for English, Maths, History, Geography and Sciences in the following can used to assess students for the 11+ and in KS3, KS4, and Year 12. Information on how to assess students in KS2, Year 13, and adult learners is at the end of this section.

English

My preferred method for assessing new students and checking students' progress at almost all levels of English analysis is **the '5 step' method**. I created this assessment as a means of checking a student's ability in the key skills required by all English courses, as well as assessing students' literacy and confidence in speaking and writing, in a flexible and informal way. If the student knows which set texts they are studying, you can use one of those texts as part of the '5 step' method – otherwise, pick an age-appropriate text from the list of resources on page 349.

- **Step 1: Reading a short extract together**. This extract should be taken from an age- and ability-appropriate text. I also usually recommend using a prose text, from a novel, as this is the simplest and least intimidating structure for students to approach. The extract can be read out loud or in the student's head, depending on their age and ability. At this stage, tutors should leave the student to read by themselves but allow time afterwards for the student to ask any questions. You can prompt questions about things like key vocabulary ('What does this word mean?' 'Could you summarise what the character says for me in your own words?') or technical terms ('What is this device called?' 'What type of word is X?') if you want to check that the student actually understands what they have read. You can also offer some contextual information about the extract at this point (which text it is from, who the author is, when it was written, etc.). The final part of this step is to ask for a quick, one- or two-sentence summary of the whole extract – students who struggle with this step may need to practise their reading comprehension before moving on to analysis skills.

- **Step 2: Mind-mapping/brain-storming/spider-diagramming key themes and 'big ideas'.** You should start this step by checking that the student knows what a theme is – if they don't, you can explain it in terms of the key or 'big' ideas of a text, which are usually expressed as abstract nouns (i.e. 'happiness', 'fear', etc.). You can give examples from popular YA novels, films, or TV shows. I like to use mind-maps/spider diagrams, which can be drawn freehand or using the template in the online Resources chapter, or a list of statements. Another way to reinforce this idea is using the binary opposite/pairing method, which can help students to make connections between key words in the texts and words they can use to describe themes (i.e. life vs death, hope vs despair, etc.). You should start the exercise by adding a couple of examples of themes from the extract you're using, leaving the examples and further themes up to the student. If the student is struggling to think of things to add, you can explain why you chose the examples you did and demonstrate where you got the inspiration from (i.e. the text describes the relationship between a mother and daughter, so one theme could be 'family').

- **Step 3: Selecting quotations from the text**. For this step, the student can select their own quotations to discuss, or you can choose quotations and ask them to explain their usefulness. Either way, the aim of this step is to see how judicious the student is in selecting evidence and how complex the reasoning behind their choice is. Some students may only select quotes with recognisable devices in (similes, metaphors, alliteration, etc.) while others may not know what devices look like and will opt for whatever 'looks interesting' – some may have no idea where to start! Whichever is the case, ask the student to explain their thoughts and choices and guide them with relevant vocabulary: word class, sounds, repetition, imagery, and so on. Students should aim to choose quotations which are no longer than a whole sentence and can choose single words.

- **Step 4: Analysing key quotations**. There are several ways to approach this step. It is usually best to start by going through the student's chosen quotations one by one, discussing their thoughts. Once you're happy that they understand the quotes and their usefulness, you can ask them to choose two or three to analyse in more detail. At this stage, tutors should not intervene in the student's choice – it should be entirely their decision. If they get stuck and want help, ask the student which quotes they feel they could say the most about, either about the meaning or effect.

- Once they have chosen the quotes they want to look at, you can begin to analyse them individually. This can be done as another round of mind-maps/spider diagrams; by breaking down the quotation and isolating individual words to discuss; or by discussing the different 'levels' of meaning within a quotation – the method you use should be based on the student's age, ability, and confidence with the task. Students should be encouraged to make short notes or bullet points about the key ideas for each quotation.

- **Step 5: Writing a paragraph**. This is a crucial step in the process, as it is the first time you will see what a student's analytical writing is like. Some students may have difficulty with basic literacy skills such as spelling and grammar, and some may seem initially confident in their language analysis but get lost trying to explain the effect on the reader, and so on.

  - A useful thing to check is if the student already has a preferred paragraph structure. These were and still are a common technique in UK schools, used to ensure that students hit all of the Assessment Objectives and cover the key information in exams. The most common by far is PEA or PEE (point, evidence, analyse/explain), but other structures include PEEL (point, evidence, explain, link), SEAL (state your point, evidence, analyse, link), PETAL (point, evidence, technique, analyse, link), and WET (words, effect, technique). In these instances, 'link' is understood to refer to both 'linking' the paragraphs together and 'linking' back to the words of the question. However, some schools and exam boards are now transitioning towards the more flexible 'What, How, Why' paragraph structure, which encourages students to write less formulaically.

  - Whichever paragraph structure the student is familiar with, you should support the student to write in that structure. It is important that tutors be familiar with as many of these different paragraph structures and techniques as possible, because you need to be able to support the student's existing understanding. You want to avoid, where possible, contradicting their teacher's methods.

  - The advantages of this method of initial assessment are that the tutor is present throughout, meaning that the student can ask any questions directly and you can get a better understanding of any of their weaknesses or sticking points and that the '5 steps' cover all of the key skills for this level and subject – ensuring that future lessons are relevant, ability appropriate, and tailored to the student.

Maths

My preferred method for assessing new students and checking students' progress in Maths is what I call the 'foundation' method. I created this assessment as a means of checking a student's ability in the topics required by most Maths courses in a format that doesn't resemble an exam paper and leaves room for tutors to pick up on the areas most in need of improvement.

- **Step 1: Pick a foundational topic**. By foundational topic, I mean an area of the curriculum that would need to be taught first so that other topics can be built on top of it. Year 9 and 10 students should already be familiar with the KS3 curriculum, which covers much of the basics of the GCSE course, so try to pick a topic which is covered in both courses – there is a list of suggestions at the end of this section. This is useful for several reasons: it is likely that the student will already be a little familiar with it, which will help them to feel confident in their first lesson, and it means there are lots of different layers of difficulty in that topic that you can work through.

- **Step 2: Work through an example question.** Choose a simple example question that uses the foundational topic you've chosen. This doesn't mean that you should just do the question for them – instead, explain what kind of question it is and what you are going to do first, and then ask questions to see if they can lead you through the steps of the example. By doing this, the student can recall the process required to find the answer, without having to worry about working it out themselves yet. If it becomes clear that they have no idea what to do with the question, you can start working on that topic right there and then, but if they take the lead and seem confident on what to do, you can then move on to the next step.

- **Step 3: Set them a question to do themselves.** Once the student has watched you complete an example, you should then set a question for them to do independently. Make it clear that they can ask as many questions as they want and offer hints if needed. That said, try not to offer any actual answers or explain the method unless they explicitly ask you to. The question shouldn't be significantly more difficult than your example, and try to avoid using example questions that are taken directly from an exam paper.

- **Step 4: Increase the difficulty until they get stuck**. Each time a student easily completes a question, you can then offer them a more difficult question until they eventually need significant help or cannot complete the question. They should then give you an idea of their general level in that key skill, as well offering the opportunity to introduce questions on that foundational topic that use other skills from all the topics on the curriculum. If a student completes all the questions you had prepared easily, you can either switch the topic to a more difficult one that is connected to the original topic, or you can offer them some questions without any support to make sure that they can complete them independently.

- **Step 5: Make a note of the topic and level they got to.** Depending on the difficulty they got to, it should be clear whether the student needs more help in this area or is confident on the topic and can move on to another. As many of the topics in Maths are connected or use similar skills, this should help you to understand their general level, but you can also repeat this assessment with other foundational topics in the same lesson or subsequent lessons to build a clearer picture of their general Maths level.

Feel free to choose whatever foundational topic feels most appropriate to you – sometimes you might need to use a topic that is given to you by the student's parent or teacher, but you can still use this assessment method.

Your initial assessment may only cover a single topic, so if you have the time, you may want to spend a few lessons getting to know the student by working through several foundational topics until you have a holistic sense of their current math level.

If you don't have the time to go through all the topics you would like to with a student, I would recommend starting with the one you consider the most fundamental to the course and combine the previous assessment with another assessment method.

Foundation topics for each age group/Key Stage could include:

KS2/11+

- **(Year 3 and 4) Fractions, decimals, and percentages** – identifying basic fractions, visually and in number form, could move into equivalence and ordering, decimal places and rounding, simple percentages, conversions, and so on.

- **(Year 5 and 6) Algebra** – simple formulae could move into sequences, simple missing number problems, solving simple equations, and so on.

- **(Any year) Geometry** – identifying basic shapes could move into the properties of shapes, 2D and 3D shapes, nets, angles, lines, symmetry and movement, missing angle/length problems, and so on.

KS3

- **Fractions, decimals, and percentages** – basic operations could move into conversion, order of operations, prime factorisation, and so on.

- **Triangles** – types of triangle could move into Pythagoras, basic trigonometry, right-angled triangles and ratios, and so on.

- **Fractions, percentages, and decimals** – basic fractions could move into conversion between the three, basic operations, rounding and estimating, standard form, and so on.

KS4 – GCSE

- **Algebra** – basic algebra could move into equations, co-ordinates and graphs, problem solving with shapes, and so on.

- **Shape** – perimeter and area of rectangles could move into triangles and Pythagoras, perimeter and area of complex shapes, problem solving with perimeter and area, and so on.

- **Triangles** – types of triangle could move into Pythagoras, trigonometry, right-angled triangles and ratios, symmetry and translations, and so on.

- **Fractions, percentages, and decimals** – basic fractions could move into conversion between the three, basic operations, rounding and estimating, standard form, and so on.

A-level

- **Algebra** – indices and surds could move into quadratic equations, simultaneous equations, inequalities, graphs of functions, and so on.

- **Trigonometry** – area of a triangle and a recap of sine, cosine, and tangent could move into key formulae, trigonometric equations, and so on.

- **Differentiation** – a recap of key symbols and basic concepts could move into topics like sketching graphs; finding gradients, tangents, and normal; differentiation using product or chain rules; basic integration; and so on.

11+

For the 11+, you can assess students using the same methods as you would for KS2 English and Maths.

While I would generally not advise using exam papers straight away with most subjects/students, because of the nature of the Verbal Reasoning and Non-Verbal Reasoning topics, you will need to use exam-style materials.

You will need to find as many online worksheets and resources as you can before you begin assessing your student in VR and NVR to ensure that you use materials they have not already seen.

It is unlikely that younger students, aged 8 to 9, will have been practising VR and NVR, even if they are starting to prepare for English/Maths, so you may need to start teaching these subjects from scratch. You may find that, once you have assessed their English and Maths, you have a good idea of their general working level and may not need to assess for these skills specifically. However, if you do decide to, you can use a small set of simple questions and make a note of which skills they find most difficult.

With older students, aged 10 to 11, you can start by discussing VR and NVR with them and find out how much they have seen and practised previously. You can then assess them using exam-style materials, working through each of the topics using collated papers of different question styles. It should quickly become clear which they are confident on and which they will need more help with.

History

You are looking for them to be able to draw connections, comparisons, and conclusions in the topics they are studying, as well as using a range of own knowledge.

If you are working with a student who is being home-schooled and you are going to begin tutoring them in History, you may find it easier to assess their general writing ability with an English assessment and then use a mind map–style exercise to ascertain a sense of their historical knowledge of the period you want to teach first.

To assess a student in History, you can use the following methods:

- **KS2 – Years 3 and 4** – a short quiz on the topic they are studying and then either multiple-choice questions or short answer questions to complete independently

- **KS2 – Years 5 and 6** – a short quiz on the topic they are studying and then a worksheet with reading comprehension and some basic inference questions

- **KS3 – Year 7/8/9** – a RAG sheet, a short quiz or mind map–style exercise on the topic they are studying and then either a worksheet or a long answer question

- **GCSE – Year 10** – a RAG sheet, a short quiz or mind map–style exercise on each of their topics, then look at an individual long answer question from each of their papers to see how they would go about planning and writing their answer. If they have covered source analysis already, you can offer them a question of that style as well

- **A-level – Year 12** – same as Year 10

Geography

You are looking for them to be able to identify trends and links and articulate their conclusions in the topics they are studying, as well as using a range of own knowledge.

If you are working with a student who is being home-schooled and you are going to begin tutoring them in Geography, you may find it easier to assess their general writing ability with an English assessment and then use a mind map–style exercise to ascertain a sense of their geographical knowledge of the topic you want to teach first.

To assess a student in Geography, you can use the following methods:

- **KS2 – Years 3 and 4** – a short quiz on the topic they are studying and then either multiple-choice questions or short answer questions to complete independently

- **KS2 – Years 5 and 6** – a short quiz on the topic they are studying and then a worksheet with reading comprehension and some basic inference questions

- **KS3 – Year 7/8/9** – a RAG sheet, short quiz, or mind map–style exercise to establish what they know about each of their topics and then either a worksheet or a long answer question

- **GCSE – Year 10** – a RAG sheet, short quiz or mind map–style exercise on each of their topics, then look at an individual long answer question from each of their papers to see how they would go about planning and writing their answer. If they have covered source analysis or case studies in school, you can offer them a question of that style as well – if not, then you can explore source analysis in a later lesson

- **A-level – Year 12** – same as Year 10

Sciences

In Science, much like History and Geography, there are two key elements to test – their knowledge and their analytical skills.

If you are working with a student who is being home-schooled and you are going to begin tutoring them in Science, you may find it easier to assess their general writing ability with an English assessment and then use a mind map–style exercise to ascertain a sense of their knowledge of the topic you want to teach first.

To assess a student in one or all of the Sciences, you can use the following methods:

- **KS2 – Years 3 and 4** – a short quiz on the topic they are studying and then either multiple-choice questions or short answer questions to complete independently

- **KS2 – Years 5 and 6** – a short quiz on the topic they are studying and then a worksheet with reading comprehension and some basic inference questions

- **KS3 – Year 7 and 8** – a RAG sheet or short quiz on the topic they are studying and then either a worksheet or a long answer question from a topic they marked as a 'Green'

- **KS3 – Year 9** – a RAG sheet or short quiz on the topic they are studying and then a partial exam-style paper

- **GCSE – Year 10** – a RAG sheet, short quiz, or mind map–style exercise on each of their topics, then look at an individual long answer question from each of their papers to see how they would go about planning and writing their answer

- **A-level – Year 12** – a RAG sheet and a partial or compilation paper (a sample paper made up with questions from all of the topics in that subject)

For GCSE/A-level students or those whose schools teach differentiated Science lessons, you will need to repeat this assessment in each of the Science subjects – Biology, Chemistry, Physics – that they are studying.

Alternatively, with students who have only just begun their courses or students who are really struggling, you may find it easier to do a general Science quiz or RAG sheet on the whole range of topics and then ask them to work through a short compilation paper to see which question styles they are least familiar with.

EFL

For EFL students who are following a qualification or proficiency test, you can use the methods of assessment for English outlined previously. With older students and adult learners, you can go straight to using past papers if you want.

With all non-qualification EFL students, I like to start with an all-round assessment: one that gives me the opportunity to assess their reading, writing, speaking, and listening.

I usually use the following format, in these three sections:

1. **A written language test**, with sections on spelling, vocabulary, grammar, and punctuation. You can either create your own or find one online – there are lots of free and paid resources to choose from, with recommendations at the end of this chapter.

2. **A reading comprehension test**, with a short extract to read and a range of short and long answer questions. Similarly, you can make your own using an extract from a text and a series of basic comprehension and inference questions or find one online.

3. **A short discussion**, 5–10 minutes where the student will need to talk without receiving any prompts or using any resources, with a series of questions to structure the conversation around a common topic, like holidays or food. These questions should be simple and open ended.

The first two components can be completed before or during the first lesson, depending on the student's preferences. If they are not confident in their English ability, you may want to do the assessment in the lesson so you can answer questions and make notes on areas of difficulty.

All the components should be conducted in an informal manner, to reassure the student and create a comfortable environment for them to perform.

ASSESSING YOUNGER STUDENTS

Some of these assessment methods will be too demanding for young students at KS2 or below.

With these students, in any subject, you can use any combination of:

- **Speaking to the parent and getting their most recent school assessed level**. Depending on a student's age and experience, they may already be very familiar with in-class assessments, or they may have never been formally assessed. However, there are some limitations to this method: some parents may not have this information or may not want to share it, and some students may be learning within a non-standard school framework that uses an assessment format that you are not familiar with. Either way, it is always worth asking if a parent has this information.

- **Offering a simple in-lesson assessment**. There are a number of pre-existing workbook or worksheet compilations, available both online and in print, or you can devise your own assessment using basic, age-appropriate materials. There should be a section each on reading, writing, spelling, punctuation, and grammar, which can either be marked outside of the lesson or as part of the student's completion of the assessment. With KS2 students, this assessment should be as informal as possible to avoid confusing or intimidating students.

- **Starting from a simple topic and working through it until you can see where they are getting stuck**. If you don't feel confident that your assessment has given you the information you need, or you had trouble getting the student to complete it, then another option is to just pick a topic to get started on that you think they'll be able to manage and then work your way up through more difficult tasks until they are clearly struggling.

- **Having a conversation with the student about what they've worked on or read recently and using that as a starting point**. If your student is very articulate, they may want to tell you a bit about what they've done in school recently and what they found easier or more difficult, which can be a helpful guide to what they might need help with or want to look at next. This method isn't suited to every student, but for students who can be clear about their strengths and weaknesses, it's a good way to see where to start and will make the student feel heard and respected.

- **Picking an age-appropriate book and devising a series of exercises from it.** From a single book, you can do a variety of reading exercises, comprehension questions, creative writing prompts, spelling and grammar exercises, inference questions, mind maps, and more! Some parents ask for reading recommendations for their child, so this can be a great way to introduce more reading to reluctant students. It is also a useful method of assessment which is creative and, hopefully, fun for the student.

ASSESSING YEAR 13 AND ADULT LEARNERS

These students are usually seeking tutoring themselves rather than their parents arranging it for them, so they should have a good idea about what they want to focus on or what they are worried about. That said, it is still important to get some kind of assessment of their current level in your first lessons together, so you can see how accurately they have interpreted their own level and what they may have missed.

- **If they can confidently tell you all of the details of their exam and can tell you which topics they have looked at and what they would like to work on next,** then start with a full past paper or compilation practice paper, taking a question or two from each area of the exam, and set them to complete it before or during your first lesson together. You can tell them to leave any topics they haven't started yet and ask them to add any notes about areas of the course they know well or want help with.

- **If they can't,** then use the methods as outlined previously in each subject section for Year 12s. After two or three lessons working through foundational topics, you should be able to plan lessons on a range of topics with an understanding of their level.

Generic assessment methods

There are also a few assessment methods you can use with any student in any subject at your discretion. You may wish to combine one or more of these methods with the subject- and age-specific methods outlined previously to get a more concrete understanding of your student's ability.

Any subject

- Discussing the student's most recent in-school assessment results if available from their parent or teacher

- Having a discussion with the student about which topics they feel are their strongest and which are their weakest

- Working through a RAG sheet of all the essential topics and of the key skills, content, and vocabulary

- Setting them a worksheet or compilation paper to complete independently

Maths/Geography/Sciences, etc.

- Creating a collated paper of questions from a range of difficulties and topics to go through in your first lesson together – there are a number of websites that can help you do this in the Resources section

- Picking a single example question and encouraging the student to lead you through the process of solving/answering it

English/History

- Setting a short writing homework to answer an essay-style question or a set of short and long exam-style questions to be handed in before the first lesson

- Using a supported writing framework for the student to write a longer response (see 'Resources' for template)

- Setting an essay question and asking them to write a detailed bullet-point plan if they don't have time to write a full essay answer

- Asking the student to identify the text/texts they are least confident about and why to use in your early lessons together

- Asking the student to annotate a short poem or extract, either one from their syllabus if you know it or one you have chosen if not

TOP TIP

While some parents will want you to skip straight to lesson content, you should always make time for an initial assessment. It will make your life so much easier when it comes to planning lessons! If students won't complete it before lessons begin, you may need to spend the first lesson or two on it.

QUESTION

Which assessment techniques will you use with your students?

Chapter 7

How do I plan and deliver a lesson?

This chapter will cover all of the basic principles of starting with a new student, from gathering the important information to checking their progress.

Once you've got all the logistics of what and how you'll tutor your new student out of the way, there are three more steps you will need to follow. In this chapter, you'll find Steps 3, 4, and 5:

3. Learn how to plan lessons

4. Learn some basic lesson techniques

5. Check on their progress

3. Learn how to plan lessons

Once you have assessed the student's ability and understanding, you can then decide how and what to teach in the next few lessons.

As discussed in the 'time management' section, most tutoring lessons are around 50 minutes to an hour, so planning enough content to make efficient use of your time with each student is important.

Usually, my lessons look like this:

Lesson stage	Activity	Timing
Starter: getting the student ready to learn or recapping knowledge from homework or previous lesson	You can use this time to check up on ongoing memorisation learning, to mark homework, or to recap key information from the previous lesson.	0–10 minutes

(Continued)

DOI: 10.4324/9781003211648-9

(Continued)

Lesson stage	Activity	Timing
Explanation/Demonstration: outlining what will be covered in the lesson and explaining the key learning	You should always try to involve the student in the explanation by asking them questions as a form of recall or asking them to infer what the next step might be.	10–20 minutes
Main activity: giving the student an opportunity for practice and feedback	You can use this time to work through a series of increasingly difficult small exercises or set a larger task with writing or planning time.	20–50 minutes
Plenary: ending the lesson with a recap or summary	This should be an opportunity to consolidate the learning from the lesson, discuss any questions or issues, and get some feedback from the student on how they found the lesson.	50–60 minutes
Homework: opportunity for additional writing or practice outside of the lesson	This is the student's chance to do a full written answer, to practice something they are struggling with, or to memorise some key information.	In addition to lesson time (can take up to 30–60 minutes)

This may vary, but I find that it's a useful guide for a basic lesson format. All the chapters in Section 2 contain a set of lesson techniques which are sorted under these headings, so you can easily use this format and those techniques to build simple, effective lesson plans.

It's important to remember here that tutors are not students' primary teachers, so tutoring sessions can be structured in a more flexible way than lessons that would be taught in school. At all stages, but especially KS2 and KS3, there are likely to be some skills or areas which students feel much less confident in, often because they haven't covered them in school yet. Being flexible, adapting your lesson plans on a week-to-week basis, will allow your students to guide you on what they would like to cover while also leaving space for you to recap topics you think the student needs more support with.

Some key things to remember when planning lessons:

- **Plan your lessons using a calendar or table.** I would recommend using either a series of Word documents or Google Docs, one for each student or day of lessons, or a calendar app or spreadsheet. Alternatively, you can use a program like Notion (which is free for university students and educators) or OneNote, which allows you to create and organise notes within customisable calendars. You can keep a running timetable of when the lessons are, what you'll do in each lesson, and what homework you set. Doing this digitally, in a spreadsheet or document, will allow you to change your plans if a student does particularly well in a lesson or asks to go over the same topic again, for example.

- **Always plan more work than you need to fill the hour**. It can be unsettling if your student speeds through your lesson content and you don't feel that you have enough to really challenge them, so always create a couple of extension tasks just in case they're more confident or capable at a topic than they previously thought. You can always use leftover lesson material as homework or carry it over into the next lesson's starter!

- **Don't rush through the lesson**. While you may have planned a whole hour of work, some students may need to cover the same topic or lesson several times over several weeks or have something explained or demonstrated a few times before they're confident about it. Make sure to go at the student's pace, not your own. Especially for non-exam students, building their confidence on the basics is as important, if not more so, than covering all the content.

- **Starters and plenaries are generally very useful, but don't worry if you don't have time every lesson**. Starter exercises especially can be useful to get students in the right mood and mindset to learn, but they should only last 5 or 10 minutes rather than half the lesson. Same with plenaries: they're good for summarising that day's learning and checking the student understands, but don't rush the main bulk of the lesson just to fit one in. They're a helpful tool but not a mandatory part of lessons, and you can always do the plenary activity as the next lesson's starter.

- **Use homework wisely**. Head to the 'Homework' section for more details on this, but it is worth remembering that homework can be a valuable tool for many students. Trying to fit long writing exercises or reading work into your lesson is rarely the most efficient use of lesson time, so think about opportunities to set these as preparatory or follow-up work outside of the lesson time to make the most of what you can do with the student directly.

4. Learn some basic lesson techniques

In each chapter of Section 2, you will find lots of lesson techniques that have been designed specifically for that age group and subject. However, there are also lots of fool-proof techniques that I have developed and tested that will work for just about any student! Mastering these basic lesson techniques means you will always have a set of exercises to fall back on if you need to plan a lesson in a rush or jump into a cover lesson at the last minute.

As well as the basic lesson techniques, there are a couple of other things you should know. The first thing that every tutor should remember is that there are so many resources available online! There are quite literally hundreds of websites containing thousands of extracts, worksheets, practice papers, and more, and you should absolutely use them. Over time, you will find the resources that work for you and build up a bank of materials that you can use with every new student. There are lots of resource recommendations at the end of this chapter, both free and paid. I won't spend too much time in this chapter discussing worksheets and pro-forma lesson content, because they're all fairly self-explanatory, but it is worth noting that it is absolutely fine to use premade lesson materials with your students to help you cover all of the content and find age- and exam-board–appropriate materials to use. When teaching STEM subjects like Maths and Science, worksheets will be your best friend, as much of the material you can find online will have been made by expert teachers, examiners, or content sites that takes all the stress out of planning work for your student. Indeed, you may find that you rely more heavily on worksheets and preprepared resources in subjects like Maths and Science than you might in other subjects, but that's not a problem – it's much harder to write your own resources in Maths than in, say, English or History.

You can find hundreds of resources by just typing the name of your subject, the qualification/key stage, and the word 'worksheets' into Google. You will also find past and sample assessment resources on all the exam board websites. However, some initial recommendations for resource banks are:

- Tes Resources – www.tes.com/teaching-resources

- Twinkl – www.twinkl.co.uk/

- Teachit – www.teachit.co.uk/

- Busy Teacher – https://busyteacher.org/

- Primary Resources – www.primaryresources.co.uk/

- Easy Teacher Worksheets – www.easyteacherworksheets.com/

- Education.com – www.education.com/

- Shmoop – www.shmoop.com/

Other subject-specific resource banks are linked in the online Resources chapter, Chapter 21. You can also find print and e-book resources, like textbooks or practice tests, for all ages and assessments from several educational publishers, like Collins, Letts, and CGP, all of which I would recommend.

However, this book isn't just about getting you tutoring – it's about making you the best tutor you can be. If every lesson is a long series of worksheets, students will learn some things, but they won't be tailored to all their individual needs. More importantly, you're a new tutor: you don't have that big bank of materials built up yet. This chapter should give you lots of ideas for the kinds of lesson techniques you can use now and in all your future lesson planning, so you can tutor confidently while you find your favourite materials.

The second thing to remember is that every student will have different likes and dislikes and attention spans. It's up to you to find ways to make the lessons interesting and engaging while also ensuring they get all of the important information they need. The rest of the chapter is full of tried-and-tested lesson techniques that I have used with lots of students of different ages and stages, but that doesn't mean you can just pick your favourites and use them with everyone. You'll need to think carefully about what will suit each of your students and find a balance of fun and informative. You'll notice variation according to what age they are, what their usual schooling is like, what their interests are, and what their ability is. KS2 students work best with a variety of short exercises interspersed with discussions and games. Year 7 students who are just starting out in secondary school will likely want some fun activities but also need to see a variety of texts, questions, and exercises to benefit them later in school, especially if they're not that keen on reading outside of the classroom. Year 9s, on the other hand, may already be gearing up for their GCSE courses and may want an introduction to their set texts, syllabi, and some of the more formal techniques they'll need to succeed. Year 11s and up usually need you to cut to the chase, tell them what they need to know, and give them opportunities to practise exam questions. Not every lesson and lesson technique will go perfectly, but being patient and finding the ones that work for your students will be rewarding for both you and them.

Starters

Discussion

This may sound obvious, but setting aside time to have discussions with students can be valuable, even if you feel you should simply be packing knowledge into every minute of lesson time. Discussions can help you learn more about what a student has already studied, what they like or dislike in lessons, when their next school assessment or exam is, or how they feel about your plan for the lesson. It can give them a sense of control over their learning and over the lesson environment, which in turn can help them to engage better with you and the lesson materials.

My favourite topics for discussion starters are:

- If they need lesson time for help with school homework or to revise for a test

- If they have a preference for the order of topics we look at in lessons, that is, to align with lessons or assessments at schools

- If they already know their strengths and weaknesses in a particular area or topic

- For them to RAG a set of texts or topics

- For them to give feedback on how the tutoring lessons are going

I usually schedule a discussion for the starter of our first lesson, so they have a chance to ask any questions or share any worries or nervousness, and then occasionally as a plenary once we've been working together for a while or if the student requests it.

Matching exercises

Matching exercises are a great way to start a lesson because they offer some of the information for students to grasp without having to do too much with it. Matching exercises involve showing students a set of examples and a set of definitions or labels, which they then need to match either verbally or by drawing on the online whiteboard. I like to use colour, font, or punctuation to show which items are examples and which are definitions to help distinguish them on the screen. This can also help make the exercise more accessible for students with colour-blindness or dyslexia.

personification   "as fast as the wind"

metaphor   alliteration   simile

"She laughed and laughed   "the door groaned"
and laughed"

                                    "a sea of grass"
"the cold cat coughed"

"the wand fizzed and glowed   onomatopoeia
and crackled"

repetition   triple   "the vase crashed onto
the floor"

Sorting exercises

Sorting exercises are useful in much the same way as matching exercises, in that they push students to recall the relationship between the items rather than the items themselves. Sorting exercises should feature sets of information that need to be aligned to identify categories or types. Again, you can use colour, font, or punctuation to show the different categories.

2D shapes   3D shapes

triangle
      rectangle

cylinder
      pyramid

circle

cuboid
      cube

square   sphere   octagon

Word searches

Word searches are great for any students looking for a fun way to practise their spelling and vocabulary. They can be tedious if made too long or too difficult, but they are also fun and effective if used properly. I like to offer fun starters to disengaged students, who may enjoy a slightly less formal style of learning. Word searches are a good way to reinforce key vocabulary, so they are best used either for spellings or for learning technical terminology like language devices or word class.

To create a word search, I usually use a free online tool, like https://thewordsearch.com/maker/. I write out a list of key words, type them into the format, and produce a PDF or image of the result which students can then draw on using the digital whiteboard. Always make sure to proofread them before you use them in a lesson to catch any accidental swear words or inappropriate language that may appear.

Crosswords

Like word searches, crosswords are a great way to practise spelling and vocabulary. Crosswords introduce the added difficulty of inferring the answer from a clue, so they can be a useful tool for stretching strong students' skills.

To create a crossword, I again usually use a free online tool, like https://worksheets.theteacherscorner.net/make-your-own/crossword/. I start by writing out the list of key words I want them to practise and then quickly summarise a clue for each: this can be the definition or meaning of the word, a 'fill the gap' clue, an anagram, a question, or something else entirely.

Mind maps

Mind maps, or spider diagrams, can be a great starter, especially when thinking about specific texts or broad topics requiring recall. You can put almost anything in the middle of a mind map: a quotation, a character, a lesson topic, a prompt for a set of ideas (genres, types of experiments, a historical time period, etc.). You can use this to ask students to recall a previous lesson or to demonstrate their knowledge on a topic they say they are confident on. I usually try to give students a few minutes to add things themselves, and then once they're stuck, we can discuss any crucial ideas they may have missed so they can add them in their own words. You shouldn't simply give students answers but rather give them a chance to formulate notes of their own. This will help with their recall of key ideas in future.

If the software is available, some students like to draw the mind map themselves, but with younger students I tend to offer a template like that in the online Resources chapter.

Where possible, I offer the student the opportunity to download the mind map we've drawn, so they can keep it and refer to it later.

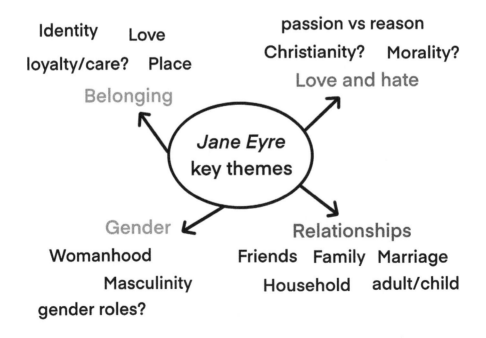

Quickfire questions

Quickfire questions are an easy starter designed to get a student focused and ready for the lesson while you prepare your slides or load your worksheet on the whiteboard. These questions should only take a maximum of a few minutes each to complete, but you can decide what topics to cover and how many to include. These questions work best with the recall of functional information, such as formulae, names and dates, or sentence starters. To keep it simple and ensure a variety of questions, you could make a PowerPoint slide or PDF with a series of sets of short questions, with a maximum of 5 or 10 depending on the level of complexity and with a mix of short and long answers if needed.

It's up to you whether you want to pick random topics or write questions that recall the previous lesson. Any questions students get wrong, you can recap in that lesson or plan to cover it again in a future one.

Homework review

By having dedicated time for starters each lesson, you can make time to check over the homework you set last lesson with the student or answer any questions they have about your homework, their school homework, or their classwork. You will need to keep an eye on the time during this starter, as it can easily take up half the lesson, but it is important that students have regular opportunities to ask questions or tell you how they are finding the work.

You can also use this time to look at specific questions they got wrong in homework you have marked outside of the lesson or to do a recap question from the previous lesson. Alternatively, you can do homework review as an explanation/demonstration if there's a useful example you want to draw on in more detail.

A rough structure for this starter might be:

1. Read through question or paragraph from the homework together

2. Give them a WWW/EBI and an opportunity to ask questions

3. Quickly walk through a similar example or some model answers together to illustrate your feedback

EXPLANATIONS/DEMONSTRATIONS

Slideshows

Slideshows is here used as a generic name for preprepared MS PowerPoints, PDFs, and images that you can use in lessons to deliver explanations or demonstrations of key material. Slideshows can be incredibly useful, helping tutors to structure lessons with prompts, strategies for writing essays, and examples all together in one file.

That said, slideshows are better suited to certain topics than others. Slideshows work best in:

- **English** – exploring the plot, characters, and themes of a set text; explaining the steps of a technique (explaining how to write a paragraph or essay, for example); compiling a series of short extracts or poems for analysis; exploring the structure of the papers or the AOs; holding templates for exercises like mind maps that aren't always easy to draw on the spot; types of exam questions

- **Maths** – explanations of common topics that you don't want to have to draw repeatedly; circle theorems, shapes, and any elements that rely on a diagram or visual; collating past paper questions on particular topics; visual explanations of topics, like factorisation trees; any topic that uses graphs or charts, as these can be hard to draw or edit during the lesson

- **Science** – images, photos, and other visual elements, especially the periodic table or pictures of equipment; atom structures, cell structures, and any elements that rely on a diagram or visual; collating past paper questions on particular topics; sentence starters, key phrases, and writing structures for 6-mark answers

- **History** – timelines and other common diagrams; sources, paintings/photos, and any other visual elements; types of exam questions

- **Geography** – diagrams of phenomena; photos of key events; sentence starters, key phrases, and writing structures for longer answer questions; types of exam questions

- **EFL** – verb tenses, persons, and conjugations; grammatical structures; visual clues and prompts for vocabulary recall; questions, speaking exercises, or conversation prompts; extracts and passages for reading comprehension; types of exam questions

However, with other topics, you may find that the slide order will restrict your opportunities to explore the student's understanding or limit the questions you can work on together. Worst of all, the slides may end up as a long set of paragraphs. Heavy slideshow use can result in a lot of lecture-style talking from the tutor and not a lot of student engagement, so slideshows should always incorporate recall questions or other response requirements. You can also build in activities from the other lesson plan sections if you want, like writing practice, tables, and mind maps. Alternatively, you can use materials like pages from worksheets or textbooks, which have activities and recall exercises incorporated between their examples.

It can also be worth preparing a script to run alongside your slideshow. You can have this script open in a document to the side of your online classroom as a guide for the information you want to give the student. I like to include bullet points with all the important ideas I want to bring up or a list of ideas that students commonly miss.

YouTube videos

Videos, such as those found on YouTube, can be a great tool for tutors.

They can be used in most subjects, for a range of activities:

- **English** – animated or Lego versions of plot summaries with students who are reluctant to engage or want just a quick recap of the text; introducing students to clips from stage productions when they begin studying a play; using clips from documentaries or educational videos about a certain historical period, character, or author; video quizzes

- **Maths/Science** – tutorials with explanations of question structures and answers; worked examples of tricky topics; demonstrations of how to link key skills and processes together; videos of experiments

- **History/Geography** – watching clips from documentaries or animations of key processes; video quizzes

Videos should never be shown at length – longer than 5 minutes or so – and should always be accompanied with another activity: a discussion afterwards, a series of recall questions throughout, or an investigative worksheet that requires students to look out for key details as they watch.

Model answers

Sometimes, when a student is particularly struggling with a topic and needs an in-depth demonstration, it can be easier to focus on one question in lots of detail and spend a longer time going over it, rather than trying several examples. Students may need a topic covered several times before they understand it and are confident to try questions independently. This is also a useful technique for introducing students to exam papers for the first time, so you can discuss the format and requirements.

For this technique, you can either write your own model answers or use ones you find online or in textbooks/resources. You should try to make/find answers for a variety of questions from past papers or exam-style questions, so students can see how to approach a range of question types. You can use the model answer technique differently depending on the subject you're tutoring.

Humanities subjects (i.e. English, History, etc.)

This technique works well for long and extended answer questions and essay questions. You can also use this technique for any writing questions in STEM subjects, such as the GCSE Science 6-mark questions, and for creative writing tasks.

Once you've written or found some questions and model answers and discussed with your student what the question is asking them to do, you can then read through the model answer and:

- Create a tick-list of essential criteria for a successful answer and ask the student to tell you which they think it has achieved

- Ask the student to create a WWW/EBI list, with three points for each

- Discuss the strengths and weaknesses of the answer, and what your student would do differently

- Evaluate the model answer against the AOs/level criteria and ask the student to 'mark' it

- Ask the student to use it as a model to write their own answer, picking out their favourite vocabulary and sentence starters

STEM subjects (i.e. Maths, Sciences, etc.)

This technique works well for multi-step questions or problem-solving questions.

Once you've written or found some questions and model answers and discussed with your student what the question is asking them to do, you can then:

- Ask the student to solve it and explain their thought process as they work, stopping to modify or correct if necessary

- Look at the solution/workings for a question and discuss it together

- Show a student an incorrect working and as them to identify the mistakes

You may need to model more than one question, but the idea of this method is to take your time going over typical questions individually until the student has a good grasp of the topic.

Live modelling

While the model answer technique generally involves looking at an existing answer and discussing it, live-modelling involves you writing or finding answers while the student watches. This technique allows to see, in real-time, what they should be aiming for and how to achieve it. It also gives them a chance to ask questions, make notes, and learn new vocabulary or skills. It works essentially the same way in all subjects, with a few necessary tweaks.

Some key things to remember when live modelling are:

- **Ask students lots of questions as you go** – they need to be actively listening and engaged with the lesson

- **Give students to opportunity to ask questions and make notes** – remind them that they can interrupt you if needed

- **Be understanding and show your own learning** – you can talk about the aspects that you find difficult and demonstrate that it's okay to make mistakes

- **Make sure your model is as accurate as possible** – even if you occasionally have to stop to Google a spelling or check a date

- **Show the student a range of models and examples** – they need to see all of the different ways that they can write or solve answers

- **Once confident, give the student an opportunity to model an answer** – you can then give immediate feedback

Humanities subjects (i.e. English, History, etc.)

The most common use for live modelling in writing subjects is to demonstrate 'academic writing' – both the vocabulary and skills needed to write answers in the style best suited to exams.

While it is important to remind students that they can express their ideas about a text, source or idea however they want to in your lessons, and that any language they choose is valid, it is also important to recognise that achieving well in Humanities subjects requires a certain kind of writing style and vocabulary.

This is especially true at GCSE level and above, where specific question types give way to more general essay questions.

To use this technique, you write your own questions or use worksheets and past papers to find example questions, sources and texts. Once you have selected them, you can them walk the student through how you would plan and write the answer.

Key academic writing skills you can live model include:

- **Whole essay structure** – introductions and conclusions; paragraph structures (i.e. thesis statements, concluding sentences); order of paragraphs; linking paragraphs

- **Sentence structure** – complex punctuation; avoiding run-on sentences; embedded quotations

- **Answer structures** – past exam question on their set text (i.e. *A Christmas Carol*); question styles and formats; choosing most effective quotes to create answer plans

- **General writing skills** – essay planning and preparation; paraphrasing and summarising; quoting; concision; nominalisation; formality; avoiding hedging language; third-person perspective; avoiding generalisations, speculation, and vague language (i.e. unspecified 'they' and 'it', using 'we' or 'you'); proofreading; formatting

- **Analysis** – building interpretations; critical thinking; balancing source/text analysis and use of own knowledge; considering the effect on the reader

- **Vocabulary** – formal tone; relevant terminology (avoiding jargon); avoiding repetition

- **Referencing** – using and evaluating sources; referencing styles (i.e. Harvard, MHRA, APA, etc.), in-text referencing; bibliographies

When live modelling writing answers, you can also provide examples of sentence starters, subject terminology (i.e. language features, historical phenomena), answer scaffolds or templates, and additional guidance on punctuation and grammar.

You can also use this technique to demonstrate creative writing. When live modelling creative writing, you can use many of the same skills mentioned previously but also include plotting, characterisation, using language and structural features, and paragraphing.

STEM subjects (i.e. Maths, Sciences, etc.)

The format of STEM exams remains essentially the same from KS2 up, so you can use live modelling to help students improve their workings and find solutions to more complex problems.

To live model a Maths-based answer, you will need to write your own questions or, more likely, use worksheets and past papers to find example questions. I would encourage you to use several different questions from the same topic/ skill at increasing levels of difficulty. Once you've shown the student the question, you can discuss with them what they think needs to be done to solve it and then model the method for them on the screen – showing your working and explaining each step. You will need to 'think out loud' so the student can follow along.

When live modelling writing answers, you can also provide formulae and diagrams, answer scaffolds or templates, and demonstrations of multi-step problems that may require multiple skills in a single question.

Worksheets and scanned resources

Worksheets and other external resources can be a great way to structure the explanation portion of the lesson. Lots of resources produced by schools, exam boards, or educational writers are well suited to use in the online classroom and can be a great guide for new tutors who aren't sure how to work through a particular topic. You can find recommendations for worksheets and content sites at the end of this chapter, or use the key words from the content breakdown at the beginning to search for worksheets on specific topics.

In the explanation portion of the lesson, I like to use worksheets that feature question progression: simple one-step questions, trickier questions, and then a multi-step question. That way, I can demonstrate the key skills with the earlier questions while keeping multi-step questions for the main activity to push the student's problem-solving skills.

As long as you vary the kind of worksheets that you use, and make sure that you pick tailored resources for different students, then worksheets can become a core part of your lesson time.

MAIN ACTIVITIES

Past papers

There are several ways to use past papers as part of a main lesson activity to practice extended reading, which should be varied and adapted according to students' needs.

When using past paper questions in lesson, the first thing to consider is the stage that the student is at in the course.

Past papers are an important main activity for students of all years, but they should be introduced sparingly with students in non-exam year groups until you are confident that they recognise the material and won't be put off by the question styles. All students need to learn about how exam questions are written and what skills and content each is asking for, but this is more of a priority for students who are revising directly for the exam that year.

With students who are revising close to the exam, it is often best to use whole papers to work out which questions they are most confident with and then break the paper down to focus on the ones they are least confident with. For example, you can make collated packs of questions to write essay plans for in English or History or a paper with only calculation questions in Chemistry.

You can spend an entire lesson working through an official past paper or compilation paper, using individual questions, modelling an answer to a question, or reading through model answers together, providing a supportive framework or plan for them to write an answer, the student writing an answer independently and then marking the paragraph together, collaboratively planning answers for a variety of questions, demonstrating effective comparison to suit a range of essay questions, the student writing an answer independently and then marking it together, and so on.

You may find that diligent parents and students have already looked at or used all the official past papers from the exam board websites, so it can be worth looking at content sites that produce their own papers or making compilation papers to ensure that the students won't have seen the questions before.

Annotation

Annotation is a useful technique in many subjects, especially when looking at text or images.

You can use annotation in:

- **English** – working through unseen material, helping students practise identifying language and structural features, building sets of notes that they can use for further study

- **History** – labelling and annotating sources, highlighting and note-taking, identifying demands of exam questions

- **Geography/Sciences** – labelling diagrams, highlighting and note-taking, identifying demands of exam questions

- **Maths** – annotating example workings to see what steps were taken, identifying demands of exam questions

You can also ask students to annotate material as part of pre-reading or reading homework to help them read carefully and make notes that can be used in the lesson.

Worksheets

Using worksheets as a main activity is pretty self-explanatory: the student works through the questions, and you offer help when needed. You can use this technique in any subject, and it is not a problem if you rely heavily on this technique in early lessons. It is generally more useful in Maths and Science than in Humanities, because it is harder to write your own questions in those subjects, and you will also likely use them more with younger students than older ones.

You want to pick work of an appropriate difficulty, which is relevant to their subject and exam board and that can be easily completed on the online whiteboard.

Question-guessing

The reality is that, with the way most exams are written, there is a finite number of ways exam questions can be phrased. While they'll never be able to predict exactly what will come up, this 'question-guessing' technique encourages students to think about the content of their exams and find the most common or most useful question focuses.

If you are not familiar with this technique from your own study, it might not be obvious what you can 'guess' at, so the best way to work out how to 'question-guess' is to go back and read all the past papers available in that student's subject. Make notes on the format and topic of the questions, and you will quickly notice patterns emerge.

An example might be that, in GCSE English Literature exams, the questions on extracts and whole texts usually focus on either a key theme ('love', 'betrayal', etc.), a plot point (the opening/closing scene, the important fight, etc.), or a character (Inspector Goole, Macbeth, or Paris, just to name a few!). Together, you and the student can create a list of the main characters, plot points, or themes that haven't come up in an exam paper in the last few years. Students can centre their revision notes around these elements, and consequently they will be prepared for a wider range of potential questions.

Alternatively, in Science, the type of content on GCSE and A-level specifications means there are only a small number of topics that are regularly used for the longer answer questions – the process of cloning, for example, or the history of the atom – so students can practise answer structures and key phrases on these topics.

I like to use lists or mind maps for this exercise, because they can be easily re-written or re-organised after you and the student have discussed your initial ideas.

PLENARIES

Mind maps

Mind maps are a great plenary: students can either write down everything they remember from the lesson, or you can give a more directed prompt using a quote or phrase in the middle ('types of non-fiction texts', 'types of energy', 'tips to improve my SPAG', etc.).

This can help you to see which pieces of information stuck in the student's brain most clearly and what you might need to recap in next lesson's starter.

Lists

Lists are another way for students to round off the lesson, by writing down either everything they remember about the topic from the lesson or something more specific, like '3 things to remember next time I write a paragraph' or 'themes from *An Inspector Calls*'.

Again, this is an easy way to see what the student remembers best and what might need to be revised.

WWW/EBI

'What Went Well/Even Better If' is commonly used in schools, and I find that it structures marking well for students and provides an effective feedback tool. Balancing positive and negative feedback is important, because students who are receiving tutoring are often doing so because they are struggling with a particular subject, and it can be easy for tutors to focus only on what needs to be improved without offering enough praise.

'What Went Well' should always be positive, with specific examples of things you liked or that the student did well. 'Even Better If' feedback should be honest but always be structured with proactive, practical suggestions, and where possible tutors should demonstrate how they are going to plan future lessons to help students improve in line with the feedback given.

There are two main ways to use this plenary: one is for the tutor to provide all the feedback, so the student can either download or make note of the 'EBIs' for next time and enjoy receiving positive feedback from the 'WWWs'. The other option is for the tutor and student to take in turn offering a piece of feedback or to have the student self-assess. Whatever way you use this format, ensure that students get positive feedback and praise as well as being pointed in the direction of improvements.

RAG

RAG stands for 'Red/Amber/Green', like the colours on a traffic light, and it can be used by students to self-evaluate their understanding of a topic. If they don't feel confident about the topic at all, it's 'Red'. If they have some idea but would like to go over it again, it's 'Amber'. If they're completely happy with it and could answer questions on it independently, it's 'Green'. Students can either say a colour or draw one on the online whiteboard.

Instead of the traffic light image, you can also use a simple thumbs up/in the middle/down with younger students.

Once you know how the student feels, you can discuss with them what you could do in the next lesson.

Summary questions

Summary questions are set of short questions covering the topic that you've done in that lesson, giving students a final recall opportunity, and serving as a check-in for you to see any areas where they might need more time to feel confident on the topic. This can be similar to the quick-fire questions activity, but it can be useful to use slightly more complex questions or to use one long multi part question rather than many shorter questions. Another difference is that students should be given the opportunity to ask questions, and you can make notes together on any areas that you would like to spend more time on.

Quiz questions

This plenary helps to reinforce key knowledge between lessons by ensuring that students are regularly practising their recall.

For this plenary, you need to ask your student to write three to five quiz questions, with the answers being important information they learned in today's lesson. It can be a new piece of vocabulary, a top tip for analysing or solving a particular question, or a summary of a topic.

You then save the questions they wrote and bring them up as a starter at the beginning of the next lesson for them to answer. If they get any wrong, you can recap that answer from the previous lesson.

Quick exam question

This plenary is essentially what it says on the tin: you just need to pick an exam-style question for the student to complete. It should be relevant to the topic of the lesson and not take more than 5–10 minutes to complete. For STEM subjects, I usually use questions from the first half of the exam paper, and for Humanities I'll either use a short answer question or ask the student to plan an essay answer.

You can either mark there and then, mark after the lesson, or carry it over into the starter for the following lesson.

HOMEWORK

NOTE: As explained in Chapter 4, if you choose to set homework, then you can set almost any task you like, but it should aim to be less than 30 minutes of work. This keeps it fair to the student, who may have other work or commitments, and to you, who will have to mark it or incorporate it into the next lesson. The average homework task I set takes around 20 minutes to complete.

Worksheets and resources

Worksheets and other external resources can also be used for homework, as they are often designed with hints and tips for students to use and have several key questions in short sections to help them recall what they've learned in the lesson with you.

Wherever possible, try to choose worksheets with an 'easy to difficult' progression, so students are practising their skills against a range of question styles.

Again, varying the kind of worksheets you use for homework, ensuring whatever you set is relevant, and making sure that whatever you set won't take the student more than half an hour will help them get the most out of the homework. I would also advise against setting long, repetitive sets of questions unless the student specifically asks for it or you think it will be helpful for them, as I tend to find that this homework does not get done and can be a big strain on students' time if they already have other work from school. Even just one side of challenging questions can be enough to reinforce their learning.

Past papers

Past papers can be used as homework for any students studying for an exam: start by using just one or two questions for students in the early part of a course, all the way up to a short compilation paper for students who are getting ready to revise. Short answer questions can be practised in lesson, so ask students to complete long and extended answer questions, or multi-step questions, to ensure that they are practising all question types.

In Humanities/essay subjects, you can also ask students to write plans for answers rather the whole thing if they don't have time to complete it in full.

If you are setting past paper questions, make sure to give yourself enough to mark the answers, or mark them as a starter in lesson.

5. Check on their progress

If you are going to be working with a student for a significant length of time – my longest-running student was over 2 years – then it can be worth building in regular progress checks to ensure that they are making improvements over time. This is especially important for students who are being home-schooled, who may not be assessed at any other time. These checks should not take too much additional time or formal marking but can be used to gain a sense of your student's progress. In addition, some parents like to receive updates of how their student is doing in your lessons, so it can be useful to have something concrete to refer to when they ask.

My preferred method is setting 'mini-assessments' every few weeks/ months. This reliable method builds in 'mini-assessments' at regular intervals in your tutoring: this might be a past paper question that the student completes independently as a starter or a piece of homework that you mark in detail. I like to set one every 1–2 months for students I see every week, so they're on Week 5 of the 10-week timetables, but you can move this around to suit your own planning. You can then keep a spreadsheet or note of how they do in each 'mini-assessment' and use it to determine what you need to revise in more detail.

There are several other ways you can keep track of your students' progress:

- **Ask about school tests or assessments** – if your student is in school, they will be tested regularly by their class teachers. Asking students and parents for these grades can be a useful way to keep tabs on their level. However, this is not always reliable, as students and parents may not be given this information regularly and students are not always keen to share their results.

- **Repeat exercises to see if they have improved** – a simple method to check a student's progress is to repeat an exercise after a few lessons to see if they have improved. This can be asking them to answer a similar question or to write a similar kind of paragraph: not the same question, but one that tests the same skills and knowledge. You can keep copies of these paragraphs in a folder and date them, using them as a reference to ensure that your student is improving over time.

- **Introduce 'pop quizzes'** – alongside assessing their essay skills, this kind of assessment can be used to check content knowledge for the texts or historical periods that the student needs to know well, as well as any significant dates, characters, facts, and other information. This can either be done in lesson, as part of something like a 'quickfire questions' starter, or as a homework task which they complete and send to you afterwards.

Another more passive method is to write lesson reports after every lesson, with details of what you taught that student, what their strengths and weaknesses were, and what you will want to cover in the future as a result. This can help you to see whether the same issues are coming up repeatedly over time and track progress on specific topics.

I usually only use this method if the site or agency I'm working for requires it or if a parent specifically requests it, as it can be time consuming, but if you have lots of students, it can make it easier to keep track of what you have taught with whom, so you don't accidentally repeat a lesson with the same student.

TOP TIP

Once you've got more experience, feel free to play with the lesson structure, content, and format. These are guides to help you get started and feel confident, not rules you have to follow, and you will develop your style and preferences. As long as you are always covering the content you need to, in a varied and interesting manner, have fun with it!

QUESTION

Which are your favourite lesson techniques so far?

Chapter 8

KS2

Lesson techniques

So, you've assessed your student's progress and you know what they need to work on – so how do you plan your first lesson?

First, you'll need to look online and in textbooks for resources and worksheets related to the student's subject and topics. Second, you'll need to learn some lesson techniques. These are the activities you'll use with students to help develop their skills and understanding.

The rest of this chapter is divided into English and Maths. You will find an additional chapter, covering History, Geography and Science, online using the key at the front of the book. In each section, you'll find a detailed list of basic lesson techniques in the 'Online tutoring basics' chapter (pages 7–26), which are all applicable to any age and subject. In the following, you'll find them listed in the relevant section alongside more specific exercises and techniques that I feel work best for each KS2 subject.

I've divided the techniques into the key parts of a lesson, as outlined in Chapter 7, so you can find lists of exercises to use with your students. Once you've learned some techniques, you can use the different categories to create quick and easy lesson plans. There's a sample lesson at the end of each subject section to show you how to do that.

How to tutor: KS2 English

Starters

Basic lesson techniques

- Matching exercises (p. 84)

- Sorting exercises (p. 85)

 DOI: 10.4324/9781003211648-10

- Word searches (p. 85)

- Crosswords (p. 85)

- Mind maps (p. 86)

- Quickfire questions (p. 87)

- Homework review (p. 87)

Plus

'Speedy reads'

'Speedy reads' is my name for small extracts with reading comprehension tasks and short answer questions. 'Speedy reads' work well for students who are worried about reading comprehension. By using unseen texts, it helps expose students who are not keen readers to a wide variety of types and styles of texts.

To create a 'Speedy read', you take a short extract – no longer than a dozen lines – from an unseen text. Next, you write several identification questions – 'What is the main character's job?' and so on – and then, if the student is confident, a few inference questions – 'How does the main character feel about losing their job?'.

I try to keep the extract fairly short and encourage students to draw directly on the text rather than from their own knowledge or guesses.

Connect four

'Connect four' is the name of a popular game where you match four shapes of the same colour in a row. The same concept applies to this vocabulary practice starter. You will need to create a 4 × 4 grid and fill in each box with a key word (either from a generic KS2 vocabulary list or from their weekly spelling tests).

To begin the game, the student must choose a word, define it, and use it in a sentence accurately. If they get it right, they can cross it out. Between you, take turns until one of you gets four boxes in a row or it is impossible to do so.

This exercise encourages students to understand their new vocabulary, not just learn to spell it, as well as creating an opportunity for a fun game against their tutor. This can also be used a plenary or game later in the lesson.

position	decide	quarter	various
island	circle	peculiar	early
trouble	refresh	especially	develop
begin	queue	narrator	achieve

Punctuation exercises

To make these exercises, I take a short passage from an unseen text and remove all of the punctuation, including full stops, capital letters, commas, apostrophes, and so on. If the student is struggling, I will put the removed punctuation in a list at the end of the extract for them to use, but if not, I will simply present the extract minus the punctuation and see how many mistakes they can spot. This can be a useful way to test how familiar a student is with the rules of punctuation, highlighting any that they don't spot or add incorrectly.

The punctuation you use in these extracts should only be from a selection that a KS2 student could reasonably be expected to understand, so start simple with commas and question marks and work up towards colons, semicolons, and brackets.

jane gasped and ran toward the balcony she could see the fire growing in the next field it was bright and burning orange against the night sky how did it get so big so fast she wondered aloud

Add any punctuation you think is missing: capital letters, full stops, commas, speech marks, question marks

'Fill the gap'/'Finish the sentence'

'Fill the gap', or 'Finish the sentence' if the gap is always at the end, can be an interesting way to prompt students to recall key information. 'Fill the gap' can be used in lots of ways:

- Removing the conjugated verbs from a piece of writing and only offering the root verb so students have to infer which person and tense to use

- Removing all of the technical terminology from an analytical paragraph so students have to remember the key terms

- Offering partial definitions for key words

- Removing the dialogue from a piece of fiction writing so students can write their own as a creative exercise

Feel free to develop your own uses as well. It is up to you, depending on the level of the student, whether to offer correct or model answers alongside the exercise – I generally don't unless a student is really struggling, as it is more effective for them to recall or imagine the answers themselves.

You can also use 'Fill the gap' exercises as main activities if you make the answers required longer or more complex.

Explanations/demonstrations

Basic lesson techniques

- Slideshows (p. 87)

- YouTube videos (p. 89)

- Model answers (p. 89)

- Live modelling (p. 91)

- Worksheets (p. 93)

Plus

Reading together

If you are working with a student who is being home-schooled, taking time out of school for an illness or other absence or struggling to commit to reading an entire set text, reading together can be a great way to demonstrate active reading strategies and make the most of time spent reading for practising other skills.

Reading together can take several forms: you can work through short sections of a text lesson by lesson, read a long section of a text for a portion of a lesson, set reading and recall questions as homework, and decide whether you want students to read out loud or in their heads depending on their ability and confidence.

Reading together can take up a lot of lesson time, so it shouldn't be used too heavily, but it can be a useful technique for students who don't engage well with reading, and some parents may even request that you spend a lesson or part of a lesson a week reading with the student if they don't have time to read with them themselves.

'Layers of meaning'

The 'layers of meaning' exercise involves taking a short quotation or phrase and then moving down the page by writing in the different 'layers' of meaning each word could have within the extract. This can help students to understand the difference between connotation and denotation, as well as developing their understanding of alternative interpretations. At KS2 level, these 'layers' can be fairly simple, as illustrated in the following, but they can help to model how students can start to think about writer's choice of language and its meaning.

This demonstration can transition into an activity, where the student takes over and has a go at it themselves.

"The wind howled through the tall dark trees."

Layer 1 Language feature	**Personification? Alliteration?** **Wind can't howl - but what can?**
Layer 2 Sounds	**'ow' sound** **Pain? Fear? Animal noises?**
Layer 3 Themes/associations	**"tall dark trees"** **nighttime, creepy, lost in woods?**

Main activities

Basic lesson techniques

- Past papers (p. 93)

- Worksheets (p. 95)

- Annotation (p. 94)

- Question-guessing (p. 95)

Plus

Basic reading comprehension

Basic reading comprehension is a skill to practise with KS2 students of all ages, especially students who are non-native English speakers or who don't read widely outside of school.

With this technique, you can use any age-appropriate text, divided into short extracts – I like to use between a paragraph and a page out of an average paperback. You can also use simple poems. Once you have chosen an extract, you will need to write a series of questions to accompany it. With basic comprehension, I like to use multiple-choice answers and short answer questions, much like those used in the SATs or 11+ exams. These questions should focus on eliciting close reading and simple inferences by asking students about details from the text ('How many children are present?'), their effect on the reader ('What effect does the adjective 'grey' have?'), and why they think the writer might have included or omitted them ('Why has the writer told us that the character's mother is ill?'). This provides a supportive structure for students to start thinking about more complex answers at a later stage.

As well as making your own, you can also find lots of worksheets with this format available online with the extracts preprepared, some with model answers as guides. These are useful as homework sheets or for new students where you haven't planned out all of your lessons yet.

Advanced reading comprehension

With more advanced reading comprehension, I like to use long answer questions, requiring paragraph answers with analysis where possible. These questions should contain more challenging inferences and ideas about effect and language and encourage students to link their answers to evidence from the text.

This exercise can also be used as a homework or starter.

Paragraphing practice

Unsurprisingly, this exercise simply involves the student practising writing paragraphs in a variety of different settings. This can be as part of an exam-style answer, in response to a question you have designed, or as part of a worksheet or online resource.

It is always best to start with a discussion of how your student is used to writing paragraphs and what methods they have been taught. As I discuss during the assessment section, some students are taught to use an acronym like PEA or PEEL, while others use a more fluid format like 'What, How, Why?' Whatever the student has been taught, you should try to work with, as you are likely to confuse them if you try to use a different acronym. However, if the student is really struggling with the method they are taught in school and asks you for a different one, you can demonstrate a few to give them the chance to find one that works better for them.

Prompted paragraphs

With students who are still very new to writing at length but who need analytical writing practice, I like to use a series of sentence prompts to help them structure their paragraphs.

These prompts can be a variation on one of the existing paragraph formats used in KS3 and GCSE. I like 'What, How, Why' with younger students, as they are usually familiar with these questions from conversation or other areas of learning and can easily apply it to this new context. These prompts also give tutors to discuss the analysis in detail with students before anything gets written down, so you can build a more detailed plan with the student to help them feel more confident to write.

If students are really struggling, you can give them an answer scaffold or template to fill in while they get used to building their own ideas. Once students get older and more confident, you can give them more freedom with paragraph structures by discussing planning strategies and more open-ended questions.

'Layers of meaning'

As outlined previously in the 'Explanations/Demonstrations' section, 'layers of meaning' is an analytical exercise which helps students to understand the different levels or layers of meaning that a quotation might contain.

It is up to you whether to label or guide the layers of their analysis: with students who are struggling to unpick quotes, prompting them to think about identifying rhetorical devices, structural analysis, contextual information about the author or period, language and sounds, or other elements of analysis can help them to see how many different ways there are to approach a quotation. With more confident students, I might leave them to see how many different layers they can think of on their own and then offer prompts once they run out of ideas.

You can offer students a worksheet or template with lines to write their ideas on, or you can simply draw lines onto the online whiteboard.

Postcard prompts

Postcard prompts is a really fun exercise that can be used to combine geographical knowledge, or memories of students' family holidays, with a writing practice that can push them to think about writing concisely and creatively.

I like to make my own postcards using a simple graphic designer software, like MS Paint or Publisher, but you can just as easily find fun vintage postcards from all over the world on Google Images. When I'm looking for postcards, I usually go for ones with pictures of landmarks, cities, or iconic food or weather on, so that students who don't know the location can infer some information about it.

These postcard prompts can be used in a number of ways: my favourite technique is to ask the student to imagine they're on holiday in the place on the postcard, discuss what they know or can infer about the place, and then ask them to write the postcard as if they were going to send it to their family to tell them what they've been up to. The other option is to ask the student to imagine that someone else is on holiday in the place and then work out what they would want to know if they were to receive a postcard from that person.

Photograph inspiration

This can be photos of non-specific places (a random tall building, for example, rather than the Empire State Building), which can be used as the prompt for the setting of a story, or photos of individuals or small groups. The people in the pictures can be used as the inspiration for a story: who are they? What do/ did they do? Where do they live? This exercise encourages students to flesh out their characters and settings, while giving them a visual prompt to work from.

Photograph inspiration works especially well with old photos: I usually choose old black-and-white or sepia photographs to encourage them to use their historical knowledge and imagination.

'Finish the story'

'Finish the story' tasks take a text that the student has read, either a book or a short extract, and asks them to imagine, 'What happened next?' The student will need to plan and then write an 'extra' chapter of the story. This technique is especially useful for students who are less confident inventing their own creative plots, which is a skill that can require practice. This technique allows them to use the setting, characters, and existing story arc of a story they are familiar with but to extend themselves using their own ideas.

Silent film

'Silent film' can be another fun exercise for students, giving them the opportunity to write a script or story from a short YouTube clip or video you show them where you have removed or muted the sound. Watching the video encourages students to think creatively without having to come up with too many ideas themselves, allowing them to practise dialogue and descriptions from visual prompts as they will be required to in the exam.

How to tutor

I like to pick clips they may be unfamiliar with, like black-and-white films or Charlie Chaplin sketches, as well as clips from stage productions, animations, or modern films.

If they choose to write a script, I like to give them the opportunity at the end of the lesson to read their script over the top of watching the video together, so we can enjoy the story they have created.

Again, like with any clip or video you show them, be sure to watch it all the way through before you see it with the student to make sure that it is safe and does not contain any age-inappropriate language or humour.

Plenaries

Basic lesson techniques

- Mind maps (p. 96)

- Lists (p. 96)

- WWW/EBI (p. 97)

- RAG (p. 97)

- Summary questions (p. 97)

- Quiz questions (p. 98)

- Quick exam question (p. 98)

Plus

'Give me five'

This plenary involves asking the student to hold up their hand and count down five pieces of information of your choosing. This can be five things they learned in the lesson or five things they want to go over again in future, or you can set up five different things: one thing they knew already, one thing they learned, and so on.

Headlines

Breaking down key information into bite-sized chunks can make recalling it in the future easier. This plenary asks students to create 'headlines', like the short phrases that top newspaper articles, to capture the most significant information they learned that lesson. You can ask for two to five, depending on how much content you covered in the lesson.

If needed, you can then return to the 'headlines' they wrote in a future lesson and ask them to create a mind map of that topic as a starter.

Homework

Basic lesson techniques

- Worksheets (p. 98)

- Past papers (p. 99)

Plus:

Pre-reading

Pre-reading is fairly self-explanatory, in that it is an opportunity for students to do some reading before the lesson to save time in the lesson. This can be part of a book they're already reading outside of the lesson or an extract or text you have set.

If the parent has requested a particular focus on reading, you can ask for a book report or set of bullet-pointed notes on the reading that they have done. You can also do a mind-map starter or set of summary questions to help them recall as much as possible from their reading.

Paragraph practice

Paragraph practice does what it says on the tin: it's an opportunity for students to practise their paragraph writing outside of the lesson time. I often find that with students I only see once a week, we just don't have enough time to write the paragraphs they need to practise, so setting just one or two to write at home can be a real help for them. I try to set paragraphs that are closely connected to what we've looked at in the rest of the lesson, so they shouldn't need too much support or preparation time to write the paragraph, and they will know the extract they need to write about well.

Depending on their level, you can ask students to write paragraphs independently, or you can provide a template or framework for them to fill in.

You can then mark the paragraph before the next lesson or mark it together as a starter or main activity.

Putting together a KS2 English lesson plan

To give you an idea of how that framework could be filled out with some of the lesson techniques I've discussed in this chapter, I've written out a sample KS2 English lesson:

Table 8.1 A sample KS2 English lesson

Date	Starter	Explanation/demonstration	Main activity	Plenary	Homework
07/11	Spelling test: 10 words learned the previous week	Slideshow: 1. Go through the rules of different types of punctuation – commas, semicolons, colons, etc. 2. Show some example sentences using each, explaining why it is used and occasionally asking the student to explain why	Worksheets: 1. Show example sentences without punctuation and ask where each should be put, correcting where necessary 2. Set punctuation exercises to complete independently	Connect four game: key vocabulary from previous spelling tests as revision	Punctuation practice: paragraph with all punctuation removed, must be added back in correctly, 20 minutes

A full 10-week timetable of lesson plans that can be adapted or used for any of your students can be found in the 'Lesson plans' chapter of this book.

Common issues

Regardless of the age, ability, or confidence of your student, they are never going to get everything right the first time. Every student is unique, so each will find different things easier or more difficult.

However, there are some consistent issues that I have noticed in my time as a tutor, which it can help to watch out for so you can offer your students advice when they need it.

The most common issues I've come across when tutoring KS2 English are:

1. **Lack of confidence**

    The KS2 students you find yourself working with might seem young, but if their parents are aiming for selective schools or the 11+, they may have very high expectations put on them. This can lead to the students feel tired or worried in lesson. I have had far too many students say 'I don't know if this is the right answer, but . . .' or 'this might be wrong, but is it . . .', and then give an amazing answer. This fear translates onto their exam paper, too – it might be the difference between them writing down a brilliant idea or not.

I have also noted a general reticence around unseen texts, so it can help to work on a wide variety of new texts in your lessons together to get them used to working closely on material they are unfamiliar with.

I have noticed that this lack of confidence is more common with young women, who are not usually as confident giving answers as their male counterparts, so a special effort should be made to reassure female students when their answers are good but also to remind them that it's okay to make mistakes and learn from them in your space.

2. Unwillingness to write at length

The second common issue I have come across at this age and stage is students being unwilling to complete classwork or homework in full, either avoiding writing in full sentences or writing very short answers and paragraphs.

This can be due to the previous issue, lack of confidence, which can lead students to write sparingly for fear of getting the answer wrong.

It may also be down to a simple lack of motivation or a short attention span – sometimes, students just don't want to work, no matter their age! If this happens on the odd occasion, you can adjust the lesson plan, set new homework, or move the writing to a future lesson, but if it is happening regularly, you may need to discuss the issue with their parent or school and ask them to speak to the student or supervise the completion of homework.

Finally, it may also be caused by tiredness, which can be seen in students who are having multiple tutoring sessions a week on top of school, holiday crash courses, and homework. If you suspect the student is struggling because of this oversubscription, it can be worth discussing it with their parent or school to see if they can prioritise their classes.

You may also want to consider offering parents of KS2 students the option of half hour or 45-minute lessons twice a week rather than the full hour once a week, so they don't need to concentrate for such an extended period.

3. Inconsistent SPAG

SPAG is an important part of the exam mark-schemes, but it often gets overlooked by students at this stage who are more worried about what to write than how to write. Using starters to do regular SPAG exercises, picking up on SPAG errors consistently in your lessons, and marking SPAG alongside content in any feedback you provide will help to highlight any particular issues the student is having. If you notice that the student's SPAG is becoming a bigger problem than you initially anticipated, you can always speak to the student's parent and school and ask that they be given more support with it in class.

4. **Finding creative writing difficult**

On the whole, I find that English students fall into two groups: ones who are already writing creatively in their own time and simply need their writing adapted to fit the exam and ones who dislike writing creatively. With the first group, you can focus on giving KS2 students confidence, inspiration, and opportunity to write, to boost their confidence, before starting to introduce some of the technical expectations from the SATs around punctuation, language features, paragraphing, and so on.

The second group can be more of a challenge for tutors, as they may struggle to come up with their own ideas or refuse to write extended creative answers. I find that using prompted exercises, like those listed previously, can help them to focus on the key techniques of creative writing without having to invent too much themselves in the first instance. I also like to introduce the ideas from analytical writing – effect on the reader, language devices, and so on – into their planning stage, so they can use ideas that they are familiar with from their analytical writing in the creative writing questions.

How to tutor: KS2 Maths

LESSON TECHNIQUES

Starters

Basic lesson techniques

- Matching exercises (p. 84)

- Sorting exercises (p. 85)

- Mind maps (p. 86)

- Quickfire questions (p. 87)

- Homework review (p. 87)

Plus

Quick activity starter

For this starter, you'll need to generate some quick Maths/reasoning puzzles for the student to solve. These test skills like mental Maths, visual reasoning, basic content like place value/fractions/decimals, and so on.

You can use an online puzzle generator or question bank to create screenshots, or paste them onto a slideshow to use again with another student. You can find recommendations in the Resources section at the end of this book.

Countdown

If you're not familiar with the TV show, Countdown is a Maths challenge where five random numbers are generated and students have to use them to make another random three-digit number. They can use any of the basic Maths skills – addition, subtraction, division, multiplication – to manipulate the numbers and can only use each number once.

Students often enjoy exercises that the tutor does with them, so you can try playing against each other to see who can get the answer fastest or get the most right answers. This also works really well with groups, as the competitive element can encourage students to engage, and the challenges are rarely impossible to solve.

There are a number of websites and online generators that can help you to make the numbers: I often generate several and save them as images to use with different students.

Explanations/demonstrations

Basic lesson techniques

- Slideshows (p. 87)

- YouTube videos (p. 89)

- Model answers (p. 89)

- Live modelling (p. 91)

- Worksheets (p. 93)

Plus

Maths tools

You may find that drawing graphs or diagrams can be tricky on an online whiteboard, especially without a graphics tablet or touchscreen, so digital Maths tools – like those listed in the 'Tutoring Tech' chapter – can make this much easier.

You can use graphing paper, protractors, rulers, and other virtual equipment, as well as accessing customisable diagrams of shapes and formulae.

Always ensure that students are engaged in the demonstration, not just watching you, by asking recall questions and responses while you explain the topic.

Tick-list

For some students, the focus will simply be on passing their maths tests rather than understanding the complexities of the topics. As their tutor, you can help them to create 'tick-lists', or step-by-step guides, for the question types they find difficult, which they can then practise until they can apply them to any question of that style.

First, you walk the student through a demonstration of an example question. Then, once they are happy they understand what you did, you work with them to create a list of instructions for them to follow for that style of question.

For example, for missing number problems, the list might look like:

1. Identify all of the missing numbers

2. Simplify by dividing

3. Isolate a and find value

4. Substitute in a in find value of b

5. Calculate value of the new number by substituting in known values

Students can use their 'tick-list' to solve problems independently until they are confident in the method.

Main activities

Basic lesson techniques

- Past papers (p. 93)

- Worksheets (p. 95)

- Annotation (p. 94)

- Question-guessing (p. 95)

Plus

Murder mystery

Murder mystery activities can be a great way to make a lesson a bit more exciting, though they should obviously be made age-appropriate for KS2 students!

There are two ways to run this activity: download a preprepared template or slideshow or write your own.

While it will be more time consuming, the advantage of writing your own murder mystery activity is that you can make it as easy or difficult as you want, and you can make different versions with different topics. I have previously used a slideshow, which makes it really simple to write and is easily imported to an online whiteboard. You can write a simple story with questions to solve to move onto the next slide or do a 'choose your own adventure'–style story with different questions to answer depending on what action the student wants to take.

Board game

This activity generally works best with students in Years 4 and 5, where it's important for them to practise key skills until they're completely confident with them. Answering lots of questions on a worksheet can be dull for the student, so a simple board game–style activity can make it more fun. This also works well to get students engaged, as most like to play with the tutor, and competition can encourage them.

I like to use a basic 'roll a die and move around a board' game with an online template that I fill out with questions from the topic we're studying. It means we don't waste any lesson time discussing complicated rules and they have a fair chance at winning. When they land on a question, you can use a timer of 30 seconds or a minute to push them to solve the question more quickly, or do them untimed if the questions are more complex.

If the student gets a question very wrong, you can either plan a lesson around that topic or take some time out of the game to explore why they found it difficult.

24 END $\frac{1}{3}-\frac{1}{6}=?$	23 $\frac{2}{5}+\frac{1}{4}=?$	22 $\frac{1}{4}\times\frac{1}{2}=?$	21 $5\frac{4}{5}=\frac{?}{5}$	20 GO BACK 2 SPACES ←	19 $12\frac{3}{4}=\frac{?}{4}$
9 $\frac{1}{6}\,?\,\frac{2}{5}$	8 GO BACK 3 SPACES	7 $\frac{3}{8}\times\frac{2}{3}=?$	6 $\frac{5}{7}+\frac{1}{7}=?$	5 GO BACK 2 SPACES ↑	18 $\frac{1}{6}\,?\,\frac{2}{5}$
10 ↓ $2\frac{1}{7}=\frac{?}{7}$	1 START $\frac{9}{2}=\frac{?}{4}$	2 $\frac{7}{5}=\frac{?}{20}$	3 $\frac{9}{2}=\frac{36}{?}$	4 $\frac{1}{4}\times\frac{1}{2}=?$	17 $\frac{2}{3}-\frac{3}{7}=?$
11 $\frac{1}{3}\times\frac{1}{6}=?$	12 $\frac{5}{7}+\frac{8}{21}=?$	13 $\frac{1}{8}\,?\,\frac{3}{4}$	14 $2\frac{3}{4}=\frac{?}{4}$	15 $8\frac{1}{5}=\frac{?}{5}$	16 GO FORWARD 3 SPACES

Real-world learning

Students generally engage better, particularly in subjects they find less interesting, when it is given a significance in everyday life. Maths is a good candidate for this technique, since it is essential in so many areas of life.

Applying this to tutoring lessons can be as simple as finding a worksheet that uses real-life examples – applying angles to architecture or exploring financial Maths – or using videos, images, and other media to contextualise the use of certain skills.

At KS2 level, you can also introduce more game-like formats, such as exploring temperatures and their relationship to climate using photos, or playing shop with financial Maths, as a way of engaging younger students. It can be easy to feel like worksheets are the only way that students will learn in your lessons, but fun and engaging activities as part of a rounded lesson plan can be a good break from the routine for students and motivate them for the less exciting exercises.

Plenaries

Basic lesson techniques

- Mind maps (p. 96)
- Lists (p. 96)
- WWW/EBI (p. 97)
- RAG (p. 97)
- Summary questions (p. 97)
- Quiz questions (p. 98)
- Quick exam question (p. 98)

Plus

'Spot the mistake'

'Spot the mistake' is a good plenary for older or very confident students, because it encourages them to look critically at the material and methods in front of them. It works especially well with the 'wordy' problem-solving questions or multi-step questions, because they have to practise reading the question carefully in order to see the mistake.

To create this plenary, you write out the workings and answer to an example question, but make a deliberate error in the process. This may be a simple miscalculation, like a wrong multiplication in the first step, or a bigger mistake, like drawing the wrong shape or a point on a graph in the wrong place. The more confident the student, the more subtle the error should be. The student then needs to read the question carefully, find the mistake, and correct the workings.

If the student is doing well or you have more time, you can always do a series of these exercises of increasing difficulty. You can also give a particularly tricky one to a group of students to see if they can work together to find the mistake.

Instruction manual

Instruction manual is a plenary which involves asking the student to write out the 'instructions' on how to solve a particular type of question in their own words, as if they were going to give them to another student to follow. They can number or order the steps any way they like, as long as they cover all of the important information.

This plenary works well for topics with more formulaic approaches, like solving or simplifying equations or working out terms in a sequence. I like to keep downloads or screengrabs of the students' manuals once they've finished, so if they're ever struggling on the same topic in future, they can see the method in their own words first to help with their recall.

If you are tutoring a group, you can get them to do this plenary independently and then swap their instructions around next lesson and have them attempt a question according to the instructions they've been given as a starter!

Homework

Basic lesson techniques

- Worksheets (p. 98)

- Past papers (p. 99)

Plus

Additional Maths questions

With particularly able students, you can use more complex problem-solving questions taken from age- and ability-appropriate sources to push them to think in more connected ways. These can be questions you find online, questions from textbooks, or, my favourite, questions taken from past papers of the Primary Team Maths and Junior Mathematical Challenge competitions. Lots of schools offer these competitions, so your student may already be familiar with them, but if not, they can help stretch their learning.

You can offer students the opportunity to use the starter time to discuss any questions they struggle with or to mark their work, so they have an opportunity for feedback.

Planning a KS2 Maths lesson

A sample KS2 Maths lesson might look like this:

Table 8.2 A sample KS2 Maths lesson

Date	Starter	Explanation/demon-stration	Main activity	Plenary	Homework
14/06	Quickfire questions: five questions on the topic from the previous week	Model questions: 1. Model a multi-step question, asking what they think needs to be done and then demonstrating the steps 2. Ask the student for input for the calculations to keep them engaged	Worksheet: 1. Once the student is happy to try questions, work through a few together to see if they understand the method 2. Offer individual questions to work on independently, helping when needed	Spot the mistake: offer a model answer and ask the student to spot the mistake, correcting if needed	Worksheet: questions to complete independently, 20 minutes

A full 10-week timetable of lesson plans that can be adapted or used for any of your students can be found in the 'Lesson plans' chapter of this book.

Common issues

Regardless of the age, ability, or confidence of your student, they are never going to get everything right the first time. Every student is unique, so each will find different things easier or more difficult.

However, there are some consistent issues that I have noticed in my time as a tutor, which it can help to watch out for so you can offer your students advice when they need it.

The most common issues I've come across when tutoring KS2 Maths are:

1. **Lack of confidence**

   See KS2 English for details

2. **Lack of motivation**

   See KS2 English for details

3. **Having significant knowledge gaps**

Tutoring should always be seen as an addition to students' opportunities to learn, on top of their in-school lessons, their teachers, and their school homework. However, due to a range of reasons – serious illness, bereavement, personal issues, or, most common recently, the disruptions caused by the COVID-19 pandemic – students can easily end up missing a chunk of consecutive lessons in school. Because much of Maths teaching is sequential, this can mean that students can have major gaps in their knowledge that you may not necessarily be able to anticipate. Tutors are a great way for students to fill these gaps, but it can be a challenge if you end up having to essentially teach a student a significant part of a topic or even a whole topic that they haven't previously had the chance to learn.

Part of your initial assessment with a student can be a discussion of the topics they have and haven't covered, and you can also ask their parents or teachers if you notice any major issues with a particular area of learning.

4. **Problem-solving questions**

Problem-solving questions consistently seem to cause Maths students issues at all stages of school, but especially in KS2 when they are fairly new to students. Problem-solving and reasoning skills are a core part of what is tested in SATs and the 11+ and other tests at this level, and they can be difficult for young students to grasp initially. They're designed to be challenging – any mistakes in the early parts of the question will be carried forward – but the biggest issue is when the questions combine two or more pieces of information or skills of different types. Students who are not familiar with this style of question or who aren't confident inferring what skill is needed can really struggle with these multi-step questions.

Tutors need to make sure that they are demonstrating the connections between the different skills and units, showing how concepts like shape and algebra can be used as a tool more broadly in Maths rather than just covering the requirements of the specification. You also need to introduce a wide range of question styles into their lessons to ensure that your students are exposed to the many different ways a question could be written. Finally, you will need to ensure that sufficient time is spent on multi-step questions once confidence in a topic has been established.

These questions can take up a significant amount of time, so they can be set as homework in the first instance and then gone through at the start of the next lesson if needed.

TOP TIP

You may find that behaviour management and attention spans are a more significant issue with this age group that any other. Try to find incentives for students to complete the work – the promise of a favourite game, or using fun images or ideas in exercises – and then be sure to reward them and include lots of praise. Alternatively, you may need to consider shorter lesson times.

QUESTION

Which games or activities does your student enjoy the most? How can you make them more challenging?

11+

So, you've assessed your student's progress and you know what they need to work on – so how do you plan your first lesson?

First, you'll need to look online and in textbooks for resources and worksheets related to the student's subject and topics. Second, you'll need to learn some lesson techniques. These are the activities you'll use with students to help develop their skills and understanding.

You'll find all of the details for the Maths and English sections in the KS2 chapter, as these are essentially the same. The rest of this chapter covers Verbal Reasoning and Non-Verbal Reasoning. In each section, you'll find a detailed list of basic lesson techniques in the 'Online tutoring basics' chapter (pages 7–26), which are all applicable to any age and subject, alongside more specific recommendations for 11+ tutoring specifically.

I've divided the techniques into the key parts of a lesson, as outlined in Chapter 7, so you can find lists of exercises to use with your students. Once you've learned some techniques, you can use the different categories to create quick and easy lesson plans. There's a sample lesson plan for English, Maths, NV, and NVR at the end of this chapter to show you how to do that.

Lesson techniques

Starters

Basic lesson techniques

- Matching exercises (p. 84)

- Sorting exercises (p. 85)

- Word searches (p. 85)

- Crosswords (p. 85)

How to tutor

- Mind maps (p. 86)

- Quickfire questions (p. 87)

- Homework review (p. 87)

Plus

Quick activity starter

For this starter, you'll need to generate some quick Maths/reasoning puzzles for the student to solve. These don't necessarily need to be in the style of NVR or VR questions but should test similar skills like mental Maths, visual and word-based reasoning, and so on.

You can use an online puzzle generator or question bank to create screenshots or paste them onto a slideshow to use again with another student. You can find recommendations in the Resources section at the end of this book.

Vocabulary/spelling starters

One of the biggest challenges for 11+ students in VR is building their vocabulary, so regular spelling tests should be introduced along with a range of starters that will expose them to new words.

You can use word searches or crosswords for these, but other spelling-based starters could include:

- Removing the vowels from 10 or more words and asking the student to work out what the original spellings were

- Giving the student a long base word and asking them to remove a letter at a time and make a new word with what's left

- Setting a series of anagrams for them to solve

- Asking them to describe a picture or photo using only new words they find using a thesaurus

- Using a worksheet or mind map to explore homophones, synonyms/antonyms, and other easily confused words

Explanations/demonstrations

Basic lesson techniques

- Slideshows (p. 87)

- YouTube videos (p. 89)

- Model answers (p. 89)

- Live modelling (p. 91)

- Worksheets (p. 93)

Plus

Specific question styles

GL papers are usually made using question banks, so there are specific styles of question that are used in VR and NVR that are identifiable by their format. The number and type of question styles varies each year, so you will need to stay up to date with the sample and past papers that are available online. There are usually between 8 and 10 different styles of question for each of VR and NVR, and there are several sites which offer guides to the different question styles which are updated regularly.

One useful tactic is to create compilation papers of each of the different types of question that is used regularly in the papers you find, either by copy and pasting sections from different papers or by using pre-made compilation papers from resource banks.

CEM papers tend to vary more widely, so you may need to rely more on sample and past papers to see trends in the types of questions they write, but ultimately all VR and NVR papers are testing similar skills, and most resources should be applicable to your student.

Main activities

Basic lesson techniques

- Past papers (p. 93)

- Worksheets (p. 95)

- Annotation (p. 94)

- Question-guessing (p. 95)

Plus

Murder mystery

Murder mystery activities can be a great way to make a lesson a bit more exciting, especially with fairly repetitive content like VR and NVR questions.

There are two ways to run this activity: download a preprepared template or slideshow, or write your own. Either way, it's worth having a look online at how others have written theirs to get some inspiration.

How to tutor

While it will be more time consuming, the advantage of writing your own murder mystery activity is that you can make it as easy or difficult as you want, and you can make different versions with different topics. I have previously used a slideshow, which makes it really simple to write and is easily imported to an online whiteboard. You can write a simple story with questions to solve to move onto the next slide, or do a 'choose your own adventure'–style story with different questions to answer depending on what action the student wants to take.

Plenaries

Basic lesson techniques

- Mind maps (p. 96)
- Lists (p. 96)
- WWW/EBI (p. 97)
- RAG (p. 97)
- Summary questions (p. 97)
- Quiz questions (p. 98)
- Quick exam question (p. 98)

Plus

Memory game

This plenary can be especially useful with students who have trouble with vocabulary, which is an essential part of VR. To create this game, you'll need to write a dozen or more key words – varying length and complexity – on a slide, give the student 30 seconds to memorise it, and then ask them to write out as many words as they can remember.

For bonus points, you can ask the student to give you a definition of each word.

Instruction manual

Instruction manual is a plenary which involves asking the student to write out the 'instructions' on how to solve a particular type of question in their own words, as if they were going to give them to another student to follow. They can number or order the steps any way they like, as long as they cover all of the important information.

This plenary works well for topics with more formulaic approaches, like solving or simplifying equations or working out terms in a sequence. I like to keep downloads or screengrabs of the students' manuals once they've finished, so if they're ever struggling on the same topic in future, they can see the method in their own words first to help with their recall.

If you are tutoring a group, you can get them to do this plenary independently and then swap their instructions around next lesson and have them attempt a question according to the instructions they've been given as a starter!

Homework

Basic lesson techniques

- Worksheets (p. 98)

- Past papers (p. 99)

Plus
Memorisation tasks

The best preparation students can get for the 11+ is practising lots of past papers and memorising key information – spellings, times tables, common mental Maths problems, shapes, and so on.

These tasks can be set in the form of worksheets or simply lists. You can also use some of the lesson time to discuss strategies for memorising information, finding new vocabulary, or testing their mental Maths.

Planning an 11+ lesson

To give you an idea of how that framework could be filled out with some of the lesson techniques I've discussed in this chapter, I've written out a sample lesson for each area of the 11+.

A full 10-week timetable of lesson plans that can be adapted or used for any of your students can be found in the 'Lesson plans' chapter of this book.

How to tutor

Table 9.1 English

Date	Starter	Explanation/ demonstration	Main activity	Plenary	Homework
07/11	Matching exercise: word class, matching examples to terms (i.e. noun, verb, adjective, etc.)	Reading comprehension: 1. Read through a short extract together 2. Show examples of question types, starting with multiple-choice and short answer questions and building towards paragraphs 3. Identify what is being asked by each question type and ask student what style of answer each requires, correcting when necessary	Reading comprehension: 1. Read second extract 2. Answer question types independently 3. Discuss how to answer long answer question in paragraphs 4. Plan answer	Mind map: recall different types of questions and styles of answers	Paragraph practice: write planned answer

Table 9.2 Maths

Date	Starter	Explanation/demon- stration	Main activity	Plenary	Homework
07/11	Sorting starter: prime, cube, and square numbers (calculator allowed)	Slideshow: 1. Work through slideshow about HCF and LCM 2. Discuss effective strategies for calculating them 3. Model answers in style of 11+, showing workings and asking for input where confident	Practice paper: 1. Work through a variety of questions of increasing difficulty 2. Mark as you go	Listing: list as many details as they can about HCF and LCM, 2 minutes	Worksheet: questions about HCF and LCM, 20 minutes

Table 9.3 VR

Date	Starter	Explanation/ demonstration	Main activity	Plenary	Homework
07/11	Sorting exercise: distinguishing adjectives from adverbs	Specific question styles (GL): 1. Work through slideshow of three new question styles 2. Offer model answer and explanation for several examples, asking student for prompts if confident	Specific question styles (GL): 1. Work through a collated paper of the three new question styles with the student, only offering help when needed	Discussion: allow student time for any questions and discuss which style they need most help with	Worksheet: One page of questions of question styles found most difficult, 20 minutes

Table 9.4 NVR

Date	Starter	Explanation/demon- stration	Main activity	Plenary	Homework
07/11	Quick activity starter: series of five shape-based puzzles	Specific question styles (GL): 1. Work through slideshow of three new question styles 2. Offer model answer and explanation for several examples, asking student for prompts if confident	Specific question styles (GL): 1. Work through a collated paper of the three new question styles with the student, only offering help when needed	Discussion: allow student time for any questions and discuss which style they need most help with	Worksheet: One page of questions of question styles found most difficult, 20 minutes

Common issues

The most common issues I've come across when tutoring the 11+ are:

1. **English: Poor grammar and weak analysis**

Not all schools include the English section, but the schools that do are generally more competitive, so it is important that even the youngest students have a good grasp of these skills.

In particular, poor grammar can affect both the analytical and creative sections of the paper. Students need to be confident using a range of sentence types and complex punctuation without making significant mistakes, as well using paragraphing for both function and effect. This may mean giving students some guidance around paragraph structures for both analytical and creative writing.

Students can also struggle with the inference or analytical elements of the paper, as these skills are tested more thoroughly by the 11+ than by the SATs and often require a broader vocabulary. This will require regular writing practice and exposure to a range of texts, both fiction and non-fiction.

2. **Maths: 'Wordy' questions and problem-solving**

Increasingly, the style of question examiners like to use in the 11+ has strayed further and further from the typical KS2 curriculum, often featuring questions that require inference from text as much as integers, which can be a real challenge for students.

Once you are confident that your student has mastered the basic skills and operations, you should try to include practice of 'wordy' questions with more description, which are not commonly taught in school at Year 5 or 6, as well as problem-solving style questions with multiple parts. Given that previous years' papers have imitated KS3 or even GCSE Maths, these may seem advanced for this age group, but they will need to be familiar with a wide range of question styles for the most competitive 11+ exams.

3. **Verbal Reasoning: Poor vocabulary**

A common problem I have seen among students practising VR is that they simply don't know enough words: the questions often rely on the student's familiarity with a range of language, or at least the linguistic rules that underpin them, so more archaic or obscure words can trip up even the most intelligent students.

This can be tackled in a number of ways, both in and out of lessons.

Students should be encouraged to read widely, and you can provide reading recommendations for parents. This is probably the best thing students can do for both the English and VR sections.

You should also institute a regular spelling test and use a range of vocabulary starters. Students will need to understand the definitions of new words as well as the spellings for some questions.

4. **Non-Verbal Reasoning: Time management**

The four sections of the 11+ may be formatted differently year to year and school to school, but they are usually of a similar length in terms of questions and time allotted. However, students do seem to particularly struggle to manage their time keeping in the VR and NVR sections, either rushing through the questions without checking their answers or spending too much time on questions they don't understand.

Students should always be encouraged to read back through their answers before they commit to finishing their work, even in lessons, as it helps to build good habits. In addition, if your student is close to the exam, you can offer them timed practice on short sets of questions to help them work out how much time they will have for each question.

TOP TIP

Tutoring all the topics for the 11+ can be a challenge, so many tutors specialise in just one or two sections – for example, I specialised in English and Verbal Reasoning. Make it clear to parents which sections you're most confident with and recommend another tutor for the other topics.

QUESTION

How will you mix games and activities into your worksheet practice for these topics?

Chapter 10

KS3

So, you've assessed your student's progress and you know what they need to work on – so how do you plan your first lesson?

First, you'll need to look online and in textbooks for resources and work-sheets related to the student's subject and topics. Second, you'll need to learn some lesson techniques. These are the activities you'll use with students to help develop their skills and understanding.

The rest of this chapter is divided in English and Maths. You will find an additional chapter, covering History, Geography, and Science, online using the key at the front of the book. In each section, you'll find a detailed list of basic lesson techniques in the 'Online tutoring basics' chapter (pages 7–26), which are all applicable to any age and subject. In the following, you'll find them listed in the relevant section alongside more specific exercises and techniques that I feel work best for each KS3 subject.

I've divided the techniques into the key parts of a lesson, as outlined in Chapter 7, so you can find lists of exercises to use with your students. Once you've learned some techniques, you can use the different categories to create quick and easy lesson plans. There's a sample lesson at the end of each subject section to show you how to do that.

How to tutor: KS3 English

LESSON TECHNIQUES

Starters

Basic lesson techniques

- Matching exercises (p. 84)

- Sorting exercises (p. 85)

 DOI: 10.4324/9781003211648-13

- Word searches (p. 85)

- Crosswords (p. 85)

- Mind maps (p. 86)

- Quickfire questions (p. 87)

- Homework review (p. 87)

Plus

'Speedy reads'

'Speedy reads' is my name for small extracts with reading comprehension tasks and short answer questions. 'Speedy reads' work well for students who are worried about reading comprehension. By using unseen texts, it helps expose students who are not keen readers to a wide variety of types and styles of texts.

To create a 'Speedy read', you take a short extract – no longer than a dozen lines – from an unseen text. Next, you write several identification questions – 'What is the main character's job?' and so on – and then, if the student is confident, a few inference questions – 'How does the main character feel about losing their job?'

I try to keep the extract fairly short and encourage students to draw directly on the text rather than from their own knowledge or guesses.

Missing boxes

This exercise involves finding or making a chart or table with headings like 'name of technique', 'analysis', 'examples', and 'effect on the reader', filling in the boxes yourself or choosing sample answers, and then hiding a selection of boxes by removing the text or superimposing a white square over the top. Students then need to fill in the empty boxes themselves, using the visible answers as a guide.

By providing some answers but not others, students have a model to follow for their additions without having too much information given to them straight away. The headings also provide them with the vocabulary to ask questions about the task and the opportunity to guess if they aren't sure.

This exercise works particularly well when asking students to identify and analyse examples of different language features (simile, alliteration, etc.) or structural features (listing, short sentences, etc.), or when they need to analyse a number of key quotes from a text.

With older students, I remove many more of the boxes, especially all of the ones about 'effect on the reader', to push them to make their own conclusions without a model. With younger students, I'll remove fewer boxes and sometimes tell a little story about how another student accidentally rubbed out some of the answers or a cat stole them!

Device	Example	Effect
Simile	"My heart pounded like a bass drum"	Loud, strong and musical - like the rhythm of the heart
	"The tiny tortoise tiptoed away"	
	"The boy was a cheetah, dashing for the finish line"	Very fast, chasing, trying to survive?
Repetition	"They climbed and climbed but got no closer"	

Punctuation exercises

To make these exercises, I take a short passage from an unseen text and remove all of the punctuation, including full stops, capital letters, commas, apostrophes, and so on. If the student is struggling, I will put all of the removed punctuation in a list at the end of the extract for them to use, but if not I will simply present the extract minus the punctuation and see how many mistakes they can spot. This can be a useful way to test how familiar a student is with the rules of punctuation, highlighting any that they don't spot or add incorrectly.

stop i cant keep up shouted jemima
panting loudly and leaning on a tree for
support the rest of her hiking team had
already reached the top of the hill jemima
was worried that they would begin to
disappear over the other side i dont know
where i am she grumbled she was not
very good at reading maps

Add any punctuation you think is missing: capital letters, full stops, commas, colons, speech marks, exclamation marks, semi-colons, apostrophes

Explanations/demonstrations

Basic lesson techniques

- Slideshows (p. 87)

- YouTube videos (p. 89)

- Model answers (p. 89)

- Live modelling (p. 91)

- Worksheets (p. 93)

Plus

Reading together

If you are working with a student who is being home-schooled, taking time out of school for an illness or other absence, or is struggling to commit to reading an entire set text, reading together can be a great way to demonstrate active reading strategies and make the most of time spent reading for practising other skills.

Reading together can take several forms: you can work through short sections of a text lesson by lesson; read a long section of a text for a portion of a lesson; set reading and recall questions as homework; and decide whether you want students to read out loud or in their heads depending on their ability and confidence.

I especially like using reading together as a strategy for tackling poems when you're working with a student who struggles with or dislikes poetry. So many poems were written to be read out loud, and it's often easier for students who struggle to identify language and structural devices to hear them when they are read aloud. If we're going to be working on a poem in a lesson, I usually start that lesson by having the student read the poem aloud or, if it is particularly long, reading alternating paragraphs with the student.

'Layers of meaning'

The 'layers of meaning' exercise involves taking a short quotation or phrase and then moving down the page by writing in the different 'layers' of meaning each word could have within the extract. This can help students to understand the difference between connotation and denotation, as well as developing their understanding of alternative interpretations. You can use prompts for the different layers, like 'context', 'language', 'structure', and so on.

This demonstration can transition into an activity, where the student takes over and has a go at it themselves.

"Deep in the heart of the forest, something was stirring."

Layer 1 Language feature	Personification? "heart of the forest" - centre? Origin/beginning? "heart" - alive? Ancient, angry, passion?
Layer 2 Sounds	Repeated 't' sound - hearT, foresT, sTirring Strong consonants contrasted with sibilant 's' - like wind through trees?
Layer 3 Themes/ associations	Trope of spooky ancient untouched forests with powerful inhabitants - Lord of the Rings etc Modern story, ideas about ecology and power?
Layer 4 Tense	Present 'ing' tense makes it feel current and happening - reminder of climate change?

Main activities

Basic lesson techniques

- Past papers (p. 93)

- Worksheets (p. 95)

- Annotation (p. 94)

- Question-guessing (p. 95)

Plus

Basic reading comprehension

Basic reading comprehension is a skill that I like to continually practise with KS3 students of all ages, especially Year 7 and 8 students who are non-native English speakers or who don't read widely outside of school. It is an essential skill in English and exposes students to a greater range of texts, genres, and authors.

With this technique, you can use any age-appropriate text, divided into short extracts – I like to use between a paragraph and a page out of an average paper-back. You can also use simple poems. Once you have chosen an extract, you will need to write a series of questions to accompany it. With basic comprehension,

I like to use multiple-choice answers and short answer questions, much like those used in the GCSE Language exams. These questions should focus on eliciting close reading and simple inferences, by asking students about details from the text ('How many children are present?'), their effect on the reader ('What effect does the adjective 'grey' have?'), and why they think the writer might have included or omitted them ('Why has the writer told us that the character's mother is ill?'). This provides a supportive structure for students to start thinking about more complex answers at a later stage.

As well as making your own, you can also find lots of worksheets with this format available online with the extracts preprepared, some with model answers as guides. These are useful as homework sheets or for new students where you haven't planned out all of your lessons yet.

'Fill the gap'/'Finish the sentence'

'Fill the gap', or 'Finish the sentence' if the gap is always at the end, can be an interesting way to prompt students to recall key information. 'Fill the gap' can be used in lots of ways:

- Removing the conjugated verbs from a piece of writing and only offering the root verb so students have to infer which person and tense to use

- Removing all of the technical terminology from an analytical paragraph so students have to remember the key terms

- Offering partial definitions for key words

- Removing the dialogue from a piece of fiction writing so students can write their own as a creative exercise

Feel free to develop your own uses as well. It is up to you, depending on the level of the student, whether to offer correct or model answers alongside the exercise – I generally don't unless a student is really struggling, as it is more effective for them to recall or imagine the answers themselves.

You can also use 'Fill the gap' exercises as a starter.

Advanced reading comprehension

Once students have mastered the basic skills, they can then move onto the more difficult skills, such as inference and analysis. Advanced reading comprehension should require students to both read and write more than the basic version. These questions should contain more challenging inferences and ideas about effect and language and encourage students to link their answers to evidence from the text. They should mimic the format of the later questions in the GCSE Language paper.

With more advanced reading comprehension, I like to use long answer questions, requiring paragraph answers with analysis where possible.

Again, you can also find lots of worksheets with this format available online with the extracts preprepared, some with model answers as guides. This exercise can also be used as a homework or starter, with the marking done either in or out of the lesson.

Paragraphing practice

Unsurprisingly, this exercise simply involves the student practising writing paragraphs, in a variety of different settings. This can be as part of an exam-style answer, in response to a question you have designed, or as part of a worksheet or online resource.

It is always best to start with a discussion of how your student is used to writing paragraphs and what methods they have been taught. As I discuss during the assessment section, some students are taught to use an acronym like PEA or PEEL, while others use a more fluid format like 'What, How, Why?' Whatever the student has been taught, you should try to work with, as you are likely to confuse them if you try to use a different acronym. However, if the student is really struggling with the method they are taught in school and asks you for a different one, you can demonstrate a few to give them the chance to find one that works better for them.

'Layers of meaning'

As outlined previously in the Explanations/Demonstrations section, 'layers of meaning' is an analytical exercise which helps students to understand the different levels or layers of meaning that a quotation might contain.

It is up to you whether to label or guide the layers of their analysis: with students who are struggling to unpick quotes, prompting them to think about identifying rhetorical devices, structural analysis, contextual information about the author or period, language and sounds, or other elements of analysis can help them to see how many different ways there are to approach a quotation. With more confident students, I might leave them to see how many different layers they can think of on their own and then offer prompts once they run out of ideas.

You can offer students a worksheet or template with lines to write their ideas on, or you can simply draw lines onto the online whiteboard.

If the student is revising key quotations for use in the exam, I always give them the opportunity to screengrab or download their notes so they can compile a list of quotes and ideas for later.

SWAT/key word analysis mind maps

As explained previously, SWAT or 'Keyword Analysis' is an essential part of writing exam answers for GCSE English students. Once you have demonstrated how to unpick a quotation using your own mind maps, it can be useful to hand this technique over to students so they can practise for themselves. I find that students who are less confident about SWAT find the mind map format less intimidating, because their ideas are not put in a hierarchy or order and they can link their ideas together in whatever way they choose. Placing the quotation in the middle also encourages them to pick out individual words and think about the context of them within the sentence or quotation they chose.

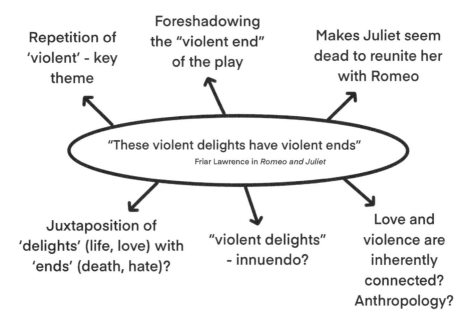

Table of quotes

Tables of quotes can be constructed in a number of ways: this is especially useful exercise for tutors, as it allows students to cover large amounts of text in a relatively short time and provides lots of fodder for producing practice paragraphs at another time or for homework. It is also often appreciated by students, as they can download or screenshot their tables to build banks of quotations about a particular text or anthology, saving them time in homework or revision.

For students who need practise identifying and explaining rhetorical devices, it can be useful to table in the names of several devices and ask them to look for them throughout and extract and offer brief explanations of their effect.

For students who need help identifying themes, tables can prompt them to look for quotations or ideas related to a particular theme and explore the relevance of these key ideas.

For students who need help introducing context into their paragraphs, you can label the various areas of the table using key social or historical ideas and ask them to look for key ideas or quotations that align with them.

For students who are in the later stages of revision and are looking to build banks of key quotes, tables can be a great way to organise their quotations and code them according to theme, character, plot point, device, or other element of the text.

Table 10.1 Key quotes from *A Christmas Carol* by Charles Dickens

Quotes from Stave One	Device	Themes	Effect
'Old Marley was as dead as a door-nail.'	Simile	Death, old age, loneliness	Common idiom, links to the door with 'Scrooge and Marley' over it. Later discusses comparison to 'coffin-nail'?
'a squeezing, wrenching, grasping, scraping, clutching, covetous, old sinner!'	Listing, metaphor	Greed, old age, morality	Long list suggests narrator's exasperation and anger. Lots of synonyms for greedy, which multiplies the effect. Biblical language – 'sinner'
'It was cold, bleak, biting weather: foggy withal'	Pathetic fallacy	Winter, cruelty	

Photograph inspiration

One of the most common, and useful, exercises for KS3 English students who are struggling with creative writing is to use photo prompts – just like the ones they will see in their exam booklets. This can be photos of non-specific places (a random tall building, for example, rather than the Empire State Building), which can be used as the prompt for the setting of a story, or photos of individuals or small groups. The people in the pictures can be used as the inspiration for a story: who are they? What do/did they do? Where do they live? This exercise encourages students to flesh out their characters and settings while giving them a visual prompt to work from.

This works especially well with old photos: I usually choose old black-and-white or sepia photographs to encourage them to use their historical knowledge and imagination.

Debate speech

Debate speech gives students the opportunity to practise their persuasive writing construction of arguments in a format that practises the key skills from the exam.

When working with confident students, you can offer them the option to write a speech about any topic they desire, but with most students, it can be useful to offer them something to argue against. This can be either something you have written or an example of a debate speech you have found online.

If you want to, you can offer students a template or script to help them write their speech, with sentence starters and other guidance, but with confident creative writers, you can leave them to write in whatever format they desire. You can also try introducing other writing formats, like newspaper articles.

With these kinds of open-ended tasks, it can be useful to end the lesson by marking what they have written against the expectations of the exam mark scheme, so they can start to see how their own creative writing lines up with the grade boundaries they will be expected to meet.

Silent film

'Silent film' can be a really fun exercise for students, giving them the opportunity to write a script or story from a short YouTube clip or video you show them where you have removed or muted the sound. Watching the video encourages students to think creatively without having to come up with too many ideas themselves, allowing them to practise dialogue and descriptions from visual prompts as they will be required to in the exam.

It can be fun to pick clips they may be unfamiliar with, like black-and-white films or Charlie Chaplin sketches, as well as clips from stage productions, animations, or modern films.

If they choose to write a script, I like to give them the opportunity at the end of the lesson to read their script over the top of watching the video together, so we can enjoy the story they have created.

Again, like with any clip or video you show them, be sure to watch it all the way through before you see it with the student to make sure that it is safe and does not contain any age-inappropriate language or humour.

Postcard prompts

Postcard prompts is a really fun exercise that can be used to combine geographical knowledge, or memories of students' family holidays, with a writing practice that can really push them to think about writing concisely and creatively.

I like to make my own postcards using a simple graphic designer software, like MS Paint or Publisher, but you can just as easily find fun vintage postcards from all over the world on Google Images. When I'm looking for postcards, I usually go for ones with pictures of landmarks, cities, or iconic food or weather on so that students who don't know the location can infer some information about it.

These postcard prompts can be used in a number of ways: my favourite technique is to ask the student to imagine they're on holiday in the place on the postcard, discuss what they know or can infer about the place, and then ask them to write the postcard as if they were going to send it to their family to tell them what they've been up to. The other option is to ask the student to imagine that someone else is on holiday in the place and then work out what they would want to know if they were to receive a postcard from that person.

Plenaries

Basic lesson techniques

- Mind maps (p. 96)

- Lists (p. 96)

- WWW/EBI (p. 97)

- RAG (p. 97)

- Summary questions (p. 97)

- Quiz questions (p. 98)

- Quick exam question (p. 98)

Plus

Dictionary definitions

For this plenary, the student will need to list any new vocabulary that they learned in the lesson, spell them correctly, and provide an accurate definition.

This can be normal vocabulary but works especially well with technical terminology, like the names of language or structure devices.

If creative writing is a focus for the student, you can also ask them to provide an example of the word or device used in a sentence. Alternatively, you can create an example sentence and ask them to quickly analyse the effect of that word/device.

Headlines

Breaking down key information into bite-sized chunks can make recalling it in the future easier. This plenary asks students to create 'headlines', like the short phrases that top newspaper articles, to capture the most significant information they learned that lesson. You can ask for two to five, depending on how much content you covered in the lesson.

If needed, you can then return to the 'headlines' they wrote in a future lesson and ask them to create a mind map of that topic as a starter.

Homework

Basic lesson techniques

- Worksheets (p. 98)

- Past papers (p. 99)

Plus

Pre-reading and annotation

This really serves as preparatory work rather than homework, by giving students the chance to read a long extract or poem outside of the lesson and make notes on themes, structural features, language devices, and types of vocab. I always encourage students to practise using their technical terminology while they're annotating, to ensure that they can spot the relevant features, and asking them to take additional notes means that they can write down the effect as well.

This can be a useful homework because some students dislike the pressure of being watched while they read, while others simply don't have enough lesson time to spend a significant portion of it reading.

Paragraph practice

Paragraph practice does what it says on the tin: it's an opportunity for students to practise their paragraph writing outside of the lesson time. I often find that with students I only see once a week, we just don't have enough time to write the paragraphs they need to practise, so setting just one or two to write at home can be a real help for them. I try to set paragraphs that are closely connected to what we've looked at in the rest of the lesson, so they shouldn't need too much support or preparation time to write the paragraph, and they will know the extract they need to write about well.

Depending on their level, you can ask students to write paragraphs independently, or you can provide a template or framework for them to fill in.

You can then mark the paragraph before the next lesson or mark it together as a starter or main activity.

Planning a KS3 English lesson

A sample KS3 English lesson might look like this:

Table 10.2 A sample KS3 English lesson

Date	Starter	Explanation/ demonstration	Main activity	Plenary	Homework
07/11	Crossword starter: language feature terminology (i.e. simile, metaphor, alliteration, etc.)	Reading together: 1. Reading a short extract from a text they're studying at school (i.e. *A Christmas Carol*) 2. Identifying language features, character motivations, plot points, and other key details, adding annotations where necessary	Basic reading comprehension: 1. Select next extract and read together 2. Set a series of multiple-choice and short answer questions to complete independently 3. Final question requires short paragraph to begin to discuss longer writing strategies	Summary questions: Five quick questions on the reading completed together	Reading: read the next extract of the text independently and make notes on areas for follow up in the following lesson

Common issues

The most common issues I've come across when tutoring GCSE English Literature are:

1. **Lack of confidence**

At GCSE level, the lack of confidence is often about their knowledge of their set texts, especially now exams are closed book, but at KS3, it's often about their basic analysis skills. I have had far too many students say, 'I don't know if this is the right answer, but . . .' or 'This might be wrong, but is it . . .', and then give an amazing answer. This fear translates onto their exam paper, too – it might be the difference between them writing down a brilliant idea or not. I have also noted a general reticence around unseen poems or texts, so it can help to work on a wide variety of new texts in your lessons together to get them used to working closely on material they are unfamiliar with.

I have noticed that this lack of confidence is more common with young women, who are not usually as confident giving answers as their male counterparts, so a special effort should be made to reassure female students when their answers are good but also to remind them that it's okay to make mistakes and learn from them in your space.

2. **Struggling to understand process and language of characterisation**

This will obviously vary between students, but a topic I often end up having to go over multiple times with students is characterisation. This can be an issue at GCSE level but is especially common with KS3 students who are just learning about this process. The sticking point is usually that students write about characters like they're people, not characters: they say 'Jane feels sad' or 'Sheila is angry', but they don't show evidence how they know that, why it's important, or how the writer has created that feeling. I recommend that students get into the habit of describing 'the character of Jane' or 'Sheila's character' to create some distance between the character as a person they relate to and the character as a construction by the writer and then using a formula like 'What, How, Why' to help them to map the writer's language onto the effect on the reader.

3. **Inconsistent SPAG**

SPAG is an important part of the exam mark schemes, but it often gets overlooked by students at this stage who are more worried about what to write than how to write. Using starters to do regular SPAG exercises, picking up on SPAG errors consistently in your lessons, and marking SPAG alongside content in any feedback you provide will help to highlight any particular issues the student is having. It can be worth pointing out to students how many marks they can get for the SPAG elements of the papers so they understand how valuable they are. If you notice that the student's SPAG is becoming a bigger problem than you initially anticipated, you can always speak to the student's parent and school and ask that they be given more support with it in class.

4. **Finding creative writing difficult**

On the whole, I find that English students fall into two groups: ones who are already writing creatively in their own time and simply need their writing adapted to fit the exam, and ones who dislike writing creatively and prefer the analytical questions in the exam. With the first group, you have plenty of time before the GCSE courses start so you can focus on giving students confidence, inspiration, and opportunity to write rather than on the technical expectations of the exam.

The second group can be more of a challenge for tutors, as they may struggle to come up with their own ideas or refuse to write extended creative answers. I find that using prompted exercises, like those listed previously, can help them to focus on the key techniques of creative writing without having to invent too much themselves in the first instance. I also like to introduce the ideas from analytical writing – effect on the reader, language devices, and so on – into their planning stage, so they can use ideas that they are familiar with from their analytical writing in the creative writing questions.

How to tutor: KS3 Maths

LESSON TECHNIQUES

Starters

Basic lesson techniques

- Matching exercises (p. 84)

- Sorting exercises (p. 85)

- Mind maps (p. 86)

- Quickfire questions (p. 87)

- Homework review (p. 87)

Plus

Quick activity starter

For this starter, you'll need to generate some quick Maths/reasoning puzzles for the student to solve. These test skills like mental Maths, visual reasoning, basic content like place value/fractions/decimals, and so on.

You can use an online puzzle generator or question bank to create screenshots or paste them onto a slideshow to use again with another student. You can find recommendations in the Resources section at the end of this book.

Countdown

If you're not familiar with the TV show, Countdown is a Maths challenge where five random numbers are generated, and students have to use them to make another random, three-digit number. They can use any of the basic Maths skills – addition, subtraction, division, multiplication – to manipulate the numbers and can only use each number once.

Students often enjoy exercises that the tutor does with them, so you can try playing against each other to see who can get the answer fastest or get the most right answers. This also works really well with groups, as the competitive element can encourage students to engage, and the challenges are rarely impossible to solve.

There are a number of websites and online generators that can help you to make the numbers: I often generate several and save them as images to use with different students.

Explanations/demonstrations

Basic lesson techniques

- Slideshows (p. 87)

- YouTube videos (p. 89)

- Model answers (p. 89)

- Live modelling (p. 91)

- Worksheets (p. 93)

Plus

Maths tools

You may find that drawing graphs or diagrams can be tricky on an online whiteboard, especially without a graphics tablet or touchscreen, so digital Maths tools – like those listed in the 'Tutoring Tech' chapter – can make this much easier.

You can use graphing paper, protractors, rulers, and other virtual equipment, as well as accessing customisable diagrams of shapes and formulae.

Always ensure that students are engaged in the demonstration, not just watching you, by asking recall questions and responses while you explain the topic.

Tick-list

For some students, the focus will simply be on passing their Maths tests rather than understanding the complexities of the topics. As their tutor, you can help them to create 'tick-lists', or step-by-step guides, for the question types they find difficult, which they can then practise until they can apply them to any question of that style.

First, you walk the student through a demonstration of an example question. Then, once they are happy they understand what you did, you work with them to create a list of instructions for them to follow for that style of question.

For example, for missing number problems, the list might look like:

1. Identify all of the missing numbers

2. Simplify by dividing

3. Isolate a and find value

4. Substitute in a and find value of b

5. Calculate value of the new number by substituting in known values

Students can use their 'tick-list' to solve problems independently until they are confident on the method.

Main activities

Basic lesson techniques

- Past papers (p. 93)

- Worksheets (p. 95)

- Annotation (p. 94)

- Question-guessing (p. 95)

Plus

Murder mystery

Murder mystery activities can be a great way to make a lesson a bit more exciting.

There are two ways to run this activity: download a preprepared template or slideshow, or write your own. Either way, it's worth having a look online at how others have written theirs to get some inspiration.

While it will be more time consuming, the advantage of writing your own murder mystery activity is that you can make it as easy or difficult as you want, and you can make different versions with different topics. I have previously used a slideshow, which makes it really simple to write and is easily imported to an online whiteboard. You can write a simple story with questions to solve to move on to the next slide, or do a 'choose your own adventure'–style story with different questions to answer depending on what action the student wants to take.

Board game

This activity generally works best with students in the early stages of KS3, where it's important for them to practise key skills until they're completely confident with them. Answering lots of questions on a worksheet can be a little dull for the student, so a simple board game–style activity can make it a little more fun. This also works well to get students engaged, as most like to play with the tutor, and a little competition can encourage them.

24 END What is the ratio of fingers to thumbs?	23 Simplify 16:20:24	22 Ratio of black to white?	21 Simplify 24:56:96	20 GO BACK 2 SPACES ←	19 3 hours : 30 mins = ?
9 4:5 = ?:10	8 GO BACK 3 SPACES	7 Simplify 20:120	6 Split £70 between Mr X and Mr Y by ratio 3:2	5 GO BACK 2 SPACES ↑	18 Simplify 15:300
10 ↓ Write the ratio of dogs' tails to paws	1 START Simplify 48:60	2 2 hours : 30 mins = ?	3 Write the ratio of heads to eyes	4 Simplify 36:96	17 Split 2.8kg of flour into 3 using ratio 4:3:7
11 2 hours : 20 mins = ?	12 Simplify 21:35	13 1:6 = ?:12	14 Simplify 28:16	15 Ratio of black to white?	16 GO FORWARD 3 SPACES

I like to use a basic 'roll a die and move around a board' game with an online template that I fill out with questions from the topic we're studying. It means we don't waste any lesson time discussing complicated rules, and they have a fair chance at winning. When they land on a question, you can use a timer of 30 seconds or a minute to push them to solve the question more quickly, or do them untimed if the questions are more complex.

If the student gets a question very wrong, you can either plan a lesson around that topic or take some time out of the game to explore why they found it difficult.

Real-world learning

Students generally engage better, particularly in subjects they find less interesting, when it is given a significance in everyday life. Maths is a good candidate for this technique, since it is essential in so many areas of life.

As a current or former STEM student, you can also give students ability-appropriate information from your course of study. You can share ideas or experiments from your labs or classes and show how their learning links to Maths study at a higher level.

Applying this to tutoring lessons can be as simple as finding a worksheet that uses real-life examples – applying angles to architecture or exploring financial Maths – or using videos, images, and other media to contextualise the use of certain skills. The examples should always be relevant to their required learning and help them to build or practise the skills they need at KS3.

Plenaries

Basic lesson techniques

- Mind maps (p. 96)

- Lists (p. 96)

- WWW/EBI (p. 97)

- RAG (p. 97)

- Summary questions (p. 97)

- Quiz questions (p. 98)

- Quick exam question (p. 98)

Plus

'Spot the mistake'

'Spot the mistake' is a good plenary for older or very confident students, because it encourages them to look critically at the material and methods in front of them. It works especially well with the 'wordy' problem-solving questions or multi-step questions, because they have to practise reading the question carefully in order to see the mistake.

To create this plenary, you write out the workings and answer to an example question, but make a deliberate error in the process. This may be a simple miscalculation, like a wrong multiplication in the first step, or a bigger mistake, like drawing the wrong shape or a point on a graph in the wrong place. The more confident the student, the more subtle the error should be. The student then needs to read the question carefully, find the mistake, and correct the workings.

If the student is doing well or you have more time, you can always do a series of these exercises of increasing difficulty. You can also give a particularly tricky one to a group of students to see if they can work together to find the mistake.

Instruction manual

Instruction manual is a plenary which involves asking the student to write out the 'instructions' on how to solve a particular type of question in their own words, as if they were going to give them to another student to follow. They can number or order the steps any way they like, as long as they cover all of the important information.

This plenary works well for topics with more formulaic approaches, like solving or simplifying equations or working out terms in a sequence. I like to keep downloads or screengrabs of the students' manuals once they've finished, so if they're ever struggling on the same topic in future, they can see the method in their own words first to help with their recall.

If you are tutoring a group, you can get them to do this plenary independently and then swap their instructions around next lesson and have them attempt a question according to the instructions they've been given as a starter!

Homework

Basic lesson techniques

- Worksheets (p. 98)

- Past papers (p. 99)

Plus

Additional Maths questions

With particularly able students, you can use more complex problem-solving questions taken from age- and ability-appropriate sources to push them to think in more connected ways. These can be questions you find online, questions from textbooks, or, my favourite, questions taken from past papers of the UK Maths Challenge and Maths Olympiad competitions. Lots of schools offer these competitions, so your student may already be familiar with them, but if not, they can help stretch their learning.

You can offer students the opportunity to use the starter time to discuss any questions they struggle with or to mark their work, so they have an opportunity for feedback.

Planning a KS3 Maths lesson

A sample KS3 Maths lesson might look like this:

Table 10.3 A sample KS3 Maths lesson

Date	Starter	Explanation/ demonstration	Main activity	Plenary	Homework
14/06	Countdown: choose a slide with several preprepared sets of random numbers, use 30-second timer with confident students	Slideshow: 1. Explain any helpful rules, tips, and ideas for approaching simultaneous equation questions 2. Explore examples and model answers to several questions 3. Offer the student the opportunity to work through a question with support by asking for input at different stages	Worksheet: 1. Start with simple equation solving and rearranging questions, working independently 2. Move to more difficult questions, offering support where needed	RAG: give student the opportunity to RAG this topic, explain their answer, and discuss what to move on to next	Worksheet: a short page of more difficult questions to complete independently, 20 minutes

A full 10-week timetable of lesson plans that can be adapted or used for any of your students can be found in the 'Lesson plans' chapter of this book.

Common issues

The most common issues I've come across when tutoring KS3 Maths are:

1. **Lack of confidence**

    See KS3 English for details.

2. **Forgetting or choosing not to write their workings**

    All major exam boards require students to write out their workings to get full marks so that examiners can be sure that students fully understand the topic for the question they are doing. Not writing out their workings can result in a drop in marks, even if their final answers are correct. This means that if students get used to not writing their workings in KS3, it will be even harder to build that habit once they get into Year 10. Students who are reticent to write out their workings should be encouraged during lessons to explain their thinking and shown how to write out the steps of each question.

3. **Having significant knowledge gaps**

    Tutoring should always be seen as an addition to students' opportunities to learn, on top of their in-school lessons, their teachers, and their school homework. However, due to a range of reasons – serious illness, bereavement, personal issues, or, most common recently, the disruptions caused by the COVID-19 pandemic – students can easily end up missing a chunk of consecutive lessons in school. Because much of Maths teaching is sequential, this can mean that students can have major gaps in their knowledge that you may not necessarily be able to anticipate. Tutors are a great way for students to fill these gaps, but it can be a challenge if you end up having to essentially teach a student a significant part of a topic or even a whole topic that they haven't previously had the chance to learn.

    Part of your initial assessment with a student can be a discussion of the topics they have and haven't covered, and you can also ask their parents or teachers if you notice any major issues with a particular area of learning.

4. Problem-solving questions

Problem-solving questions consistently seem to cause Maths students issues at all stages of school, but especially in KS3 when they are fairly new to students. They're designed to be challenging – any mistakes in the early parts of the question will be carried forward – but the biggest issue is when the questions combine two or more skills from different units and don't necessarily indicate when a new skill will be needed. An example of this could be a question that features an image of a shape but actually needs algebra to be used to solve it or a particularly wordy question that requires some inference from the instructions. Students who are not familiar with this style of question or who aren't confident inferring what skill is needed can really struggle with these multi-step questions.

Tutors need to make sure that they are demonstrating the connections between the different skills and units, showing how concepts like algebra can be used a tool more broadly in Maths rather than just covering the requirements of the specification. You also need to introduce a wide range of question styles into their lessons to ensure that your students are exposed to the many ways a question could be written. Finally, you will need to ensure that sufficient time is spent on multi-step questions once confidence in a topic has been established. These questions can take up a significant amount of time, so they can be set as homework in the first instance and then gone through at the start of the next lesson if needed.

TOP TIP

KS3 can be a challenge, as you will need to balance the parent's ideas, their school curriculum, and your own lesson planning in order to work out what to tutor. Make sure to set firm goals with the student and parent before starting tutor, which can then be changed or refreshed after a few months.

QUESTION

How will you adjust your lesson plans between Year 7, 8, and 9?

Chapter 11

GCSE English

GCSE English

GCSE English is split into two qualifications, English Literature and English Language. Each GCSE is composed of two papers, Paper 1 and Paper 2, each of which tests a different set of skills with a variety of questions. As a tutor, you will need to be familiar with the exam board the student is studying for so that you know which papers, questions, and texts they will need to study.

A list of the set texts for each exam board can be found on their websites. All students should have to study, at minimum, a Shakespeare play, a 19th-century novel, a modern (post-1914) drama or prose text, and a poetry anthology.

Table 11.1 GCSE English Literature

	Paper 1	Paper 2
AQA	**Section A** **Shakespeare** • 1 long answer question – part a) on an extract and part b) on the whole text (30 marks + 4 for SPAG) **Section B** **19th-Century Novel** • 1 long answer question – part a) on an extract and part b) on the whole text (30 marks) 1 hour 45 minutes **64 marks** 40%	**Section A** **Modern texts** • 1 essay question (30 marks + 4 for SPAG) **Section B** **Poetry** • 1 comparative question – on one named poem and one other poem of their choice from the anthology (30 marks) **Section C** **Unseen poetry** • 1 essay question – on unseen poem (24 marks) • 1 comparative question – comparing the previous unseen poem to another (8 marks) 2 hours 15 minutes **96 marks** 60%

(Continued)

DOI: 10.4324/9781003211648-15

Table 11.1 (Continued)

	Paper 1	Paper 2
Edexcel	**Section A** **Shakespeare** • 1 long answer question – part a) on an extract and part b) on the whole text (2 × 20 marks) **Section B** **Modern texts** • 1 essay question (40 marks) 1 hour 45 minutes **80 marks** 50%	**Section A** **19th-Century Novel** • 1 long answer question – part a) on an extract and part b) on the whole text (2 × 20 marks) **Section B, Part 1** **Poetry** • 1 comparative question – comparing one named poem and one other poem of their choice (20 marks) **Section B, Part 2** **Unseen poetry** • 1 comparative question – comparing two unseen contemporary poems (20 marks) 2 hours 15 minutes **80 marks** 50%
OCR	**Section A** **Modern texts** • 1 long answer question – part a) on an extract and part b) on the whole text (2 × 20 marks) **Section B** **19th-Century Novel** • 1 essay question (40 marks) 2 hours **80 marks** 50%	**Section A** **Poetry** • 1 comparative question – part a) comparing one named poem with an unseen poem and part b) analysing another poem of their choice (2 × 20 marks) **Section B** **Shakespeare** • 1 essay question (40 marks) 2 hours **80 marks** 50%
Eduqas	**Section A** **Shakespeare** • 1 long answer question – on an extract (1 × 15 marks) • 1 essay question – on the whole text (1 × 25 marks) **Section B** **Poetry** • 1 long answer question – on a named poem (1 × 15 marks) • 1 comparative question – comparing a poem of their choice to the named poem (1 × 25 marks) 2 hours **80 marks** 40%	**Section A** **Modern texts** • 1 long answer question – on both an extract and the whole text (40 marks) **Section B** **19th-Century Novel** • 1 long answer question – on both an extract and the whole text (40 marks) **Section C** **Unseen poetry** • 1 long answer question – on an unseen poem (1 × 15 marks) • 1 comparative question – comparing the unseen poem to another unseen poem (1 × 25 marks) 2 hours 30 minutes **80 marks** 60%

Having tutored hundreds of students and spoken to many teachers, the most common set texts, across all exam boards, appear to be:

- Shakespeare play: *Macbeth* and *Romeo and Juliet*
- Modern drama: *An Inspector Calls*
- 19th-century novel: *A Christmas Carol* and *Jekyll and Hyde*

Reading and familiarising yourself with these texts is a great way to ensure that you're ready to support any GCSE English Literature student. However, this is only the most common GCSE texts, not a comprehensive list, so be aware that you will to check the exam boards' text lists and be clear with parents if they want you to look at a text you are not familiar with.

Table 11.2 GCSE English Language

	Paper 1	Paper 2
AQA	**Section A** **Reading (fiction)** • 1 short answer question (1 × 4 marks) • 2 long answer questions (2 × 8 marks) • 1 extended answer question (1 × 20 marks) **Section B** **Writing (descriptive or narrative writing)** • 1 creative writing question (24 marks + 16 marks for SPAG) 1 hour 45 minutes **80 marks** 50%	**Section A** **Reading (non-fiction and literary non-fiction)** • 1 short answer question (1 × 4 marks) • 2 longer answer questions (1 × 8, 1 × 12 marks) • 1 extended answer question (1 × 16 marks) **Section B** **Writing (persuasive writing)** • 1 extended writing question (24 marks + 16 marks for SPAG) 1 hour 45 minutes **80 marks** 50%
Edexcel	**Section A** **Reading (19th-century fiction)** • 2 short answer questions (1 × 1 mark, 1 × 2 marks) • 1 long answer question (1 × 6 marks) • 1 extended answer question (1 × 15 marks) **Section B** **Writing (descriptive or narrative writing)** • 1 extended answer question (1 × 40 marks) 1 hour 45 minutes **64 marks** 40%	**Section A** **Reading (non-fiction and literary non-fiction)** • 2 short answer questions (2 × 2 marks) • 1 extended answer question (1 × 15 marks) • 2 short answer questions (2 × 1 mark) • 1 extended answer question (1 × 15 marks) • 1 long answer question (1 × 6 marks) • 1 extended answer question (1 × 14 marks) **Section B** **Writing (persuasive writing)** • 1 extended answer question (1 × 40 marks) 2 hours 5 minutes **96 marks** 60%

(Continued)

Table 11.2 (Continued)

	Paper 1	Paper 2
OCR	**Section A** **Reading (19th- and 20th-century fiction)** • 2 short answer questions (1 × 2 marks, 2 × 1 mark) • 1 long answer question (1 × 6 marks) • 2 extended answer question (1 × 12 marks, 1 × 18 marks) **Section B** **Writing (descriptive or narrative writing)** • 1 extended answer question (1 × 40 marks) 2 hours **80 marks** 50%	**Section A** **Reading (fiction and literary non-fiction)** • 2 short answer questions (1 × 2 marks, 2 × 1 mark) • 1 long answer question (1 × 6 marks) • 2 extended answer question (1 × 12 marks, 1 × 18 marks) **Section B** **Writing (descriptive or narrative writing)** • 1 extended answer question (1 × 40 marks) 2 hours **80 marks** 50%
Eduqas	**Section A** **Reading (20th-century fiction)** • 2 short answer questions (2 × 5 marks) • 3 long answer question (3 × 10 marks) **Section B** **Writing (descriptive or narrative writing)** • 1 extended answer question (1 × 40 marks) 1 hour 45 minutes **80 marks** 40%	**Section A** **Reading (19th- and 21st-century fiction)** • 7 short answer questions (6 × 1 mark, 1 × 4 marks) • 3 long answer question (3 × 10 marks) **Section B** **Writing (persuasive or transactional writing)** • 2 extended answer question (2 × 20 marks) 2 hours **80 marks** 60%

Changes in 2022

In 2022, there will be some significant changes to the GCSE English Literature exam structures and content. These changes have been introduced as a result of the COVID-19 pandemic and may potentially be reversed in future.

Table 11.3 Changes to each of the major exam boards' English Literature exams in 2022

AQA	All students to study for Paper 1 Section A (Shakespeare) **and** Paper 2 Section C (Unseen Poems) in one exam, then any **two** of the **three** remaining units: 19th-Century Novel, Modern Texts, and Poetry
Edexcel	All students to study for Paper 1 in full and then **either** Section A or Section B of Paper 2

OCR	All students to study for Paper 2 Section B (Shakespeare) and then any **two** of the **three** remaining units: 19th-Century Novel, Modern Texts, and Poetry
Eduqas	All students to study for Paper 1 Section A (Shakespeare) **and** Paper 2 Section A (Modern Texts) as two separate 1-hour exams, then any **two** of the **three** remaining units: Poetry Anthology, 19th-Century Prose, and Unseen Poetry.

Some of the timings and marks available in each paper may vary depending on the exam board, but the question styles should remain the same.

The GCSE Language papers will remain the same in 2022.

So, you've assessed your student's progress and you know what they need to work on – so how do you plan your first lesson?

First, you'll need to look online and in textbooks for resources and worksheets related to the student's subject and topics. Second, you'll need to learn some lesson techniques. These are the activities you'll use with students to help develop their skills and understanding.

The rest of this chapter is divided into the sections of the lesson plan. In each section, you'll find a detailed list of basic lesson techniques in the 'Online tutoring basics' chapter (pages 7–26), which are all applicable to any age and subject. In the following, you'll find them listed in the relevant section alongside more specific exercises and techniques that I feel work best for each GCSE subject.

I've divided the techniques into the key parts of a lesson, as outlined in Chapter 7, so you can find lists of exercises to use with your students. Once you've learned some techniques, you can use the different categories to create quick and easy lesson plans. There's a sample lesson at the end of each subject section to show you how to do that.

Lesson techniques

Starters

Basic lesson techniques

- Matching exercises (p. 84)

- Sorting exercises (p. 85)

- Word searches (p. 85)

- Crosswords (p. 85)

- Mind maps (p. 86)

How to tutor

- Quickfire questions (p. 87)

- Homework review (p. 87)

Plus

'Speedy reads'

'Speedy reads' is my name for small extracts with reading comprehension tasks and short answer questions. 'Speedy reads' work well for students who are worried about reading comprehension. By using unseen texts, it helps expose students who are not keen readers to a wide variety of types and styles of texts.

To create a 'Speedy read', you take a short extract – no longer than a dozen lines – from an unseen text. Next, you write several identification questions – 'What is the main character's job?' and so on – and then, if the student is confident, a few inference questions – 'How does the main character feel about losing their job?'

I try to keep the extract fairly short and encourage students to draw directly on the text rather than from their own knowledge or guesses.

'Fill the gap'/'Finish the sentence'

'Fill the gap', or 'Finish the sentence' if the gap is always at the end, can be an interesting way to prompt students to recall key information. 'Fill the gap' can be used in lots of ways:

- Removing the conjugated verbs from a piece of writing and only offering the root verb so students have to infer which person and tense to use

- Removing all of the technical terminology from an analytical paragraph so students have to remember the key terms

- Offering partial definitions for key words

- Removing the dialogue from a piece of fiction writing so students can write their own as a creative exercise

Feel free to develop your own uses as well. It is up to you, depending on the level of the student, whether to offer correct or model answers alongside the exercise – I generally don't unless a student is really struggling, as it is more effective for them to recall or imagine the answers themselves.

You can also use 'Fill the gap' exercises as main activities, if you make the answers required longer or more complex.

Punctuation exercises

To make these exercises, I take a short passage from an unseen text, or one I have written myself, and remove all of the punctuation, including full stops, capital letters, commas, apostrophes, and so on. If the student is struggling I will put all of the removed punctuation in a list at the end of the extract for them to use, but if not I will simply present the extract minus the punctuation and see how many mistakes they can spot. This can be a useful way to test how familiar a student is with the rules of punctuation, highlighting any that they don't spot or add incorrectly. Because of the sheer number of ambiguities that can exist in the English language, this is less a perfect text of proofreading accuracy and more a chance to see how your student thinks about punctuation and which elements they are most confident with.

typical of them to leave steven said softly what does that mean clare replied sticking out her chin i just mean well they arent very thoughtful he replied tactfully clare knew he was right but didnt want to admit it where are you going now she asked steven got to his feet im off to the shops now but ill be back later

Add any punctuation you think is missing: capital letters, full stops, commas, speech marks, question marks

Poetry starter

This starter is for GCSE English Literature students who are taking a Poetry unit with an anthology. Many students seem to find their anthology daunting or simply unfamiliar, so rather than working through lots of poems one after the other or spending a whole lesson on one, they may find it easier to do them one at a time over a long period.

For the poetry starter, I will change the lesson structure slightly, using the first 20 minutes or so of the lesson to get the student to read the poem out loud, discuss any significant language or structural features, contextualise it, and then pick out a few key quotes. Students can make their initial notes on the online whiteboard or in their print anthologies, which we can then return to when they want to cover the poems in more detail or revise them.

Explanations/demonstrations

Basic lesson techniques

- Slideshows (p. 87)

- YouTube videos (p. 89)

- Model answers (p. 89)

- Live modelling (p. 91)

- Worksheets (p. 93)

Plus

Reading together

If you are working with a student who is being home-schooled, taking time out of school for an illness or other absence, or struggling to commit to reading an entire set text, reading together can be a great way to demonstrate active reading strategies and make the most of time spent reading for practising other skills.

Reading together can take several forms: you can work through short sections of a text lesson by lesson, read a long section of a text for a portion of a lesson, set reading and recall questions as homework, and decide whether you want students to read out loud or in their heads depending on their ability and confidence.

I especially like using reading together as a strategy for tackling poems when you're working with a student who struggles with or dislikes poetry. So many poems were written to be read out loud, and it's often easier for students who struggle to identify language and structural devices to hear them when they are read aloud. If we're going to be working on a poem in a lesson, I usually start that lesson by having the student read the poem aloud or, if it is particularly long, reading alternating paragraphs with the student.

Reading together can take up a lot of lesson time so it shouldn't be used too heavily, but for students who aren't familiar with their texts it can be a really useful technique. Tutors should always be judicious in their selection of extracts to read together to make the most of this technique.

SWAT/key word analysis demonstration

Single Word Analysis Techniques (SWAT), sometimes called Keyword Analysis, is crucial to achieving in English, but it can be difficult for some students to grasp and is not necessarily an intuitive technique.

There are a number of ways I like to demonstrate SWAT, my favourite being the mind map demonstration: reading a short extract together; selecting a short quotation or phrase; and creating a map of connotations, links, and ideas to walk students through the process of isolating key words from within it.

This demonstration segues well into an activity where students can try the technique themselves using the same extract you've been working on together, with the opportunity to explore their ideas and ask questions.

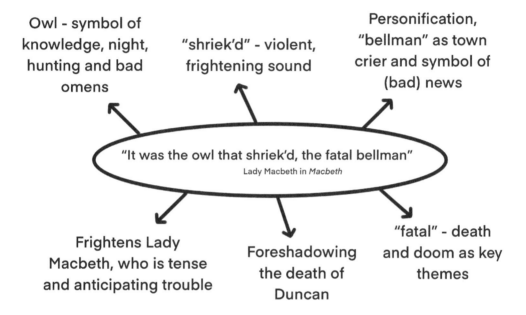

'Layers of meaning'

The 'layers of meaning' exercise involves taking a short quotation or phrase and then moving down the page by writing in the different 'layers' of meaning each word could have within the extract. This can help students to understand the difference between connotation and denotation, as well as developing their understanding of alternative interpretations. By using the layers to demonstrate how many different ways students can pick apart quotations, it can help to model how students can develop an interpretation of the writer's choice of language and structure.

This demonstration can transition into an activity, where the student takes over and has a go at it themselves.

"You really are an automaton—a calculating-machine!"

Watson in *The Sign of Four*

Layer 1 Language feature	Metaphor - depersonalisation? "automaton" - self-operating, imitation of a person Logical, reasoning, cold - detached from humanity
Layer 2 Sounds	Lots of consonants - stiff and mechanical Exclamation mark indicates excited tone
Layer 3 Context	Rapid technological development and a fascination with human/machine relationship 'Fin de siècle' anxiety about tech
Layer 4 Punctuation	Dash creates pause - gasp for air or astonishment or grasping for right words

Unseen material

Unseen material is one of the elements students can find very intimidating, so it should be used regularly. Some students may just want opportunities to write answers for these sections and have them marked, but others may want guidance on how to approach them.

Unseen prose extracts or poems can be introduced during another lesson activity, to explore a language analysis technique or plan an answer, but they can also be used on their own.

There are several activities that you can use to increase students' confidence when working with unseen material:

- **Read through the unseen material together, out loud for poems, and discuss structural ideas (rhyme/metre/paragraphing/pace, etc.)** – students are often less confident at identifying these

- **Ask the student to identify and annotate language/structural features, either as pre-reading or in lesson, before discussing their ideas** – can be used to make answer plans

- Walk through model answers and discuss WWW/EBI before the student has a go themselves

- **Give the student 10 minutes to choose five features/quotes and present their argument against a given question** – discuss any issues or obvious missed ideas

Main activities

Basic lesson techniques

- Past papers (p. 93)

- Worksheets (p. 95)

- Annotation (p. 94)

- Question guessing (p. 95)

Plus

Plot review

Plot review, as is clear from the name, is an activity that can be used to check students' familiarity with the plot of their set texts and revise the important events.

I usually ask students to create a timeline as part of a plot review, or two if the plot is in non-chronological order – one in time order and one in plot order – to help them understand what is happening. Other formats for plot review can include flow charts or tables, or you could create a series of jumbled paragraphs describing plot events which students have to put in the right order.

If students are particularly struggling, I will sometimes make or find on Google Images an infographic of the plot with labels or events removed, so they have a visual prompt of the plot which they can then fill in and download a copy of for themselves. You should try to avoid simply telling the student what happens unless they are clearly struggling, as this will undermine their recall ability later on.

If the student is more confident with the plot of their text, it can be good to introduce some ideas about theme and character as you work through it to start consolidating the key ideas they will need in their revision.

You can also use the YouTube lesson technique described previously for plot review, where you ask students to watch a short clip explaining the plot and then summarise in their own words.

Character review

Character review is much like plot review, in that it tests students' recall of the characters of a set text and provides an opportunity to fill in any gaps.

There are several ways to do character review – I usually use mind maps, with an image/illustration of the character or their name in the centre of the map, but you can also use charts, worksheets, stills from productions or movies, or other interactive resources. There are some excellent infographics and other images available for common set texts, like Shakespeare plays, available on resource websites.

Once you've covered all of the characters, you can then help the student to create individual mind maps or fact files for each one, with their name, age, relationships to other characters, motive, role, likes/dislikes, and other relevant information.

You can also use the YouTube lesson technique described previously for character review, where you ask students to watch a short clip explaining the characters and then summarise in their own words.

Paragraphing practice

Unsurprisingly, this exercise simply involves the student practising writing paragraphs, in a variety of different settings. This can be as part of an exam-style answer, in response to a question you have designed, or as part of a worksheet or online resource.

It is always best to start with a discussion of how your student is used to writing paragraphs and what methods they have been taught. As I discuss during the assessment section, some students are taught to use an acronym like PEA or PEEL, while others use a more fluid format like 'What, How, Why?' Whatever the student has been taught, you should try to work with, as you are likely to confuse them if you try to use a different acronym. However, if the student is really struggling with the method they are taught in school and asks you for a different one, you can demonstrate a few to give them the chance to find one that works better for them.

'Layers of meaning'

As outlined previously in the Explanations/Demonstrations section, 'layers of meaning' is an analytical exercise which helps students to understand the different levels or layers of meaning that a quotation might contain.

It is up to you whether to label or guide the layers of their analysis: with students who are struggling to unpick quotes, prompting them to think about identifying rhetorical devices, structural analysis, contextual information about the author or period, language and sounds, or other elements of analysis can help them to see how many different ways there are to approach a quotation. With more confident students, I might leave them to see how many different layers they can think of on their own and then offer prompts once they run out of ideas.

You can offer students a worksheet or template with lines to write their ideas on, or you can simply draw lines onto the online whiteboard.

If the student is revising key quotations for use in the exam, I always give them the opportunity to screengrab or download their notes so they can compile a list of quotes and ideas for later.

SWAT/key word analysis mind maps

As explained previously, SWAT, or 'Keyword Analysis', is an essential part of writing exam answers for GCSE English students. Once you have demonstrated how to unpick a quotation using your own mind maps, it can be useful to hand this technique over to students so they can practise for themselves. I find that students who are less confident about SWAT find the mind map format less intimidating, because their ideas are not put in a hierarchy or order and they can link their ideas together in whatever way they choose. Placing the quotation in the middle also encourages them to pick out individual words and think about the context of them within the sentence or quotation they chose.

Tables of quotes

Tables of quotes can be constructed in a number of ways: this is an especially useful exercise for tutors as it allows students to cover large amounts of text in a relatively short time and provides lots of fodder for producing practice paragraphs at another time or for homework. It is also often appreciated by students as they can download or screenshot their tables to build banks of quotations about a particular text or anthology, saving them time in homework or revision.

For students who need practise identifying and explaining rhetorical devices, it can be useful to table in the names of several devices and ask them to look for them throughout and extract and offer brief explanations of their effect.

For students who need help identifying themes, tables can prompt them to look for quotations or ideas related to a particular theme and explore the relevance of these key ideas.

For students who need help introducing context into their paragraphs, you can label the various areas of the table using key social or historical ideas and ask them to look for key ideas or quotations that align with them.

For students who are in the later stages of revision and are looking to build banks of key quotes, tables can be a great way to organise their quotations and code them according to theme, character, plot point, device, or other element of the text.

Photograph inspiration

One of the most common, and useful, exercises for GCSE English students who are struggling with creative writing is to use photo prompts – just like the ones

Table 11.4 Key quotes from *Macbeth* by William Shakespeare

Quote	Theme	Effect
'Fair is foul, and foul is fair'	Betrayal, fate	Alliteration of 'f' and chiasmus – inversion, reversal, theme of outward appearance versus inward nature
'So well thy words become thee as thy wounds;/They smack of honour both'	Masculinity, honour	
'There if I grow,/The harvest is your own'	Fate, honour	

they will see in their exam booklets. This can be photos of non-specific places (a random tall building, for example, rather than the Empire State Building), which can be used as the prompt for the setting of a story, or photos of individuals or small groups. The people in the pictures can be used as the inspiration for a story: who are they? What do/did they do? Where do they live? This exercise encourages students to flesh out their characters and settings while giving them a visual prompt to work from.

Photograph inspiration works especially well with old photos: I usually choose old black-and-white or sepia photographs to encourage them to use their historical knowledge and imagination.

Debate speech

Debate speech gives students the opportunity to practise their persuasive writing construction of arguments in a format that practises the key skills from the exam.

When working with confident students, you can offer them the option to write a speech about any topic they desire, but with most students, it can be useful to offer them something to argue against. This can be either something you have written or an example of a debate speech you have found online.

If you want to, you can offer students a template or script to help them write their speech, with sentence starters and other guidance, but with confident creative writers, you can leave them to write in whatever format they desire.

With these kinds of open-ended tasks, it can be useful to end the lesson by marking what they have written against the expectations of the exam mark scheme, so they can start to see how their own creative writing lines up with the grade boundaries they will be expected to meet.

Plenaries

Basic lesson techniques

- Mind maps (p. 96)

- Lists (p. 96)

- WWW/EBI (p. 97)

- RAG (p. 97)

- Summary questions (p. 97)

- Quiz questions (p. 98)

- Quick exam question (p. 98)

Plus

Memory game

This plenary can be especially useful with students who have trouble committing key vocabulary to memory. To create this game, you'll need to write a dozen or more key words – word classes, language or structure devices, characters, plot points, and so on – on a slide, give the student 30 seconds to memorise it, and then ask them to write out as many words as they can remember.

For bonus points, you can ask the student to give you a definition of the word or an example of the device.

Homework

Basic lesson techniques

- Worksheets (p. 98)

- Past papers (p. 99)

Plus

Pre-reading and vocab identification

This really serves as preparatory work rather than homework by giving students the chance to read a long extract or poem outside of the lesson and make notes on themes, structural features, language devices, and types of vocab. I always encourage students to practise using their technical terminology while they're annotating, to ensure that they can spot the relevant features, and asking them to take additional notes means that they can write down the effect as well.

This can be a useful homework because some students dislike the pressure of being watched while they read, while others simply don't have enough lesson time to spend a significant portion of it reading.

Paragraph practice

Paragraph practice does what it says on the tin: it's an opportunity for students to practise their paragraph writing outside of the lesson time. I often find that with students I only see once a week, we just don't have enough time to write the paragraphs they need to practise, so setting just one or two to write at home can be a real help for them.

You will need to set your student a writing task – I usually ask them to complete the writing task from the lesson so the content they need is fresh in their mind – and once it is finished, they can send it to you to mark before the next lesson, or you can mark it together as the next starter.

Planning a GCSE English lesson

To give you an idea of how that framework could be filled out with some of the lesson techniques I've discussed in this chapter, I've written out a sample of each type of lesson.

Table 11.5 A sample GCSE English Literature lesson

Date	Starter	Explanation/ demonstration	Main activity	Plenary	Homework
07/11	Punctuation exercise: – Remove all punctuation from an extract from prose text – Discuss effect of different punctuation marks	Character focus from modern play, *An Inspector Calls* – Identify all the characters in the play – Sketch relationship map between characters – Discuss key themes in relation to each character, such as Mr Birling capitalism, Inspector Goole socialism	Plan answer to essay question about a key character, Sheila Birling – Discuss question, 'In what ways does Sheila Birling mature over the course of the play?' – Mind map some key quotes/ideas – Sort ideas in paragraphs, with one or two quotes for each – Plan intro and conc – Write first paragraph of analysis	Mark the paragraph – Discuss paragraph together and how the student feels about it – Read and offer feedback – Use WWW/ EBI or similar	Write the rest of the answer, including intro and conc

Table 11.6 A sample GCSE English Language lesson

Date	Starter	Explanation/ demonstration	Main activity	Plenary	Homework
03/05	Sorting exercise: – word class (adverbs vs adjectives) – discuss significance of these words in creative writing	How to plan a creative writing answer: plot – Look at a short story together – Create a flow chart of the plot – Discuss the effect of changing the order of the plot on the reader – Relate to key skills/AOs from mark scheme	Write own creative writing answer – Choose prompt photo – Write plot ideas in chronological order – Experiment with changing the order of the plot	Mind map: – write down everything learned about importance of plot order in lesson	Write first two paragraphs of creative writing answer

A full 10-week timetable of lesson plans for each that can be adapted or used for any of your students can be found in the 'Lesson plans' chapter of this book.

Common issues

Regardless of the age, ability, or confidence of your student, they are never going to get everything right the first time. Every student is unique, so each will find different things easier or more difficult.

However, there are some consistent issues that I have noticed in my time as a tutor, which it can help to watch out for so you can offer your students advice when they need it.

The most common issues I've come across when tutoring GCSE English Literature are:

1. **Lack of confidence**

   Students can be worried about their GCSEs for all sorts of reasons, so wherever possible, tutors should try to be as supportive as possible – whether that's offering hints and tips, sharing anecdotes about your experiences at school, or just offering a bit of emotional reassurance. Lots of GCSE English Literature students seem to worry about not being able to learn the quotes, themes, and ideas for the set texts off by heart, so it can help to remind them that they don't need to know everything and that they can prioritise the information rather than trying to cover it all. Alternatively, they may be anxious about the unseen poems or texts, so it can help to work on a range of unseen texts in your lessons together to get them used to it. I would also recommend reminding your students whenever they're worried that your lessons are a safe place to make mistakes and that you're there to help, not just to test them or mark their work.

2. **Struggling to understand process and language of characterisation**

This will obviously vary between students, but a topic I often end up having to go over multiple times with students is characterisation. The sticking point is usually that students write about characters like they're people, not characters: they say 'Jane feels sad' or 'Sheila is angry', but they don't show evidence of how they know that, why it's important, or how the writer has created that feeling. I recommend that students get into the habit of describing 'the character of Jane' or 'Sheila's character' to create some distance between the character as a person they relate to and the character as a construction by the writer and then using a formula like 'What, How, Why' to help them to map the writer's language onto the effect on the reader.

3. **Inconsistent SPAG**

SPAG is an important part of the GCSE mark schemes, but it often gets overlooked by students who are more worried about what to write than how to write. Using starters to do regular SPAG exercises, picking up on SPAG errors consistently in your lessons, and marking SPAG alongside content in any feedback you provide will help to highlight any particular issues the student is having. It can be worth pointing out to students how many marks they can get for the SPAG elements of the papers, so they understand how valuable they are. If you notice that the student's SPAG is becoming a bigger problem than you initially anticipated, you can always speak to the student's parent and school and ask that they be given more support with it in class.

4. **Forgetting to use technical terminology**

Technical terminology can be a slightly contentious issue among teachers, but I think that tutoring lessons are the best time to introduce some of the names of language devices to students. Some students like to be given a list of words to learn; others just like to learn them when they are shown an example of them, but, either way, helping students to feel confident using words like simile, alliteration, or rhyme correctly can really help with their analytical writing. The key thing to remember is that technical terminology should always be linked to effect on the reader: there's no point in saying 'that's a metaphor' if the student doesn't then say what its effect is and link it to the writer's viewpoint!

The most common issues I've come across when tutoring GCSE English Language are:

1. **Lack of confidence**

   The reason I've put this one twice is that it looks different in Language: in Literature, the lack of confidence is often about their knowledge of the texts, but in Language, it's about their identifying and analysing skills. I have had far too many students say, 'I don't know if this is the right answer, but . . .' or 'this might be wrong, but is it . . .', and then give an amazing answer. This fear translates onto their exam paper, too – it might be the difference between them writing down a brilliant idea or not. I have noticed that this is often true of young women, who are not usually as confident giving answers as their male counterparts, so a special effort should be made to reassure female students when their answers are good but also to remind them that it's okay to make mistakes and learn from them in your space.

2. **Struggling to identify language features in non-fiction texts**

   Non-fiction texts also have language features in them, but some students seem to really struggle to recognise them. To help with this, I try to expose students to a wide range of non-fiction texts, especially travel writing and biographies, that are often laden with language devices, and then show them newspaper articles like the ones used in the exam paper to challenge them to pay closer attention to what language features look like in different contexts.

3. **Giving too much or too little detail in answers**

   The first few questions of the paper are usually short comprehension questions, while the last few questions ask for longer responses, but I regularly see students writing too much detail in the early questions and not enough in the later ones! Some students seem to struggle to adapt their writing to the demands of the different questions in the two papers, so they end up giving the same level of detail no matter what the question is asking for. Encouraging students to read the question carefully, check how many marks it is asking for, and then adjust their answers accordingly can help. I also like to use exercises like the 'layers of meaning' task to show students how to extend and organise their longer answers.

4. **Finding creative writing difficult**

On the whole, I find that GCSE English students fall into two groups: ones who are already writing creatively in their own time and simply need their writing adapted to fit the exam and ones who dislike writing creatively and prefer the analytical questions in the exam. The second group can be more of a challenge for tutors, as they may struggle to come up with their own ideas or refuse to write extended creative answers. I find that using prompted exercises, like those listed previously, can help them to focus on the key techniques of creative writing without having to invent too much themselves in the first instance. I also like to introduce the ideas from analytical writing – effect on the reader, language devices, and so on – into their planning stage, so they can use ideas that they are familiar with from their analytical writing in the creative writing questions.

TOP TIP

Use a wide range of texts in your examples and live modelling – including some poetry, even if the student isn't studying it for the exam because of the 2022 changes. It will help students to become more holistic critics and expose them to a wider range of writers, language, structures and styles.

QUESTION

How will your tutoring differ when working on analytical writing compared to creative writing?

Chapter 12

GCSE Maths

GCSE Maths

As a tutor, you will need to be familiar with the exam board the student is studying for, so that you know which papers and questions they will need to answer and therefore which topics to cover.

Here's a quick breakdown of the key differences between the main exam boards in the UK:

Table 12.1 Key differences between UK exam boards

	Paper 1	Paper 2	Paper 3
AQA	**Non-calculator** 1 hr 30 mins **80 marks** Mix of questions from any topics **33.3%**	**Calculator allowed** 1 hr 30 mins **80 marks** Mix of questions from any topics **33.3%**	**Calculator allowed** 1 hr 30 mins **80 marks** Mix of questions from any topics **33.3%**
Edexcel	**Non-calculator** 1 hr 30 mins **80 marks** Mix of questions from any topics **33.3%**	**Calculator allowed** 1 hr 30 mins **80 marks** Mix of questions from any topics **33.3%**	**Calculator allowed** 1 hr 30 mins **80 marks** Mix of questions from any topics **33.3%**
OCR	**Calculator allowed** 1 hr 30 mins **100 marks** Mix of questions from any topics **33.3%**	**Non-calculator** 1 hr 30 mins **100 marks** Mix of questions from any topics **33.3%**	**Calculator allowed** 1 hr 30 mins **100 marks** Mix of questions from any topics **33.3%**

(Continued)

Table 12.1 (Continued)

	Paper 1	Paper 2	Paper 3
Eduqas	Non-calculator 2 hrs 15 mins **120 marks** Mix of questions from any topics **50%**	Calculator allowed 2 hrs 15 mins **120 marks** Mix of questions from any topics **50%**	N/A

In 2022, students will be allowed a formula sheet and other advance information, unlike previous years. These changes were introduced as a result of the COVID-19 pandemic and may potentially be reversed in future years.

So, you've assessed your student's progress and you know what they need to work on – so how do you plan your first lesson?

First, you'll need to look online and in textbooks for resources and worksheets related to the student's subject and topics. Second, you'll need to learn some lesson techniques. These are the activities you'll use with students to help develop their skills and understanding.

You'll find a detailed list of basic lesson techniques in the 'Online tutoring basics' chapter (pages 7–26), which are all applicable to any age and subject. In the following, you'll find them listed in the relevant section alongside more specific exercises and techniques that I feel work best for each GCSE subject.

I've divided the techniques into the key parts of a lesson, as outlined in Chapter 7, so you can find lists of exercises to use with your students. Once you've learned some techniques, you can use the different categories to create quick and easy lesson plans. There's a sample lesson at the end of each subject section to show you how to do that.

LESSON TECHNIQUES

Starters

Basic techniques

- Matching exercises (p. 84)

- Sorting exercises (p. 85)

- Mind maps (p. 86)

- Quickfire questions (p. 87)

- Homework review (p. 87)

Plus

Quick activity starter

For this starter, you'll need to generate some quick Maths/reasoning puzzles for the student to solve. These test skills like mental Maths, visual reasoning, basic content like place value/fractions/decimals, and so on.

You can use an online puzzle generator or question bank to create screen-shots, or paste them onto a slideshow to use again with another student. You can find recommendations in the Resources section at the end of this book.

Countdown

If you're not familiar with the TV show, Countdown is a Maths challenge where five random numbers are generated, and students have to use them to make another random, three-digit number. They can use any of the basic Maths skills – addition, subtraction, division, multiplication – to manipulate the numbers and can only use each number once.

Students often enjoy exercises that the tutor does with them, so you can try playing against each other to see who can get the answer fastest or get the most right answers. This also works really well with groups, as the competitive element can encourage students to engage, and the challenges are rarely impossible to solve.

There are a number of websites and online generators that can help you to make the numbers: I often generate several and save them as images to use with different students.

Explanations/demonstrations

Basic lesson techniques

- Slideshows (p. 87)

- YouTube videos (p. 89)

- Model answers (p. 89)

- Live modelling (p. 91)

- Worksheets (p. 93)

How to tutor

Plus

Maths tools

You may find that drawing graphs or diagrams can be tricky on an online whiteboard, especially without a graphics tablet or touchscreen, so digital Maths tools – like those listed in the 'Tutoring Tech' chapter – can make this much easier.

You can use graphing paper, protractors, rulers, and other virtual equipment, as well as accessing customisable diagrams of shapes and formulae.

Always ensure that students are engaged in the demonstration, not just watching you, by asking recall questions and responses while you explain the topic.

Tick-list

For some students, the focus will simply be on passing their Maths tests rather than understanding the complexities of the topics. As their tutor, you can help them to create 'tick-lists', or step-by-step guides, for the question types they find difficult, which they can then practise until they can apply them to any question of that style.

First, you walk the student through a demonstration of an example question. Then, once they are happy they understand what you did, you work with them to create a list of instructions for them to follow for that style of question.

For example, for missing number problems, the list might look like:

1. Identify all of the missing numbers

2. Simplify by dividing

3. Isolate a and find value

4. Substitute in a in find value of b

5. Calculate value of the new number by substituting in known values

Students can use their 'tick-list' to solve problems independently until they are confident on the method.

Main activities

Basic lesson techniques

- Past papers (p. 93)

- Worksheets (p. 95)

- Annotation (p. 94)

- Question-guessing (p. 95)

Plus

Murder mystery

Murder mystery activities can be a great way to make a lesson a bit more exciting.

There are two ways to run this activity: download a preprepared template or slideshow, or write your own. Either way, it's worth having a look online at how others have written theirs to get some inspiration.

While it will be more time consuming, the advantage of writing your own murder mystery activity is that you can make it as easy or difficult as you want, and you can make different versions with different topics. I have previously used a slideshow, which makes it really simple to write and is easily imported to an online whiteboard. You can write a simple story with questions to solve to move on to the next slide, or do a 'choose your own adventure'–style story with different questions to answer depending on what action the student wants to take.

Board game

This activity generally works best with students in the early stages of the GCSE course, where it's important for them to practise key skills until they're completely confident with them. Answering lots of questions on a worksheet can be a little dull for the student, so a simple board game–style activity can make it a little more fun. This also works well to get students engaged, as most like to play with the tutor, and a little competition can encourage them.

I like to use a basic 'roll a die and move around a board' game with an online template that I fill out with questions from the topic we're studying. It means we don't waste any lesson time discussing complicated rules, and they have a fair chance at winning. When they land on a question, you can use a timer of 30 seconds or a minute to push them to solve the question more quickly, or do them untimed if the questions are more complex.

If the student gets a question very wrong, you can either plan a lesson around that topic or take some time out of the game to explore why they found it difficult.

Real-world learning

Students generally engage better, particularly in subjects they find less interesting, when it is given a significance in everyday life. Maths is a good candidate

24 END Factorise ax+bx+cx	**23** Solve $(x-1)^2 = 17$	**22** Factorise $72ab+45a^2b$	**21** Factorise $14x^2+21x^2$	**20** GO BACK 2 SPACES	**19** Solve $x^2 = 2 \times 8$
9 Solve $\frac{8}{x} = x-2$	**8** GO BACK 3 SPACES	**7** Solve $x^2 = x+2$	**6** Factorise x^2-7	**5** GO BACK 2 SPACES	**18** Factorise $12x^2y+18xy^2$
10 Factorise $4n+6mn^2$	**1** START Factorise $15+25y$	**2** Solve $\frac{3x}{5} + 3 = 7$	**3** Solve $x^2-x=0$	**4** Factorise x^2+6x+8	**17** Solve $3(x^2+x) = 6$
11 Factorise x^2-x	**12** Solve $x+2=3-x$	**13** Solve $\frac{5x-11}{3} = x$	**14** Factorise $27xy-18x^2$	**15** Solve $\frac{3}{x} = 4$	**16** GO FORWARD 3 SPACES

for this technique, since it is essential in so many areas of life. Students often like to know *why* they have to learn something, rather than just *how* to do it, and tutors have the time to answer that question that teachers often don't.

Demonstrating Maths in the real world might look like:

- **Themed worksheets that use real-life examples** – applying angles to architecture, exploring financial Maths, or linking statistics and probability to weather data

- **Roleplaying** – you and the student can play out buying things from a shop with discounts, buying a car on a finance plan with interest, getting around a map, choosing a mobile phone contract, and so on

- **Videos, images, and other media** – these could be YouTube videos, excerpts from documentaries, elements from your course

- Newspaper articles or headlines related to the topic you're working on with them

- **Puzzles and games** – exploring chess puzzles, a stock market simulator, card tricks, Sudoku, Countdown, you name it!

As a current or former STEM student, you can also give students ability-appropriate information from your course of study. You can share ideas or experiments from your labs which will contextualise their learning and help them to link abstract ideas to real-world events.

Plenaries

Basic lesson techniques

- Mind maps (p. 96)

- Lists (p. 96)

- WWW/EBI (p. 97)

- RAG (p. 97)

- Summary questions (p. 97)

- Quiz questions (p. 98)

- Quick exam question (p. 98)

Plus

'Spot the mistake'

'Spot the mistake' is a good plenary for more confident students, because it encourages them to look critically at the material and methods in front of them. It works especially well with the 'wordy' problem-solving questions or multi-step questions, because they have to practise reading the question carefully in order to see the mistake.

To create this plenary, you write out the workings and answer to an example question, but make a deliberate error in the process. This may be a simple mis-calculation, like a wrong multiplication in the first step, or a bigger mistake, like drawing the wrong shape or a point on a graph in the wrong place. The more confident the student, the more subtle the error should be. The student then needs to read the question carefully, find the mistake, and correct the workings.

If the student is doing well or you have more time, you can always do a series of these exercises of increasing difficulty. You can also give a particularly tricky one to a group of students to see if they can work together to find the mistake.

Instruction manual

Instruction manual is a plenary which involves asking the student to write out the 'instructions' on how to solve a particular type of question in their own words, as if they were going to give them to another student to follow. They can number or order the steps any way they like, as long as they cover all of the important information.

This plenary works well for topics with more formulaic approaches, like solving or simplifying equations or working out terms in a sequence. I like to keep downloads or screengrabs of the students' manuals once they've finished, so if they're ever struggling on the same topic in future, they can see the method in their own words first to help with their recall.

If you are tutoring a group, you can get them to do this plenary independently and then swap their instructions around next lesson and have them attempt a question according to the instructions they've been given as a starter!

Homework

Basic lesson techniques

- Worksheets (p. 98)

- Past papers (p. 99)

Plus

Additional Maths questions

With particularly able students, you can use more complex problem-solving questions taken from age- and ability-appropriate sources to push them to think in more connected ways. These can be questions you find online, questions from textbooks, or questions taken from past papers of the UK Maths Challenge and Maths Olympiad competitions. The student's school may already offer these competitions, so they may be familiar with them, but regardless they deliberately designed with the age and stage of GCSE students in mind and can help stretch their learning and knowledge.

Planning a GCSE Maths lesson

A sample GCSE Maths lesson might look like this:

Table 12.2 A sample GCSE Maths lesson

Date	Starter	Explanation/ demonstration	Main activity	Plenary	Homework
14/06	Quickfire questions: – fractions, decimals, and percentages questions – 10 questions total – recap previous lesson	Slideshow: – Go through examples of adding and subtracting decimals, modelling workings and asking student to offer the steps – Go through examples of multiplying and dividing decimals, following the same steps	Compilation paper: – Mix of exam-style questions on the topic – Start with simple questions and build to multi-step questions – Marking as we go	Listing: – Recall a list of all points on adding and subtracting, 1 minute – Recall a list of all points on multiplying and dividing, 1 minute	Worksheet: Short worksheet of practice questions, 20 minutes of work

A full 10 week timetable of lesson plans that can be adapted or used for any of your students can be found in the 'Lesson plans' chapter of this book.

Common issues

The most common issues I've come across when tutoring GCSE Maths are:

1. Lack of confidence

Students can be worried about their GCSEs for all sorts of reasons, so wherever possible, tutors should try to be as supportive as possible – whether that's offering hints and tips, sharing anecdotes about your experiences at GCSE, or just offering a bit of emotional reassurance. A general pattern that I have noticed when tutoring is that young women are generally less confident than their male counterparts in offering answers, especially in STEM subjects, and this translates to their performance in assessments and exams. Therefore, tutors should always encourage and praise students when they succeed and offer non-judgemental guidance and support when they are struggling with a topic.

I would also recommend reminding your students whenever they're worried that your lessons are a safe place to make mistakes and that you're there to help, not just to test them or mark their work.

2. Forgetting or choosing not to write their workings

All major exam boards require students to write out their workings to get full marks so that examiners can be sure that students fully understand the topic for the question they are doing. Not writing out their workings can result in a drop in marks, even if their final answers are correct. Students who are reticent to write out their workings should be encouraged during lessons to explain their thinking and shown how to write out the steps of each question.

3. Having significant knowledge gaps

Tutoring should always be seen as an addition to students' opportunities to learn, on top of their in-school lessons, their teachers, and their school homework. However, due to a range of reasons – serious illness, bereavement, personal issues, or, most common recently, the disruptions caused by the COVID-19 pandemic – students can easily end up missing a chunk of consecutive lessons in school. Because much of Maths teaching is sequential, this can mean that students can have major gaps in their knowledge that you may not necessarily be able to anticipate. Tutors are a great way for students to fill these gaps, but it can be a challenge if you end up having to essentially teach a student a significant part of a topic or even a whole topic that they haven't previously had the chance to learn.

Part of your initial assessment with a student can be a discussion of the topics they have and haven't covered, and you can also ask their parents or teachers if you notice any major issues with a particular area of learning.

4. Problem-solving questions

Problem-solving questions consistently seem to cause GCSE Maths students issues at all stages of the course. They're designed to be challenging – any mistakes in the early parts of the question will be carried forward – but the biggest issue is when the questions combine two or more skills from different units and don't necessarily indicate when a new skill will be needed. An example of this could be a question that features an image of a shape but actually needs algebra to be used to solve it or a particularly wordy question that requires some inference from the instructions. Students who are not familiar with this style of question or who aren't confident inferring what skill is needed can really struggle with these multi-step questions.

Tutors need to make sure that they are demonstrating the connections between the different skills and units, showing how concepts like algebra can be used a tool more broadly in Maths rather than just covering the requirements of the specification. You also need to introduce a wide range of question styles into their lessons to ensure that your students are exposed to the many different ways a question could be written. Finally, you will need to ensure that sufficient time is spent on multi-step questions once confidence in a topic has been established. These questions can take up a significant amount of time, so they can be set as homework in the first instance and then gone through at the start of the next lesson if needed.

TOP TIP

Use a range of explanations in your lessons – using diagrams, visuals like sketches or Maths tools, and multiple methods for calculating or solving. Especially when students are finding the method they've been taught at school difficult, it can help them to see another way of getting an answer.

QUESTION

How will you motivate students who dislike Maths or find it very difficult?

Chapter 13

Other GCSEs

So, you've assessed your student's progress and you know what they need to work on – so how do you plan your first lesson?

First, you'll need to look online and in textbooks for resources and worksheets related to the student's subject and topics. Second, you'll need to learn some lesson techniques. These are the activities you'll use with students to help develop their skills and understanding.

The rest of this chapter is divided in History, Geography, and Sciences. In each section, you'll find a detailed list of basic lesson techniques in the 'Online tutoring basics' chapter (pages 7–26), which are all applicable to any age and subject. In the following, you'll find them listed in the relevant section alongside more specific exercises and techniques that I feel work best for each GCSE subject.

I've divided the techniques into the key parts of a lesson, as outlined in Chapter 7, so you can find lists of exercises to use with your students. Once you've learned some techniques, you can use the different categories to create quick and easy lesson plans. There's a sample lesson at the end of each subject section to show you how to do that.

How to tutor: GCSE History

LESSON TECHNIQUES

Starters

Basic lesson techniques

- Matching exercises (p. 84)

- Sorting exercises (p. 85)

- Word searches (p. 85)

DOI: 10.4324/9781003211648-17

- Crosswords (p. 85)

- Mind maps (p. 86)

- Quickfire questions (p. 87)

- Homework review (p. 87)

Plus

Timeline recall

Timelines are a really valuable tool when tutoring History and can be used for all sorts of activities. For this starter, I like to use a template of a timeline, either blank or with some of the key dates and events/figures already filled in, which students then have to complete using their recollection of a previous unit or lesson.

For students who are really struggling, you can also do a version of this exercise that is similar to the memory exercise where you have to remember all of the items on a tray before they are removed – by showing them a completed timeline and then asking them to remember as many events and dates as possible in 5 minutes.

Headshots

Headshots is a quiz game to help students to remember names and faces. This is particularly useful for students who will have to analyse sources or learn about a period with many significant figures or monarchs. It also helps add a visual element to other information they will have to memorise.

- Offer the student a set of names and faces that they have to match up

- Show a series of faces and ask students to remember their names

- Place a picture in the middle of a mind map and ask students to recall as much information about that person as possible

- Write a list of descriptors of a significant person and ask students to pick the correct image

This exercise can also be used with any image more broadly, such as sources or famous pictures or paintings, as a prompt for recalling key information. You can use famous paintings and discuss the elements of the picture to learn about society at the time – for example, students studying the 1500s could look at Holbein's painting 'The Ambassadors' to learn contextual information about Tudor attitudes to science, music, politics, and so on. There are lots of online guides to famous images to help you with this.

Explanations/demonstrations

Basic lesson techniques

- Slideshows (p. 87)

- YouTube videos (p. 89)

- Model answers (p. 89)

- Live-modelling (p. 91)

- Worksheets (p. 93)

Plus

Source analysis

Students often struggle with primary source analysis, because it requires them to combine their inferences and own knowledge to create an interpretation.

Sources are usually images or short paragraphs but can range from photos and Punch cartoons to diary entries and woodblock prints and are often shown in pairs in worksheets or exam-style questions. Students may be required to infer beliefs or ideas from the source, discuss its provenance and reliability, and compare it to another source.

Tutors can model source analysis for students, demonstrating how to develop their inferences and providing paragraph structures, and you can then offer sources as a routine part of lessons to familiarise them with the techniques.

Different schools will use different acronyms or paragraph structures to remind students what to include in their answers to these questions – such as PANDA (Purpose, Author, Nature, Date and Audience), NOP (Nature, Origin, Purpose), or COMA (Content, Origin, Motive and Analysis), to name a few – so try to work with the acronym(s) and structure(s) the student is familiar with rather than introducing too many new ones.

You must always refer to the requirements of the exam specification, either directly or through exam board resources like textbooks, to ensure that the student is best prepared for these questions.

Main activities

Basic lesson techniques

- Past papers (p. 93)

- Worksheets (p. 95)

- Annotation (p. 94)

- Question-guessing (p. 95)

Plus

Timelines

Timelines are a great strategy to help students understand themes like change/ continuity/cause/consequence, because they allow them to directly compare events and ideas.

You can ask students to:

- Read a passage or extract and then create a timeline of the dates/events

- Put a series of events in order and recall the dates/details

- Use a completed timeline to answer a series of exam-style questions or create an essay plan

The timeline technique can be adapted for different students.

- Key dates and facts

- Descriptions of key events

- Images, like maps, diagrams, or photos

- Sources, like those used in source analysis questions

Once the student has created their timeline, they can download it to keep for revision or further study. Alternatively, they can be reused and added to in later lessons.

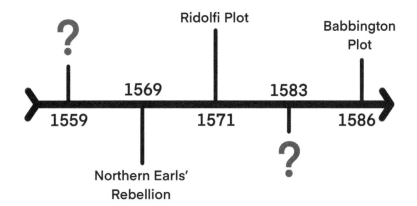

How to tutor

Tables

Using tables as a demonstration technique can help show students how to distil large amounts of information down to the key points, isolating key themes, events, and ideas. Using it as a main activity can help students to commit the information to memory and organise it usefully for further study.

It is up to you whether you put the information into the table yourself before you discuss it with the student or whether you work through paragraphs or lists of information together with the student, deciding what to put into each box together.

The first column in the table should have a heading which helps students group the most important information, like 'Date', 'Monarch', 'Law', 'Event', and so on. They can then list all of the elements under that heading, before adding a second column with 'Details', 'Themes', 'Terms', and so on. The boxes can be filled in with bullet points or phrases rather than full sentences.

Once students have created their table, they can then colour-code it, highlight key points, and download a copy to keep for revision.

Table 13.1 Key dates for medicine and public health

Date	Name	Details
400 BC	Hippocrates	Writes the Hippocratic Collection and defines the 'Four Humours' (blood, yellow bile, black bile, and phlegm)
400 BC–500 AD	Roman Empire	Introduces effective public health measures (reservoirs, baths, toilets, sewage, etc.)
162 AD	Galen	

Paragraphing practice

Unsurprisingly, this exercise simply involves the student practising writing paragraphs, in a variety of different settings. This can be as part of an exam-style answer, in response to a question you have designed, or as part of a worksheet or online resource.

It is always best to start with a discussion of how your student is used to writing paragraphs and what methods they have been taught. As I discuss during the assessment section, some students are taught to use an acronym like PEA or PEEL, while others use a more fluid format like 'What, How, Why?' Whatever the student has been taught, you should try to work with, as you are likely to confuse them if you try to use a different acronym. However, if the student is really struggling with the method they are taught in school and asks you for a different one, you can demonstrate a few to give them the chance to find one that works better for them.

Plenaries

Basic lesson techniques

- Mind maps (p. 96)

- Lists (p. 96)

- WWW/EBI (p. 97)

- RAG (p. 97)

- Summary questions (p. 97)

- Quiz questions (p. 98)

- Quick exam question (p. 98)

Plus

Sequencing

This exercise is a useful summary exercise at the end of a lesson where they have learned a range of key dates, events or facts, as well as a good discussion starter with more reticent students. The sequencing plenary is created by putting five or more words, images, items or ideas on the online whiteboard, which the student must then arrange into historical/chronological order and justify their decisions. The items could be inventions, battles, monarchs, or any number of people, objects, or events.

Homework

Basic lesson techniques

- Worksheets (p. 98)

- Past papers (p. 99)

Plus

Paragraph practice

Paragraph practice does what it says on the tin: it's an opportunity for students to practise their paragraph writing outside of the lesson time. I often find that with students I only see once a week, we just don't have enough time to write the paragraphs they need to practise, so setting just one or two to write at home can be a real help for them.

You will need to set your student a writing task – I usually ask them to complete the writing task from the lesson so the content they need is fresh in their mind – and once it is finished, they can send it to you to mark before the next lesson, or you can mark it together as the next starter.

Planning a GCSE History lesson

A sample GCSE History lesson might look like this:

Table 13.2 A sample GCSE History lesson

Date	Starter	Explanation/ demonstration	Main activity	Plenary	Homework
20/04	Sorting exercise: causes and consequences of WW1	Tables: 1. Read through a passage of key information about the interwar years, highlighting key dates and events 2. Demonstrate how to list key events in table, with details and factors, showing completed example row/column	Tables: 1. Ask the student to complete the table, noting any areas they want to go over again in future 2. Once finished, colour-code or highlight information to help with revision	Quick exam question: short or long answer question on topic covered in the lesson	Worksheet: series of long answer questions on events in table, 20–30 minutes

A full 10-week timetable of lesson plans that can be adapted or used for any of your students can be found in the 'Lesson plans' chapter of this book.

Common issues

The most common issues I've come across when tutoring GCSE History are:

1. Lack of historical knowledge

GCSE History involves a huge amount of memorisation and recall, but not all students put the work into learning the necessary own knowledge and skills for their lessons. If the student wasn't the one who asked for tutoring, they may be particularly reluctant to engage in homework or additional learning.

One common problem is that students can struggle with the way information is given to them or tested in school, so offering students a range of exercises and strategies in lessons can help to give them more control over their learning. It can also help to arrange a schedule for recall testing, assessments, and quizzes with the student to ensure that your lesson plans are made in conjunction with them and they know when to expect them.

If you feel that the student is genuinely not making any progress in your subject, this may be because they have too many other learning commitments or are focusing their energy on other core subjects like English or Maths. In this case, I would recommend speaking to their parent or teacher and discussing whether they need to limit their commitments or have more time for this subject if it is a priority.

2. **Difficulty with the format of the questions**

GCSE History exams are some of the most prescriptive exams I have personally ever faced, and several of the students I have taught in this subject have said the same. No matter which exam board students study for, they all have quite particular question styles and require the student to include a varying combination of source analysis, own knowledge, analysis, inference, and explanation. Students often find it difficult to remember what to include in each answer, on top of memorising key own knowledge and source analysis strategies.

This is particularly significant for students who are revising or starting to revise, as they will need to be completely confident on what to do before in-class assessments, mocks, and the real thing. As their tutor, I like to use techniques like slideshows and regular recall exercises to affirm the strategies for each question, as well as pop quizzes for own knowledge.

How to tutor: GCSE Geography

LESSON TECHNIQUES

Starters

Basic lesson techniques

- Matching exercises (p. 84)
- Sorting exercises (p. 85)
- Word searches (p. 85)

How to tutor

- Crosswords (p. 85)

- Mind maps (p. 86)

- Quickfire questions (p. 87)

- Homework review (p. 87)

Plus

Map starter

This starter involves putting a map, or other geographical prompt like a postcard or photo, on the screen, and the student then needs to suggest what they think the lesson is going to be about. They can make notes as a mind map or list of what information they already know about that topic and what they think they might be about to learn about.

For example, if you put a map of Argentina on the board, they might guess that the lesson is going to be about volcanoes or polar regions, the tectonic plates, Spanish-speaking countries, or South America more generally.

Likewise, a postcard from Australia or a picture of Uluru could lead to guesses of deserts and the Outback, the Aboriginal people, and so on.

Flags or countries quiz

With this starter, you'll need to prepare or find a slideshow with different countries' flags on it that the student then needs to guess which they belong to. An additional level of difficulty could be learning the countries' capital cities, populations, or other information.

The alternative is to create a slideshow with outlines of countries with no other identifying features, or countries highlighted on an otherwise blank map. This involves the student having to guess what the country is purely based on its shape or relative location.

Explanations/demonstrations

Basic lesson techniques

- Slideshows (p. 87)

- YouTube videos (p. 89)

- Model answers (p. 89)

- Live-modelling (p. 91)

- Worksheets (p. 93)

Plus

Case studies

Case studies are a core element of Geography, so students need to be confident that they understand the key information and can apply it to a real-life scenario.

Case studies for several exam boards include: hot environments, cold environments, coastal processes and sustainable management, human geography (major cities), and so on. For details on which case studies your student is expected to know and how they will be tested, check the relevant exam board's website.

To work on a case study with a student, you can start by using one of the other techniques listed here – a slideshow or video – to introduce them to the case study before using a Main Activity like 'Tables' or 'Flowcharts' to introduce them to the facts and figures. Once the student understands the case study, you can use past paper questions or worksheets to test their exam technique and offer model answers.

Some students may have a list of case studies that they have been given by their school or in their textbook, which you should try to use, but some may need to be given case study options to use. For the latter, there are plenty of guides and fact files for different case studies online, with some resource recommendations linked at the end of this section.

Main activities

Basic lesson techniques

- Past papers (p. 93)

- Worksheets (p. 95)

- Annotation (p. 94)

- Question-guessing (p. 95)

Plus

Tables

Using tables as a demonstration technique can help show students how to distil large amounts of information down to the key points, isolating key themes, events, and ideas. Using it as a main activity can help students to commit the information to memory and organise it usefully for further study.

It is up to you whether you put the information into the table yourself before you discuss it with the student or whether you work through paragraphs or lists of information together with the student, deciding what to put into each box together.

The first column in the table should have a heading which helps students group the most important information, like 'Date', 'Event, 'Impact', 'Solution', and so on. They can then list all of the elements under that heading before adding a second column with 'Details', 'Themes', 'Terms', and so on. The boxes can be filled in with bullet points or phrases rather than full sentences.

Once students have created their table, they can then colour-code it, highlight key points, and download a copy to keep for revision or further study.

Table 13.3 Types of coastal weathering

Term	Process
Freeze-thaw	Water seeps into permeable/porous rocks and freezes
Biological	Plant roots push through rock
Chemical	

Flow charts

Similar to the 'Timelines' technique in KS3 History, this technique can help students to understand themes like cause/consequence/impact/solution, because they allow them to create chronologies and connections between topics.

You can ask students to:

- Read a passage or extract and then create a chart of the dates/events

- Put a series of events in order and recall the dates/details

- Use a completed flowchart to answer a series of exam-style questions

- Summarise a case study using a flow chart

The flowchart technique can be adapted for different students.

- Key dates and facts

- Descriptions of key events or phenomena

- Images, like maps, diagrams, or photos

- Sources, charts, and graphs

Once the student has created their flowchart, they can download it to keep for revision or further study. Alternatively, they can be reused and added to in later lessons.

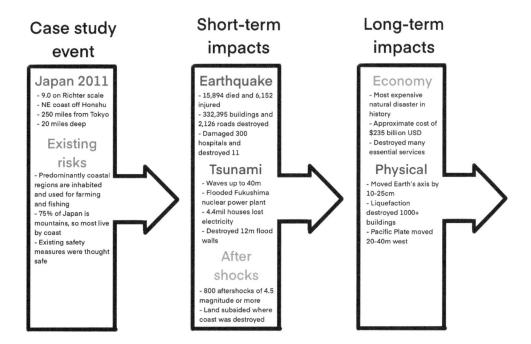

Plenaries

Basic lesson techniques

- Mind maps (p. 96)

- Lists (p. 96)

- WWW/EBI (p. 97)

- RAG (p. 97)

- Summary questions (p. 97)

- Quiz questions (p. 98)

- Quick exam question (p. 98)

How to tutor

Plus

Diagram labelling

Labelling a diagram may sound easy but can actually form a question in the exam, so it is a useful skill for occasional practice and a great starter or plenary activity.

You will need to provide an image or diagram that needs labelling. You can use diagrams of phenomena, like longshore drift or erosion, with graphs, map sections, and charts and even with photos, like identifying elements of a sustainable city.

With Year 11s, you can use past exam questions to help them feel comfortable with the format. With younger students, you can use more general diagrams and add boxes for the labels to go in so they can see how many there are.

Once they're finished, you can mark it and discuss any they missed or got wrong.

'5 Ws'

This plenary works well for lessons that focus on events or case studies. You will need to put a key image from, or related to, the lesson in the centre of the online whiteboard, and students will need to add as much information as they can under the '5 W' headings: Who? What? When? Where? Why? They can use bullet points, sentences, notes, or sketches.

This format can help to prompt recall and is a useful format for arranging their notes later.

Homework

Basic lesson techniques

- Worksheets (p. 98)

- Past papers (p. 99)

Plus

Paragraph practice

Paragraph practice does what it says on the tin: it's an opportunity for students to practise their paragraph writing outside of the lesson time. I often find that with students I only see once a week, we just don't have enough time to write the paragraphs they need to practise, so setting just one or two to write at home can be a real help for them.

You will need to set your student a writing task – I usually ask them to complete the writing task from the lesson so the content they need is fresh in their mind – and once it is finished, they can send it to you to mark before the next lesson, or you can mark it together as the next starter.

Planning a GCSE Geography lesson

A sample GCSE Geography lesson might look like this:

Table 13.4 A sample GCSE Geography lesson

Date	Starter	Explanation/ demonstration	Main activity	Plenary	Homework
20/04	Word search starter: all of the key words/ vocab from the previous lesson	Slideshow: 1. Discuss how much the student has previously studied the new topic 2. Work through slideshow of key ideas 3. Five summary questions on the key elements of the slideshow	Past paper: 1. Work through a past paper with a range of question styles on that topic 2. Make a note of any question styles the student struggles with and any areas of the topic that need a recap	'5 Ws': show a key image from the lesson topic and ask students to write down key information	Past paper: ask students to finish the rest of the past paper, 20–30 minutes

A full 10-week timetable of lesson plans that can be adapted or used for any of your students can be found in the 'Lesson plans' chapter of this book.

Common issues

The most common issues I've come across when tutoring GCSE Geography are:

1. **Struggling with question structures**

   Much like GCSE History, GCSE Geography contains a fair amount of content which has to be memorised, but the exam structure is what many students find difficult.

   Across all of the exam boards, GCSE Geography questions are divided up by the number of marks they're worth, with short answer questions worth 1 to 6 marks and long answer questions worth 9 marks or more. Each question type also features a different command word, with some asking students to 'identify', 'state', or 'define' and others asking them to 'explain', 'identify', or 'assess'.

The best thing students can do is, of course, practise the whole range of question types – with the opportunity to have their answers marked and then any issues discussed your lessons.

There are some great online guides for the different question types for each exam board, and you can also make slideshows and sets of example questions to work through in lessons.

Once your student has started to get more confident with the question structures, you can use progress checks to keep an eye on how they're improving and which types you will need to focus on.

2. **Difficulty with case studies**

While the general content is broad, many students also report difficulty with the case study sections of the exams. Case studies are essentially large-scale examples, focusing on a key event or place, which are used to explore the key concepts and apply the skills learned from the course. These sections require students to learn lots of information, facts, and elements of narrative in order to present an assessment or judgement about a key theme, like natural disasters, climate and habitat, population, and so on. They are then tested using open-ended mini-essays requiring students to recall precise information and fit their facts to the question.

Part of what can be challenging is learning the material: students need a comprehensive understanding of each case study, with good recall of the different factors, outcomes, or other details. They also need to be judicious in their selection of evidence, as they only have limited time and space to write and will be marked on the organisation and fluency of their answer. Finally, they will need to ensure that their conclusions, judgements, or suggestions fit the key words of the question appropriately and are consistent throughout their answer.

Again, tutors can help by offering students the opportunity to answer practice questions and get detailed feedback. You can also offer pop quizzes and listing exercises to encourage recall and use the specific case studies to revise the key concepts and vocabulary of the topic they're linked to.

How to tutor: GCSE Science

LESSON TECHNIQUES

Starters

Basic lesson techniques

- Matching exercises (p. 84)

- Sorting exercises (p. 85)

- Word searches (p. 85)

- Crosswords (p. 85)

- Mind maps (p. 86)

- Quickfire questions (p. 87)

- Homework review (p. 87)

Plus

Memory game

This plenary helps encourage students to commit key content to memory, with a mix of visual and word-based clues. To create this game, you'll need to write a dozen or more key words, images, diagrams, or formulae on a slide, give the student 30 seconds to memorise it, and then ask them to write out as many as they can remember.

For bonus points, you can ask the student to give you a definition of the word or an example of the device. For an extra difficult twist, you could choose all of the items from a specific topic and ask the student which topic they think they were related to.

Explanations/demonstrations

Basic lesson techniques

- Slideshows (p. 87)

- YouTube videos (p. 89)

- Model answers (p. 89)

- Live modelling (p. 91)

- Worksheets (p. 93)

How to tutor

Plus

Big picture, small picture

One of the problems students sometimes identify in Science is that they will know some terminology or recognise some concepts but don't understand how those concepts fit together or what to do with the symbols or words they've learned.

To tackle this, I recommend 'zooming out' first – moving back out to general concepts and explanations, talking through their basic understanding of the key ideas first – before 'zooming in' on the specific elements that they will need to know for that topic.

This can done using another of the methods for this section, such as a slide-show, but it can also be done more organically using a mind map, allowing students to make links between the relevant content for themselves.

Alternatively, you can find worksheets that make a similar progression through the content, using questions of increasing complexity.

Main activities

Basic lesson techniques

- Past papers (p. 93)

- Worksheets (p. 95)

- Annotation (p. 94)

- Question-guessing (p. 95)

Plus

Tables

Using tables as a demonstration technique can help show students how to distil large amounts of information down to the key points, isolating key processes, events, and ideas. Using it as a main activity can help students to commit the information to memory and organise it usefully for further study.

It is up to you whether you put the information into the table yourself before you discuss it with the student or whether you work through paragraphs or lists of information together with the student, deciding what to put into each box together.

The first column in the table should have a heading which helps students group the most important information, like 'Topic', 'Experiment', 'Event', and so on. They can then list all of the elements under that heading before adding a second column with 'Details', 'Outcomes', 'Terms', and so on. The boxes can be filled in with bullet points or phrases rather than full sentences.

Once students have created their table, they can then colour-code it, highlight key points, and download a copy to keep for revision or further study.

Table 13.5 Homologous series in Chemistry

Name of series	General formula	Details
Alkanes	$C_nH_{2n=2}$	Saturated (contain a C=C double bond) hydrocarbons (made only of C and H)
Alkenes	C_nH_{2n}	Unsaturated hydrocarbons (made only of C and H)
Alcohols	$C_nH_{2n}+_1OH$	

Plenaries

Basic lesson techniques

- Mind maps (p. 96)

- Lists (p. 96)

- WWW/EBI (p. 97)

- RAG (p. 97)

- Summary questions (p. 97)

- Quiz questions (p. 98)

- Quick exam question (p. 98)

Plus

'Spot the mistake'

'Spot the mistake' is a good plenary for more confident students, because it encourages them to look critically at the material and methods in front of them. It works especially well with the Maths-based topics in Chemistry and Physics or multi-step questions, because they have to practise reading the question carefully in order to see the mistake.

To create this plenary, you write out the workings and answer to an example question, but make a deliberate error in the process. This may be a simple miscalculation, like a wrong multiplication in the first step, or a bigger mistake, like drawing the wrong shape or a point on a graph in the wrong place. The more confident the student, the more subtle the error should be. The student then needs to read the question carefully, find the mistake, and correct the workings.

If the student is doing well or you have more time, you can always do a series of these exercises of increasing difficulty. You can also give a particularly tricky one to a group of students to see if they can work together to find the mistake.

Instruction manual

Instruction manual is a plenary which involves asking the student to write out the 'instructions' on how to solve a particular type of question in their own words, as if they were going to give them to another student to follow. They can number or order the steps any way they like, as long as they cover all of the important information.

This plenary works well for topics with more formulaic approaches, like solving or simplifying equations or working out terms in a sequence. I like to keep downloads or screengrabs of the students' manuals once they've finished, so if they're ever struggling on the same topic in future, they can see the method in their own words first to help with their recall.

If you are tutoring a group, you can get them to do this plenary independently and then swap their instructions around next lesson and have them attempt a question according to the instructions they've been given as a starter!

Homework

Basic lesson techniques

- Worksheets (p. 98)

- Past papers (p. 99)

Plus

Experiments

One of the main elements of Science lessons that is difficult to recreate or discuss in online lessons are the experiments, but students do still need to understand the equipment, methodologies, and results of common experiments.

If students want to learn more about the experiments they're learning about, or want a more interactive visual tool, you can recommend them an online experiment simulator. There are several that have been specifically tailored to the UK's KS3, GCSE, and A-level syllabi. These sites allow students to play with and explore the concepts they're learning about while learning the vocabulary and methods they will need to answer the relevant exam questions.

You can show students where to find these tools and even set them a worksheet or set of exam-style questions to complete on that experiment or topic.

Planning a GCSE Science lesson

A sample GCSE Science lesson might look like this:

Table 13.6 A sample GCSE Science lesson

Date	Starter	Explanation/ demonstration	Main activity	Plenary	Homework
20/04	Sorting exercise: elements of animal and plant cells	Worksheet: 1. Read a short passage or table with key information on the topic with the student, discussing any words/ideas they are unsure about 2. Model answers for a couple of short and long answer questions to demonstrate key question styles	Worksheet: 1. Ask the student to complete a variety of questions independently 2. Make a note of any content/question they find difficult	RAG: ask the student to RAG the content and question types covered	Worksheet: Long answer questions on the lesson topic, 20–30 minutes

A full 10-week timetable of lesson plans that can be adapted or used for any of your students can be found in the 'Lesson plans' chapter of this book.

Common issues

The most common issues I've come across when tutoring GCSE Science are:

1. **Difficulty with topics and skills from other subjects that are used in the Sciences**

   A common issue among students in all three Science GCSEs is that they all require students to have a combination of skills from other subjects: predominantly Maths skills with the use of formulae and graphs, but also fluency and confidence with descriptions of scientific concepts, diagrams, and models. If the student already finds a particular skill difficult in Maths or English, they are going to find it ever harder to apply in a new context.

With some students, this can be a literacy issue, in that some students struggle with reading comprehension and complex vocabulary, which can trip them up when trying to access Science resources.

Tutors can offer pop quizzes or spelling tests to ensure that students are confident about their key vocabulary, as well as using techniques like basic reading comprehension and worksheets to give students a framework for developing their understanding of the more complicated topics.

Alternatively, it may be a numeracy issue. All three Sciences require at least some Maths skills, especially Chemistry and Physics: reading graphs, filling out tables, calculating averages or other values. Students who are already finding Maths difficult tend to find that their confusion translates into the Sciences, so tutors who notice this concern with their students should focus on these elements and offer to cover the basic Maths topics that underlie them if needed.

If you have significant concerns about a student's numeracy, you can speak to their parent or teacher about the student accessing dedicated Maths tutoring as well to support their exam performance.

2. **Struggling with 6-mark questions**

Like in History and Geography, certain question styles in the Science exams can be very prescriptive. The most commonly reported concern is with 6-mark questions, like those used by AQA in all three subjects.

The marking for these questions relies on the presence of certain phrases or key words, so students who describe concepts in general terms may be penalised, even if their answer demonstrates a good understanding of the topic.

Tutors can use techniques like the model answer exercise to demonstrate how the answers can be written and what key words come up regularly over the years of past papers available. You can also offer to mark practice questions and use listing and mind map exercises for common topics for 6-mark questions.

TOP TIP

Even when students have chosen these subjects as their GCSE options, they may still find them difficult or be reluctant to study. Offer a range of study materials, support with revision and recall, and isolate their main weaknesses to make your lessons as effective for them as possible.

QUESTION

How will you tackle the cross-subject elements (i.e. calculations, extended writing) in these subjects?

Chapter 14

A-level English Literature

A-level Literature is composed of two papers, Paper 1 and Paper 2, each of which tests a different set of skills with a variety of questions. As a tutor, you will need to be familiar with the exam board the student is studying for so that you know which papers and questions they will need to answer.

Changes in 2022

In 2022, there may be some changes to the A-level English Literature exams, which may reduce the amount of content students are required to cover. These changes have been introduced as a result of the COVID-19 pandemic and may potentially be reversed in future.

Some of the timings and marks available in each paper may vary depending on the exam board, but the question styles should remain the same.

So, you've assessed your student's progress and you know what they need to work on – so how do you plan your first lesson?

First, you'll need to look online and in textbooks for resources and worksheets related to the student's subject and topics. Second, you'll need to learn some lesson techniques. These are the activities you'll use with students to help develop their skills and understanding.

You'll find a detailed list of basic lesson techniques in the 'Online tutoring basics' chapter (pages 7–26), which are all applicable to any age and subject. In the following, you'll find them listed in the relevant section alongside more specific exercises and techniques that I feel work best for A-level English.

I've divided the techniques into the key parts of a lesson, as outlined in Chapter 7, so you can find lists of exercises to use with your students. Once you've learned some techniques, you can use the different categories to create quick and easy lesson plans. There's a sample lesson at the end of each subject section to show you how to do that.

DOI: 10.4324/9781003211648-18

Table 14.1 A-level English Literature papers for each UK exam board

	Paper 1	Paper 2	Paper 3	Coursework
AQA (Specification A)	**Section A Shakespeare** • 1 essay question – on both an extract and the whole text (25 marks) **Section B Unseen Poetry** • 1 essay question – comparing two unseen poems (25 marks) **Section C Comparing Texts** • 1 essay question – comparing two studied poems and one studied prose text (25 marks) 3 hours **75 marks** 40%	Either **Option 2A (WW1 and its aftermath)** OR **Option 2B (Modern times: literature from 1945 to the present day)** **Section A Set Texts** • 1 essay question – on either poetry, prose or drama (2B) (25 marks) **Section B Contextual Linking** • 1 essay question – on an unseen extract (25 marks) • 1 essay question – linking two texts, either drama or poetry (25 marks) 2 hours 30 minutes **75 marks** 40%	N/A	Extended essay, comparing two texts (2500 words) **50 marks** 20%

(Continued)

Table 14.1 (Continued)

	Paper 1	Paper 2	Paper 3	Coursework
AQA (Specification B)	Either **Option 1A (Aspects of tragedy)** OR **Option 1B (Aspects of comedy)** **Section A** **Shakespeare** • 1 essay question – on both an extract and the whole text (25 marks) **Section B** **Shakespeare** • 1 essay question (25 marks) **Section C** **Comparing Texts** • 1 essay question – comparing two studied set texts, one drama and the other drama/prose/poetry (25 marks) 2 hours 30 minutes **75 marks** 40%	Either **Option 2A (Elements of crime writing)** OR **Option 2B (Elements of political and social protest writing)** **Section A** **Unseen Prose** • 1 essay question – on an extract (25 marks) **Section B** **Set Texts** • 1 essay question (25 marks) **Section C** **Comparing Texts** • 1 essay question – comparing two studied texts (25 marks) 3 hours **75 marks** 40%	N/A	Two essays, at least one academic (other can be recreative, accompanied by commentary) (1250–1500 words each) **50 marks** 20%

	Paper 1	Paper 2	Paper 3	Coursework
Edexcel	**Section A** **Shakespeare** • 1 essay question (35 marks) **Section B** **Other Drama** • 1 essay question (25 marks) 2 hours 15 minutes **60 marks** 30%	**Section A** **Prose** • 1 essay question – comparing two studied texts (40 marks) 1 hour 15 minutes **40 marks** 20%	**Section A** **Post-2000 Poetry** • 1 essay question – comparing an unseen poem to a studied poem (30 marks) **Section B** **Pre- or Post-1900 Poetry** • 1 essay question (30 marks) 2 hours 15 minutes **60 marks** 30%	Extended essay, comparing two texts (2500–3000 words) **60 marks** 20%
OCR	**Section A** **Shakespeare** • 1 essay question (35 marks) **Section B** **Pre-1900 Drama and Poetry** • 1 essay question (25 marks) 2 hours 30 minutes **60 marks** 30%	**Section A** **Close Reading** • 1 essay question – on both an extract and the whole topic (30 marks) **Section B** **Comparing Texts** • 1 essay question – comparing two studied texts (30 marks) 2 hours 30 minutes **60 marks** 30%	N/A	Two essays – one comparative, the other based on close reading or recreative accompanied by commentary (3000 words total) **40 marks** 20%

(Continued)

Table 14.1 (Continued)

	Paper 1	Paper 2	Paper 3	Coursework
Eduqas	**Section A** **Pre-1900 Poetry** • 1 essay question – on both an extract and the whole text (20 marks + 40 marks) **Section B** **Post-1900 Poetry** • 1 essay question (60 marks) 2 hours **120 marks** 30%	**Section A** **Shakespeare** • 1 essay question on both an extract and the whole text (15 marks + 45 marks) **Section B** **Drama** • 1 essay question (60 marks) 2 hours **120 marks** 30%	**Section A** **Unseen Prose** • 1 essay question – on an unseen extract (50 marks) **Section B** **Unseen Poetry** • 1 essay question – on an unseen poem (30 marks) 2 hours **80 marks** 20%	Extended essay, comparing two texts (2500–3500 words) **80 marks** 20%

LESSON TECHNIQUES

Starters

Basic lesson techniques

- Matching exercises (p. 84)

- Sorting exercises (p. 85)

- Word searches (p. 85)

- Crosswords (p. 85)

- Mind maps (p. 86)

- Quickfire questions (p. 87)

- Homework review (p. 87)

Plus

5-minute recall

This recall exercise works well for students where content familiarity is an issue and for students who are revising.

You can direct the recall with as much specificity as you want: it could be subject content like 'the characters of *A Streetcar Named Desire*' or 'central themes of the Conflict anthology', or practical knowledge like 'key quotations from *Othello*' or 'planning strategies for Paper 2'.

'Speedy reads'

'Speedy reads' is my name for small extracts with reading comprehension tasks and short answer questions. 'Speedy reads' work well for students who are worried about reading comprehension, because you can do one every lesson, and as a starter, they help students to get into the right frame of mind to begin to learn. In addition, by using unseen texts, it helps expose students who are not keen readers to a wide variety of types and styles of texts. For A-level English, I usually use this exercise to cover poems from their anthology, so they are regularly revising that content, or I pick poems that are age appropriate and sufficiently challenging to stretch their analysis skills.

'Fill the gap'/'Finish the sentence'

'Fill the gap', or 'Finish the sentence' if the gap is always at the end, can be an interesting way to prompt students to recall key information. 'Fill the gap' can be used in lots of ways:

- Removing the conjugated verbs from a piece of writing and only offering the root verb so students have to infer which person and tense to use

- Removing all of the technical terminology from an analytical paragraph so students have to remember the key terms

- Offering partial definitions for key words (i.e. 'A microcosm is a metaphorical technique where . . .')

- Asking for comparisons (i.e. 'Two poems that both feature grief and loss as central themes are . . .')

Feel free to develop your own uses as well. It is up to you, depending on the level of the student, whether to offer correct or model answers alongside the exercise – I generally don't unless a student is really struggling, as it is more effective for them to recall or imagine the answers themselves.

You can also use 'Fill the gap' exercises as main activities, if you make the answers required longer or more complex.

Explanations/demonstrations

Basic lesson techniques

- Slideshows (p. 87)

- YouTube videos (p. 89)

- Model answers (p. 89)

- Live modelling (p. 91)

- Worksheets (p. 93)

Plus

SWAT/key word analysis demonstration

Single Word Analysis Techniques (SWAT), sometimes called Keyword Analysis, is crucial to achieving in English, but it can be difficult for some students to grasp and is not necessarily an intuitive technique.

There are a number of ways I like to demonstrate SWAT, my favourite being the mind map demonstration: reading a short extract together, selecting a short quotation or phrase, and creating a map of connotations, links, and ideas to walk students through the process of isolating key words from within it.

This demonstration segues well into an activity where students can try the technique themselves using the same extract you've been working on together, with the opportunity to explore their ideas and ask questions.

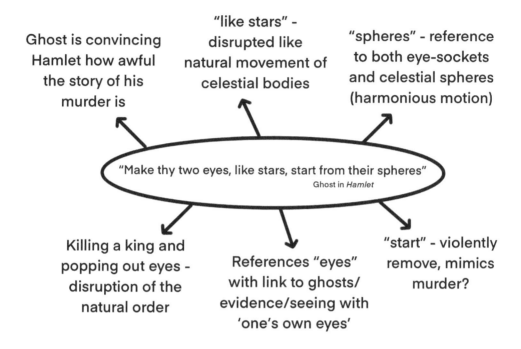

'Layers of meaning'

The 'layers of meaning' exercise involves taking a short quotation or phrase and then moving down the page by writing in the different 'layers' of meaning each word could have within the extract. This can help students to understand the difference between connotation and denotation, as well as developing their understanding of alternative interpretations. By using the layers to demonstrate how many different ways students can pick apart quotations, it can help to model how students can develop an interpretation of the writer's choice of language and structure.

This demonstration can transition into an activity, where the student takes over and has a go at it themselves.

Plot review

Plot review, as is clear from the name, is an activity that can be used to check students' familiarity with the plot of their set texts and revise the important events.

I usually ask students to create a timeline as part of a plot review, or two if the plot is in non-chronological order – one in time order and one in plot order – to help them understand what is happening. Other formats for plot review can include flow charts or tables, or you could create a series of jumbled paragraphs describing plot events which students have to put in the right order.

If students are particularly struggling, I will sometimes make or find on Google Images an infographic of the plot with labels or events removed, so they have a visual prompt of the plot which they can then fill in and download a copy of for themselves. You should try to avoid simply telling the student what happens unless they are clearly struggling, as this will undermine their recall ability later on.

If the student is more confident with the plot of their text, it can be good to introduce some ideas about theme and character as you work through it to start consolidating the key ideas they will need in their revision. At A-level, most students usually have a fairly confident grasp of the content unless they are right at the beginning of the course, so I try to incorporate an element of planning, comparison, or analysis into plot review to get the most out of the exercise.

Whatever format you use, it can help to create master documents for plot review for the student to make notes on and return to when they begin to revise. By saving successive notes onto the same document, it makes it easier to see what you have covered together, and the student can keep them to revise from later. I like to create one for each key text and each poem.

Character review

Character review is much like plot review, in that it tests students' recall of the characters of a set text and provides an opportunity to fill in any gaps.

There are several ways to do character review – I usually use mind maps, with an image/illustration of the character or their name in the centre of the map, but you can also use charts, worksheets, stills from productions or movies, or other interactive resources. There are some excellent infographics and other images available for common set texts, like Shakespeare plays, available on resource websites.

Once you've covered all of the characters, you can then help the student to create individual mind maps or fact files for each one, with their name, age, relationships to other characters, motive, role, likes/dislikes, and other relevant information.

Again, this information can be added to a master document and used for planning and writing essays later.

Main activities

Basic lesson techniques

- Past papers (p. 93)

- Worksheets (p. 95)

- Annotation (p. 94)

- Question-guessing (p. 95)

Plus

Unseen material

Unseen material is one of the elements students can find very intimidating, so it should be used regularly. Some students may just want opportunities to write answers for these sections and have them marked, but others may want guidance on how to approach them.

Unseen prose extracts or poems can be introduced during another lesson activity, to explore a language analysis technique or plan an answer, but they can also be used on their own.

There are several activities that you can use to increase students' confidence when working with unseen material:

- **Read through the unseen material together, out loud for poems, and discuss structural ideas (rhyme/metre/paragraphing/pace, etc.)** – students are often less confident at identifying these

- **Ask the student to identify and annotate language/structural features, either as pre-reading or in lesson, before discussing their ideas** – can be used to make answer plans

- Walk through model answers and discuss WWW/EBI before the student has a go themselves

- **Give the student 10 minutes to choose five features/quotes and present their argument against a given question** – discuss any issues or obvious missed ideas

Paragraphing practice

Unsurprisingly, this exercise simply involves the student practising writing paragraphs, in a variety of different settings. This can be as part of an exam-style answer, in response to a question you have designed, or as part of a worksheet or online resource.

It is always best to start with a discussion of how your student is used to writing paragraphs and what methods they have been taught. As I discuss during the assessment section, some students are taught to use an acronym like PEA or PEEL at GCSE, which they should be moving away from at A-level, while others use a more fluid format like 'What, How, Why?' Whatever the student has been taught, you should try to work with, as you are likely to confuse them if you try to use a different acronym. However, if the student is really struggling with the method they are taught in school and asks you for a different one, you can demonstrate a few to give them the chance to find one that works better for them.

'Layers of meaning'

As outlined previously in the Explanations/Demonstrations section, 'layers of meaning' is an analytical exercise which helps students to understand the different levels or layers of meaning that a quotation might contain.

It is up to you whether to label or guide the layers of their analysis: with students who are struggling to unpick quotes, prompting them to think about identifying rhetorical devices, structural analysis, contextual information about the author or period, language and sounds, or other elements of analysis can help them to see how many different ways there are to approach a quotation. With

---

"In his blue gardens men and girls came and went like moths among the whispering and the champagne and the stars."

The Great Gatsby

Layer 1 Language features	Simile - "like moths" - gentle, flittering, patterned and nocturnal, attracted to light Triple - "whispering", "champagne", "stars"
Layer 2 Sounds	Soft sibilant sounds - "moTHS", "WHISPering" Soothing and calm, like a warm evening
Layer 3 Themes/ associations	"men and girls" - infantilises the women, indicates power imbalance and youth vs age Typical image of wealth
Layer 4 Tense	"came and went" - non-specific, implies repeated event over time Past tense - pattern now over?

more confident students, I might leave them to see how many different layers they can think of on their own and then offer prompts once they run out of ideas.

You can offer students a worksheet or template with lines to write their ideas on, or you can simply draw lines onto the online whiteboard.

If the student is revising key quotations for use in the exam, I always give them the opportunity to screengrab or download their notes so they can compile a list of quotes and ideas for later.

SWAT/key word analysis mind maps

As explained previously, SWAT, or 'Keyword Analysis', is an essential part of writing exam answers for A-level English students. Once you have demonstrated how to unpick a quotation using your own mind maps, it can be useful to hand this technique over to students so they can practise for themselves. I find that students who are less confident about SWAT find the mind map format less intimidating, because their ideas are not put in a hierarchy or order and they can link their ideas together in whatever way they choose. Placing the quotation in the middle also encourages them to pick out individual words and think about the context of them within the sentence or quotation they chose.

Tables of quotes

Tables of quotes can be constructed in a number of ways: this is an especially useful exercise for tutors as it allows students to cover large amounts of text in a relatively short time and provides lots of fodder for producing practice paragraphs at another time or for homework. It is also often appreciated by students as they can download or screenshot their tables to build banks of quotations about a particular text or anthology, saving them time in homework or revision.

For students who need practise identifying and explaining rhetorical devices, it can be useful to table in the names of several devices and ask them to look for them throughout and extract and offer brief explanations of their effect.

For students who need help identifying themes, tables can prompt them to look for quotations or ideas related to a particular theme and explore the relevance of these key ideas.

For students who need help introducing context into their paragraphs, you can label the various areas of the table using key social or historical ideas and ask them to look for key ideas or quotations that align with them.

For students who are in the later stages of revision and are looking to build banks of key quotes, tables can be a great way to organise their quotations and code them according to theme, character, plot point, device, or other element of the text.

Table 14.2 Key quotes from *Othello* by William Shakespeare

Quote	Theme	Effect
'Were I the Moor, I would not be Iago'	Identity, betrayal	Initially obvious but deeper meaning – 'Iago' as synecdoche for his whole self/nature, trades in hypotheticals and negatives
'Look to your house, your daughter and your bags!'	Patriarchy, honour	Warning Brabantio about 'theft' – the idea of women/virginity as property. Triple creates order of priority/value?
'an old black ram/Is topping your white ewe'	Race, sex	

Plenaries

Basic lesson techniques

- Mind maps (p. 96)

- Lists (p. 96)

- WWW/EBI (p. 97)

- RAG (p. 97)

- Summary questions (p. 97)

- Quiz questions (p. 98)

- Quick exam question (p. 98)

Plus

Memory game

This plenary can be especially useful with students who have trouble committing key vocabulary to memory. To create this game, you'll need to write a dozen or more key words – word classes, language or structure devices, characters, plot points, and so on – on a slide, give the student 30 seconds to memorise it, and then ask them to write out as many words as they can remember.

For bonus points, you can ask the student to give you a definition of the word or an example of the device.

Homework

Basic lesson techniques

- Worksheets (p. 98)

- Past papers (p. 99)

Plus

Pre-reading and vocab identification

This really serves as preparatory work rather than homework by giving students the chance to read a long extract or poem outside of the lesson and make notes on themes, structural features, language devices, and types of vocab. I always encourage students to practise using their technical terminology while they're annotating, to ensure that they can spot the relevant features, and asking them to take additional notes means that they can write down the effect as well.

This can be a useful homework because some students dislike the pressure of being watched while they read, while others simply don't have enough lesson time to spend a significant portion of it reading.

Paragraph practice

Paragraph practice does what it says on the tin: it's an opportunity for students to practise their paragraph writing outside of the lesson time. I often find that with students I only see once a week, we just don't have enough time to write the paragraphs they need to practise, so setting just one or two to write at home can be a real help for them.

You will need to set your student a writing task – I usually ask them to complete the writing task from the lesson so the content they need is fresh in their mind – and once it is finished, they can send it to you to mark before the next lesson, or you can mark it together as the next starter.

Essay planning

Some students won't have the time to write additional essays in full for you, so you can ask them to plan essays instead. This is still good practice for the skills they need but takes less time. You can ask them to plan one question in detail or make multiple plans for a compilation paper's worth of questions. You can then either incorporate these plans into lessons, building their paragraph plans into SWAT or Layers of Meaning activities, or the student can simply keep them for revision later.

Planning an A-level English lesson

To give you an idea of how that framework could be filled out with some of the lesson techniques I've discussed in this chapter, I've written out a sample A-level English Literature lesson:

Table 14.3 A sample A-level English Literature lesson

Date	Starter	Explanation/ demonstration	Main activity	Plenary	Homework
15/10	Homework review: discuss previous essay, give feedback, and discuss next steps	'Layers of meaning': 1. Read an extract from a set text they would like to work on, discussing plot, themes, and initial ideas 2. Pick some key quotations 3. Complete the 'layers', factoring in identification of language/structural features, links to other areas of the book, themes, context, close reading/SWAT, and so on	Paragraph practice: 1. Pick one or two quotes and write a practice paragraph	WWW/EBI: both student and tutor feedback on paragraph	Paragraph practice: write an additional paragraph, from one of the quotations selected during lesson, 10–20 minutes

A full 10 week timetable of lesson plans that can be adapted or used for any of your students can be found in the 'Lesson plans' chapter of this book.

Common issues

The most common issues I've come across when tutoring A-level English Literature are:

1. Lack of confidence

Students can be worried about their A-levels for all sorts of reasons, so wherever possible, tutors should try to be as supportive as possible – whether that's offering hints and tips, sharing anecdotes about your experiences at school, or just offering a bit of emotional reassurance. There is a lot of pressure on A-level students to get the grades they need for their next step, so as a current or former undergraduate student, you are perfectly placed to discuss their worries and options with them.

In particular, lots of A-level English Literature students worry about learning the quotes, themes, and ideas for the set texts off by heart, despite the exams being open book, so it can help to remind them that they don't need to know everything and that they can prioritise the information rather than trying to cover it all.

I would also recommend reminding your students whenever they're worried that your lessons are a safe place to make mistakes and that you're there to help, not just to test them or mark their work.

2. **Poor use of contextual information**

There is a greater emphasis on the use of contextual information in A-level English Literature than there is at GCSE, but, in my experience, this often seems to lead students to throw lots of context into their essays without necessarily placing it thoughtfully or linking it to their argument well. Some students see it as almost a 'tick box' exercise, without recognising that they won't get marks for simply remembering facts about the period or author in their essay.

The AOs state that students must 'demonstrate [an] understanding of the significance and influence of the contexts in which literary texts are written and received', requiring them to link contextual information into their analysis and conclusions with purpose rather than just tacking it on at the end.

It can be difficult to break students' habits around this, especially if they are at a later stage in the course.

One technique that I use to help with this is to model answers and plans that employ context with a clear connection to the analysis, which the student and I can then evaluate together. By encouraging the student to use the model to create some rules for using context in their own words, it can help them remember what they need to do in future and to follow them more intuitively.

3. **Struggling to understand process and language of characterisation**

   This will obviously vary between students, but a topic I often end up having to go over multiple times with students is characterisation. The sticking point is usually that students write about characters like they're people, not characters: they say 'Jane feels sad' or 'Sheila is angry', but they don't show evidence of how they know that, why it's important, or how the writer has created that feeling.

   I recommend that students get into the habit of describing 'the character of Jane' or 'Sheila's character' to create some distance between the character as a person they relate to and the character as a construction by the writer and then using a formula like 'What, How, Why' to help them to map the writer's language onto the effect on the reader.

4. **Poor essay structure**

   As previously mentioned, the step up from GCSE to A-level English Literature is significant. A-level English requires exam answers as fully formed essays, which can be a difficult transition for students who are used to the more structured format of the GCSE. As a result, a common issue is poor essay structure, which particularly manifests as difficulty writing strong introductions/conclusions.

   As a tutor, there are any number of ways to tackle this problem: marking essays, discussing planning strategies, looking at model essays, and exploring the purposes of introductions/conclusions to better understand what students should be trying to achieve. There are some excellent resources available online that give good rules, sentence starters, guides, and models for these tricky paragraphs, which I have linked to at the end of this chapter.

   The best way to practise writing essays is, unfortunately for students, to write lots of essays, but because of the limited lesson time and A-level students' busy schedules, it can be difficult to get students to write additional essays for you. Instead, I have found that asking students to plan the body of the essay but write the introduction/conclusion out properly can help to them to focus on those elements and give you lots of opportunities to offer advice and guidance.

TOP TIP

The students looking for A-level English tutoring are usually aiming for the top grades, so you will need to find ways to really challenge their critical faculties while also refining the basics of their writing like grammar, single word/key word analysis, and embedding quotations.

QUESTION

What techniques will you use to improve the quality of your students' essay writing?

Chapter 15

A-level Maths

As a tutor, you will need to be familiar with the exam board the student is studying for, so that you know which papers and questions they will need to answer and therefore which topics to cover.

Here's a quick breakdown of the key differences between the main exam boards in the UK:

Table 15.1 Key differences between UK exam boards

	Paper 1	Paper 2	Paper 3
AQA	Questions on topics A–I 2 hours **100 marks** 33.3%	Questions on any topics from Paper 1, plus topics J–S 2 hours **100 marks** 33.3%	Questions on any topics from Paper 1, plus topics K–O 2 hours **100 marks** 33.3%
Edexcel	Questions on Pure Maths topics 1–10 2 hours **100 marks** 33.3%	Questions on Pure Maths topics 1–10 2 hours **100 marks** 33.3%	**Section A** **Statistics** Topics 1–5 **Section B** **Mechanics** Topics 6–9 2 hours **100 marks** 33.3%

DOI: 10.4324/9781003211648-19

	Paper 1	Paper 2	Paper 3
OCR (Specification A)	Pure Maths topics only 2 hours **100 marks** 33.3%	**Section A** **Pure Maths** (50 marks) **Section B Statistics** (50 marks) 2 hours **100 marks** 33.3%	**Section A** **Pure Maths** (50 marks) **Section B** **Mechanics** (50 marks) 2 hours **100 marks** **33.3%**
OCR (Specification B, MEI)	Mix of Pure Maths and Mechanics topics 2 hours **100 marks** 36.4%	Mix of Pure Maths and Statistics topics 2 hours **100 marks** 36.4%	Pure Maths topics only 2 hours **75 marks** 27.3%

Eduqas does not offer an A-level Maths course, although their parent board, WJEC, does offer one in Wales.

In 2022, there may be changes to the format of the exams, which may reduce the number of topics or allow students some advance information. These changes have been introduced as a result of the COVID-19 pandemic and may potentially be reversed in future years.

LESSON TECHNIQUES

Starters

- Matching exercises (p. 84)
- Sorting exercises (p. 85)
- Mind maps (p. 86)
- Quickfire questions (p. 87)
- Homework review (p. 87)

Plus

'Impossible' questions

These can be a great challenge for students who are aiming for a prestigious university application or are looking for a challenge beyond the curriculum.

You can use questions you find online, questions from textbooks, or questions taken from past papers of the UK Maths Challenge and Maths Olympiad competitions.

If the student is planning to apply to study Maths or Physics at university, you can also begin to introduce STEP, PAT, MAT, and other entrance exam questions, to familiarise them with the format and give them a chance to see what they will be expected to do.

You can also use these questions as extension work or as homework. They should be given with the caveat that students can always ask questions if they get stuck and that they are not expected to get them right straight away, as they will require practice.

Explanations/demonstrations

Basic lesson techniques

- Slideshows (p. 87)

- YouTube videos (p. 89)

- Model answers (p. 89)

- Live modelling (p. 91)

- Worksheets (p. 93)

Plus

Maths tools

You may find that drawing graphs or diagrams can be tricky on an online whiteboard, especially without a graphics tablet or touchscreen, so digital Maths tools – like those listed in the 'Tutoring tech' chapter – can make this much easier.

You can use graphing paper, protractors, rulers, and other virtual equipment, as well as accessing customisable diagrams of shapes and formulae.

Always ensure that students are engaged in the demonstration, not just watching you, by asking recall questions and responses while you explain the topic.

Tick-list

For some students, the focus will simply be on passing their Maths tests, rather than understanding the complexities of the topics. As their tutor, you can help them to create 'tick-lists', or step-by-step guides, for the question types they find difficult, which they can then practise until they can apply them to any question of that style.

First, you walk the student through a demonstration of an example question. Then, once they are happy they understand what you did, you work with them to create a list of instructions for them to follow for that style of question.

For example, for missing number problems, the list might look like:

1. Identify all of the missing numbers

2. Simplify by dividing

3. Isolate a and find value

4. Substitute in a in find value of b

5. Calculate value of the new number by substituting in known values

Students can use their 'tick-list' to solve problems independently until they are confident on the method.

Main activities

Basic lesson techniques

- Past papers (p. 93)

- Worksheets (p. 95)

- Annotation (p. 94)

- Question-guessing (p. 95)

Plus

Real-world learning

Students generally engage better, particularly in subjects they find less interesting, when it is given a significance in everyday life. Maths is a good candidate for this technique, since it is essential in so many areas of life. Students often like to know *why* they have to learn something, rather than just *how* to do it, and tutors have the time to answer that question that teachers often don't.

Demonstrating Maths in the real world might look like:

- **Themed worksheets that use real-life examples** – applying angles to architecture, exploring financial Maths, or linking statistics and probability to weather data

- **Videos, images, and other media** – these could be YouTube videos, excerpts from documentaries, elements from your course

- Newspaper articles or headlines related to the topic you're working on with them

- **Puzzles and games** – exploring chess puzzles, a stock market simulator, card tricks, Sudoku, Countdown, you name it!

As a current or former STEM student, you can also give students ability-appropriate information from your course of study. You can share ideas or experiments from your labs which will contextualise their learning and help them to link abstract ideas to real-world events.

This technique is especially useful to students who might want to study Maths or Physics at university and may want you to help them with their applications or entrance exams, as you will be able to tell them about your course and ideas about careers.

Plenaries

Basic lesson techniques

- Mind maps (p. 96)
- Lists (p. 96)
- WWW/EBI (p. 97)
- RAG (p. 97)
- Summary questions (p. 97)
- Quiz questions (p. 98)
- Quick exam question (p. 98)

Plus

'Spot the mistake'

'Spot the mistake' is a good plenary for more confident students, because it encourages them to look critically at the material and methods in front of them.

It works especially well with the 'wordy' problem-solving questions or multi-step questions, because they have to practise reading the question carefully in order to see the mistake.

To create this plenary, you write out the workings and answer to an example question, but make a deliberate error in the process. This may be a simple miscalculation, like a wrong multiplication in the first step, or a bigger mistake, like drawing the wrong shape or a point on a graph in the wrong place. The more confident the student, the more subtle the error should be. The student then needs to read the question carefully, find the mistake, and correct the workings.

If the student is doing well or you have more time, you can always do a series of these exercises of increasing difficulty. You can also give a particularly tricky one to a group of students to see if they can work together to find the mistake.

Instruction manual

Instruction manual is a plenary which involves asking the student to write out the 'instructions' on how to solve a particular type of question in their own words, as if they were going to give them to another student to follow. They can number or order the steps any way they like, as long as they cover all of the important information.

This plenary works well for topics with more formulaic approaches, like solving or simplifying equations or working out terms in a sequence. I like to keep downloads or screengrabs of the students' manuals once they've finished, so if they're ever struggling on the same topic in future, they can see the method in their own words first to help with their recall.

If you are tutoring a group, you can get them to do this plenary independently and then swap their instructions around next lesson and have them attempt a question according to the instructions they've been given as a starter.

Additional Maths questions

With particularly able students, you can use more complex problem-solving questions taken from age- and ability-appropriate sources to push them to think in more connected ways. These can be questions you find online, questions from textbooks, or questions taken from entrance exam past papers like STEP or MAT.

This is best suited to students who are thinking of or in the process of applying for Maths or another STEM-based course at university, especially students who are going to face entrance exams or interviews.

Homework

Basic lesson techniques

- Worksheets (p. 98)

- Past papers (p. 99)

Plus

Additional Maths questions

With particularly able students, you can use more complex problem-solving questions taken from age- and ability-appropriate sources to push them to think in more connected ways. These can be questions you find online, questions from textbooks, or questions taken from past papers of university entrance exams like the MAT, PAT or STEP. The student's school may already offer them tutoring in these areas if they are keen to apply, so they may be familiar with them, but regardless they deliberately designed with the age and stage of A-level students in mind and can help stretch their learning and knowledge.

Planning an A-level Maths lesson

A sample A-level Maths lesson might look like this:

Table 15.2 A sample A-level Maths lesson

Date	Starter	Explanation/ Demonstration	Main activity	Plenary	Homework
15/11	Homework review: go over any questions that were unfinished or contain mistakes, discuss any revision if needed	Slideshow: 1. Go through slideshow of key concepts 2. Model a number of examples to show different ways questions may be phrased 3. Final example can be led by student, who suggests what to do next and final answer	Practice paper: 1. Go through compilation paper of questions on that topic, with student working independently 2. Offer help and pointers if needed, encouraging the student to apply their knowledge	WWW/EBI: both student and tutor give feedback	Practice paper: compilation paper of questions from the lesson topic, to be marked before next lesson, 30 minutes

A full 10-week timetable of lesson plans that can be adapted or used for any of your students can be found in the 'Lesson plans' chapter of this book.

Common issues

The most common issues I've come across when tutoring A-level Maths are:

1. **Difficulty with making connections between skills and topics**

   One of the goals of the A-level Maths course is that students should develop an understanding of the connections between the different topics and areas within the course.

   Understanding the relationships between key concepts like circles and triangles, or formulae and their graphical representations, is a fundamental skill when approaching the A-level Maths papers. The questions provide a limited framework for the skills and method that students should use, instead leaving it up to students to infer what they should use to find the answer. If students don't have a good idea of how topics connect together, or only understand each skill in isolation, they will find it very difficult to work out how to answer the questions.

   While it can feel easier as a tutor to go through topics in order and keep them separate, especially if you are relying on textbooks or online resources, it is also important to emphasise the connections between them and look at example questions that incorporate a range of skills. Problem-solving questions in particular require students to be creative with their use of different topics and concepts and have a high mark reward as a result.

2. **Lack of confidence**

   The most common issue I have seen consistently at this age and stage is a lack of confidence, both in giving answers verbally and giving written answers. So often, I work with very able students who seem compelled to say, 'I don't know if this is right but . . .' and then give an excellent answer, and the same hesitance can affect their exam performance as well.

   I would recommend reminding your students often that your lessons are a safe place to make mistakes and that you're there to help not just to test them or mark their work. You may find yourself saying this a lot at the beginning, but it can have a marked impact on students' confidence over time.

Another general pattern that I have noticed when tutoring is that young women are generally less confident than their male counterparts in offering answers, especially in STEM subjects, and this translates to their performance in assessments and exams. Therefore, tutors should always make a point to encourage and praise students when they succeed and offer non-judgemental guidance and support when they are struggling with a topic.

3. **Missing key knowledge or understanding in basic topics**

Tutoring should always be seen as an addition to students' opportunities to learn, on top of their in-school lessons, their teachers, and their school homework. However, due to a range of reasons – serious illness, bereavement, personal issues, or, most common recently, the disruptions caused by the COVID-19 pandemic – students can easily end up missing a chunk of consecutive lessons in school. Because much of Maths teaching is sequential, this can mean that students can have major gaps in their knowledge that you may not necessarily be able to anticipate. Tutors are a great way for students to fill these gaps, but it can be a challenge if you end up having to essentially teach a student a significant part of a topic or even a whole topic that they haven't previously had the chance to learn.

Part of your initial assessment with a student can be a discussion of the topics they have and haven't covered, and you can also ask their parents or teachers if you notice any major issues with a particular area of learning.

4. **Not checking their working**

Especially once students have become more confident, it can be easy to forget to read back their workings or to check their answers before they hand them in. This is important for two reasons: catching calculation errors and ensuring they've written their workings out in full. The first reason is the most important: a little mistake in addition or subtraction can ruin a whole answer, even if the rest of the method is correct, and there is an expectation from examiners that A-level students will pay close attention to the detail of their work. In addition, marks are given for the correct workings as well as correct final answers, though in fairness there is less emphasis on this at A-level than at GCSE. Regardless, students should be encouraged to write their workings neatly and in full to maximise their opportunity for marks.

Encouraging students to get into the habit of reading their work back at the end of their classwork or homework exercise before they commit to their final answer will help them to form good habits and make their work a more accurate reflection of their strengths and weaknesses.

TOP TIP

You should try to offer high achievers opportunities to test their skills against challenge questions, especially if they are planning to apply to study Maths at university. You can also recommend resources from your course or talk them through the application process, as well as supporting them with further Maths or Physics if you are familiar with those courses.

QUESTION

How will you ensure that students are confident with the basics as well as the more complex elements of the course?

Chapter 16

Other A-levels

So, you've assessed your student's progress and you know what they need to work on – so how do you plan your first lesson?

First, you'll need to look online and in textbooks for resources and worksheets related to the student's subject and topics. Second, you'll need to learn some lesson techniques. These are the activities you'll use with students to help develop their skills and understanding.

The rest of this chapter is divided into History, Geography, and Sciences.

In each section, you'll find a detailed list of basic lesson techniques from the 'Online tutoring basics' chapter (pages 7–26), which are all applicable to any age and subject. In the following, you'll find them listed in the relevant section alongside more specific exercises and techniques that I feel work best for each A-level subject.

I've divided the techniques into the key parts of a lesson, as outlined in Chapter 7, so you can find lists of exercises to use with your students. Once you've learned some techniques, you can use the different categories to create quick and easy lesson plans. There's a sample lesson at the end of each subject section to show you how to do that.

How to tutor: A-level History

LESSON TECHNIQUES

Starters

Basic lesson techniques

- Matching exercises (p. 84)

- Sorting exercises (p. 85)

- Word searches (p. 85)

DOI: 10.4324/9781003211648-20

- Crosswords (p. 85)

- Mind maps (p. 86)

- Quickfire questions (p. 87)

- Homework review (p. 87)

Plus

Timeline recall

Timelines are a valuable tool when tutoring History and can be used for all sorts of activities. For this starter, I like to use a template of a timeline, either blank or with some of the key dates and events/figures already filled in, which students then have to complete using their recollection of a previous unit or lesson.

For students who are really struggling, you can also do a version of this exercise that is similar to the memory exercise where you have to remember all of the items on a tray before they are removed – by showing them a completed timeline and then asking them to remember as many events and dates as possible in 5 minutes.

Flowchart recall

Flowchart recall can help students practise recall and create short summaries of the causes, details, and consequences of key events.

The student will need to write all of the causes in the first arrow, the details of the event in the box, and the consequences of the event in the second arrow. Students should be encouraged to write a minimum of three points for each, and any they miss can be discussed afterwards. They should try to include key details of own knowledge, such as dates, numbers, and places, to help them to write answers on that topic.

You can create a template for students to write on or ask them to draw their own. Once the flowchart is complete, and you've added any missing elements, they can download it to revise from later.

Explanations/demonstrations

Basic lesson techniques

- Slideshows (p. 87)

- YouTube videos (p. 89)

- Model answers (p. 89)

How to tutor

- Live modelling (p. 91)

- Worksheets (p. 95)

Plus

Source analysis

Students often struggle with primary source analysis, because it requires them to combine their inferences and own knowledge to create an interpretation.

Sources are usually images or short paragraphs but can range from photos and Punch cartoons to diary entries and woodblock prints and are often shown in pairs in worksheets or exam-style questions. Students may be required to infer beliefs or ideas from the source, discuss its provenance and reliability, and compare it to another source.

Tutors can model source analysis for students, demonstrating how to develop their inferences and providing paragraph structures, and you can then offer sources as a routine part of lessons to familiarise them with the techniques.

Different schools will use different acronyms or paragraph structures to remind students what to include in their answers to these questions – such as PANDA (Purpose, Author, Nature, Date and Audience), NOP (Nature, Origin, Purpose), or COMA (Content, Origin, Motive and Analysis), to name a few – so try to work with the acronym(s) and structure(s) the student is familiar with rather than introducing too many new ones.

You must always refer to the requirements of the exam specification, either directly or through exam board resources like textbooks, to ensure that the student is best prepared for these questions.

Main activities

Basic lesson techniques

- Past papers (p. 93)

- Worksheets (p. 93)

- Annotation (p. 94)

- Question-guessing (p. 95)

Plus

Timelines

Timelines are a great strategy to help students understand themes like change/continuity/cause/consequence, because they allow them to directly compare events and ideas.

You can ask students to:

- Read a passage or extract and then create a timeline of the dates/events

- Put a series of events in order and recall the dates/details

- Use a completed timeline to answer a series of exam-style questions or create an essay plan

The timeline technique can be adapted for different students.

- Key dates and facts

- Descriptions of key events

- Images, like maps, diagrams, or photos

- Sources, like those used in source analysis questions

Once the student has created their timeline, they can download it to keep for revision or further study. Alternatively, they can be reused and added to in later lessons.

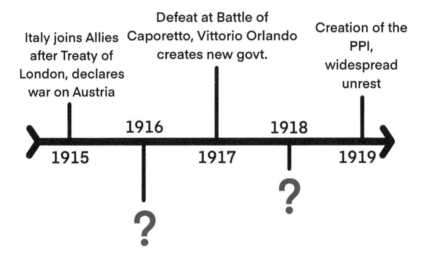

Tables

Using tables as a demonstration technique can help show students how to distil large amounts of information down to the key points, isolating key themes, events, and ideas. Using it as a main activity can help students to commit the information to memory and organise it usefully for further study.

It is up to you whether you put the information into the table yourself before you discuss it with the student or whether you work through paragraphs or lists of information together with the student, deciding what to put into each box together.

The first column in the table should have a heading which helps students group the most important information, like 'Date', 'Monarch', 'Law', 'Event', and so on. They can then list all of the elements under that heading, before adding a second column with 'Details', 'Themes', 'Terms', and so on. The boxes can be filled in with bullet points or phrases rather than full sentences.

Once students have created their table, they can then colour-code it, highlight key points, and download a copy to keep for revision or further study.

Table 16.1 Key dates from the Wars of the Roses

Date	Year	Location	Winner
May 22nd	1455	St Albans (1st)	York
September 23rd	1459	Blore Heath	York
October 12th/13th	1459	Ludford Bridge	

Paragraphing practice

Unsurprisingly, this exercise simply involves the student practising writing paragraphs, in a variety of different settings. This can be as part of an exam-style answer, in response to a question you have designed, or as part of a worksheet or online resource.

It is always best to start with a discussion of how your student is used to writing paragraphs and what methods they have been taught. As I discuss during the assessment section, some students are taught to use an acronym like PEA or PEEL, while others use a more fluid format like 'What, How, Why?' Whatever the student has been taught, you should try to work with, as you are likely to confuse them if you try to use a different acronym. However, if the student is really struggling with the method they are taught in school and asks you for a different one, you can demonstrate a few to give them the chance to find one that works better for them.

Plenaries

Basic lesson techniques

- Mind maps (p. 96)

- Lists (p. 96)

- WWW/EBI (p. 97)

- RAG (p. 97)

- Summary questions (p. 97)

- Quiz questions (p. 98)

- Quick exam question (p. 98)

Plus

Sequencing

This exercise is a useful summary exercise at the end of a lesson where they have learned a range of key dates, events or facts, as well as a good discussion starter with more reticent students. The sequencing plenary is created by putting five or more words, images, items or ideas on the online whiteboard, which the student must then arrange into historical/chronological order and justify their decisions. The items could be inventions, battles, monarchs, or any number of people, objects, or events.

Headlines

Breaking down key information into bite-sized chunks can make recalling it in the future easier. This plenary asks students to create 'headlines', like the short phrases that top newspaper articles, to capture the most significant information they learned that lesson. You can ask for two to five, depending on how much content you covered in the lesson. They can also draw a picture or diagram to accompany their headlines, if they want.

If needed, you can then return to the 'headlines' they wrote in a future lesson and ask them to create a mind map of that topic as a starter.

Homework

Basic lesson techniques

- Worksheets (p. 98)

- Past papers (p. 99)

Plus

Paragraph practice

Paragraph practice does what it says on the tin: it's an opportunity for students to practise their paragraph writing outside of the lesson time. I often find that with students I only see once a week, we just don't have enough time to write the paragraphs they need to practise, so setting just one or two to write at home can be a real help for them.

You will need to set your student a writing task – I usually ask them to complete the writing task from the lesson so the content they need is fresh in their mind – and once it is finished, they can send it to you to mark before the next lesson, or you can mark it together as the next starter.

Essay planning

Some students won't have the time to write additional essays in full for you, so you can ask them to plan essays instead. This is still good practice for the skills they need but takes less time. You can ask them to plan one question in detail or make multiple plans for a compilation paper's worth of questions. You can then either incorporate these plans into lessons, building their paragraph plans into SWAT or Layers of Meaning activities, or the student can simply keep them for revision later.

Planning an A-level History lesson

A sample A-level History lesson might look like this:

Table 16.2 A sample A-level History lesson

Date	Starter	Explanation/ demonstration	Main activity	Plenary	Homework
20/04	Summary questions: Five questions on the content from the previous lesson	Model answer: 1. Discuss two model essay answers from the exam board website, one lower-level answer and one higher 2. Ask student to evaluate WWW/ EBI for each 3. Create a list of rules for approaching this style of questions – things to do and avoid	Past paper: 1. Using a compilation paper of several examples of questions of that style, ask the student to plan answers for each 2. Once plans are complete, discuss how the introductions and conclusions would be written	RAG: ask student to explain how they feel about answering this style of question and what they would like to practise more in future	Paragraph practise: student chooses their favourite plan and writes the introduction and conclusion, 20 minutes

A full 10-week timetable of lesson plans that can be adapted or used for any of your students can be found in the 'Lesson plans' chapter of this book.

Common issues

The most common issues I've come across when tutoring A-level History are:

1. **Structuring their essays and answers**

    One of the most common complaints from students about History as a subject is that it is content heavy – there is a lot to learn, memorise, and organise in your head. However, A-level students typically seek tutoring by themselves, demonstrating a proactive approach to their learning which correlates with less of a concern about revising content.

    However, a problem that many A-level History students want help with is structuring their answers. Just as with GCSE History, A-level History questions are quite prescriptive, and there are lots of expectations around how answers should be planned and written. The skills needed to write a good A-level History essay are harder to glean from research, so many students turn to tutors who have achieved good grades themselves to learn what strategies they used.

    Having studied A-level History yourself, you will have the techniques and structures you learned at school and your opinion on how well they worked, which you should use to develop pointers for students' essays. There are also lots of useful online resources with frameworks, model answers, and other guides that your students can follow or that you can use to demonstrate with in lesson. Bear in mind that you should always try to work with the acronym or writing strategy that the student is most familiar with, like 'What, How, Why' or 'COP' (Content, Origin, Provenance), to avoid confusion, though you can offer them other strategies to use if they ask for them.

    My recommendation, regardless of exam board, would be to take a slightly different approach for each style of question.

    With source questions and shorter answer questions, students should aim to be concise and write a paragraph on each source or point, with a focus on consistent analysis, judicious selection of evidence and own knowledge, and summary sentences at the end of each paragraph.

With essay questions, students should focus on creating well-synthesised essays: rather than writing out a paragraph per idea, they should try to create a plan that accommodates both sides of the question, with each paragraph being either for or against it. No matter what, students should always include a short introduction with the key words and their stance on the question, a summary sentence at the end of each paragraph, and a conclusion which reiterates their stance and points to their most compelling evidence. Finally, encourage students to commit to making judgements! It can be hard to do, especially if they aren't confident about their answer, but it is a necessity at this level that they commit to one side of their argument.

2. **Difficulty with source analysis and comparison**

Source analysis of this kind is likely new to most History A-level students and can take time to become familiar with. It requires students to read unseen content closely, evaluate it against their own knowledge of the historical events and the viewpoint posited in the question, and then offer their own interpretation of the sources' content, context, and provenance. While the fact of previously unseen sources can be worrying, it is a question style that can be practised and prepared for.

Again, having studied A-level History yourself, you should know the skills they need fairly well, though there are also resources and guides available online if needed.

Some tips for students: stay focused on the key words of the question ('aims', 'outcomes', 'consequences', etc.), only commenting on relevant aspects from the sources; keep your quotations brief, embed if you can; and bring in your own knowledge when needed to show contrast and support inferences from the source.

How to tutor: A-level Geography

LESSON TECHNIQUES

Starters

Basic lesson techniques

- Matching exercises (p. 84)

- Sorting exercises (p. 85)

- Word searches (p. 85)

- Crosswords (p. 85)

- Mind maps (p. 86)

- Quickfire questions (p. 87)

- Homework review (p. 87)

Plus

Map starter

This starter involves putting a map, or other geographical prompt like a postcard or photo, on the screen, and the student then needs to suggest what they think the lesson is going to be about. They can make notes as a mind map or list of what information they already know about that topic and what they think they might be about to learn about.

For example, if you put a map of Argentina on the board, they might guess that the lesson is going to be about volcanoes or polar regions, the tectonic plates, Spanish-speaking countries, or South America more generally.

Likewise, a postcard from Australia or a picture of Uluru could lead to guesses of deserts and the Outback, the Aboriginal people, and so on.

Diagram labelling

Labelling a diagram may sound easy, but reading and labelling diagrams can actually form a question in the exam, so it is a useful skill for occasional practice and a great starter activity.

You will need to provide an image or diagram that needs labelling. You can use diagrams of phenomena, like longshore drift or erosion, with graphs, map sections, and charts and even with photos, like identifying elements of a sustainable city.

You can make your own questions or use past exam questions to help them feel comfortable with the format.

Once they're finished, you can mark it and discuss any they missed or got wrong.

Explanations/demonstrations

Basic lesson techniques

- Slideshows (p. 87)

- YouTube videos (p. 89)

How to tutor

- Model answers (p. 89)

- Live modelling (p. 91)

- Worksheets (p. 93)

Plus

Case studies

Case studies are a core element of Geography, so students need to be confident that they understand the key information and can apply it to a real-life scenario.

Case studies for several exam boards include: tropical rainforest, river catchment, desertification, coastal processes and sustainable management, glaciated landscapes, multi-hazardous environments and risk management, ecosystems and ecological change, human geography (population change, health, urban and rural areas), resource issues, and so on. For details on which case studies your student is expected to know and how they will be tested, check the relevant exam board's website.

To work on a case study with a student, you can start by using one of the other techniques listed here – a slideshow or video – to introduce them to the case study before using a Main Activity like 'Tables' or 'Flowcharts' to introduce them to the facts and figures. Once the student understands the case study, you can use past paper questions or worksheets to test their exam technique and offer model answers.

Some students may have a list of case studies that they have been given by their school or in their textbook, which you should try to use, but some may need to be given case study options to use. For the latter, there are plenty of guides and fact files for different case studies online, with some resource recommendations linked at the end of this section.

Main activities

Basic lesson techniques

- Past papers (p. 93)

- Worksheets (p. 95)

Plus

Tables

Using tables as a demonstration technique can help show students how to distil large amounts of information down to the key points, isolating key themes, events, and ideas.

It is up to you whether you put the information into the table yourself before you discuss it with the student or whether you work through paragraphs or lists of information together with the student, deciding what to put into each box together.

The first column in the table should have a heading which helps students group the most important information, like 'Date', 'Event', 'Impact', 'Solution', and so on. They can then list all of the elements under that heading, before adding a second column with 'Details', 'Themes', 'Terms', and so on. The boxes can be filled in with bullet points or phrases rather than full sentences.

Once students have created their table, they can then colour-code it, highlight key points, and download a copy to keep for revision or further study.

Table 16.3 Common natural hazards and their impacts

Date	Primary impact	Secondary impact	Proposed measures
Volcanic eruption	– Destruction of plants and animals – Deaths and injuries – Infrastructure damage	– Acid rain – Greenhouse gases – Fires	– Monitor volcanic activity – Create evacuation zones and procedures – Change tourist routes
Earthquake	– Infrastructure damage – Liquefaction – Building collapse	– Salinisation – Tsunamis	– Improve building codes – Destroy dangerous buildings – Create evacuation zones and procedures
Wildfires	– Pollution (i.e. smoke, ash, water) – Firefighting cost – Deaths and injuries	– Health issues (i.e. burns, smoke inhalation) – Public transport affected	

Flow charts

Similar to the 'Timelines' technique in KS3 History, this technique can help students to understand themes like cause/consequence/impact/solution, because they allow them to create chronologies and connections between topics.

You can ask students to:

- Read a passage or extract and then create a chart of the dates/events

- Put a series of events in order and recall the dates/details

How to tutor

- Use a completed flowchart to answer a series of exam-style questions

- Summarise a case study using a flow chart

The timeline technique can be adapted for different students.

- Key dates and facts

- Descriptions of key events or phenomena

- Images, like maps, diagrams, or photos

- Sources, charts, and graphs

Once the student has created their flowchart, they can download it to keep for revision or further study. Alternatively, they can be reused and added to in later lessons.

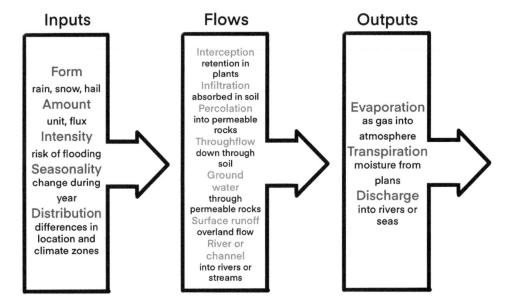

Plenaries

Basic lesson techniques

- Mind maps (p. 96)

- Lists (p. 96)

- WWW/EBI (p. 97)

- RAG (p. 97)

- Summary questions (p. 97)

- Quiz questions (p. 98)

- Quick exam question (p. 98)

Plus

Memory game

This plenary can be especially useful with students who have trouble committing key vocabulary to memory. To create this game, you'll need to write a dozen or more key words – geographical terminology, phrases or facts, and so on – on a slide, give the student 30 seconds to memorise it, and then ask them to write out as many words as they can remember.

For bonus points, you can ask the student to give you a definition of the word or an example of the phenomena.

'5 Ws'

This plenary works well for lessons that focus on events or case studies. You will need to put a key image from, or related to, the lesson in the centre of the online whiteboard, and students will need to add as much information as they can under the '5 W' headings: Who? What? When? Where? Why? They can use bullet points, sentences, notes, or sketches.

This format can help to prompt recall and is a useful format for arranging their notes later.

Homework

Basic lesson techniques

- Worksheets (p. 98)

- Past papers (p. 99)

Plus

Paragraph practice

Paragraph practice does what it says on the tin: it's an opportunity for students to practise their paragraph writing outside of the lesson time. I often find that with students I only see once a week, we just don't have enough time to write the paragraphs they need to practise, so setting just one or two to write at home can be a real help for them.

You will need to set your student a writing task – I usually ask them to complete the writing task from the lesson so the content they need is fresh in their mind – and once it is finished, they can send it to you to mark before the next lesson, or you can mark it together as the next starter.

Planning an A-level Geography lesson

A sample A-level Geography lesson might look like this:

Table 16.4 A sample A-level Geography lesson

Date	Starter	Explanation/ demonstration	Main activity	Plenary	Homework
09/05	Map starter: images of famous deserts (prompt for guesses about desertification, processes and systems, landforms, desert case study, etc.)	Slideshow: 1. Discuss key areas of content for this unit 2. Summary questions on the slides at the end of each section	Case study: 1. Read through case study factfile 2. Create a flowchart/ table for case study information 3. Encourage students to organise their information to help them revise	Quick exam question: short or long answer question on the lesson content	Worksheet: set of long and extended answer questions, 30 minutes

A full 10-week timetable of lesson plans that can be adapted or used for any of your students can be found in the 'Lesson plans' chapter of this book.

Common issues

The most common issues I've come across when tutoring A-level Geography are:

1. **Difficulty with case studies**

    While the general content is broad, many students also report difficulty with the case study sections of the exams. Case studies are essentially large-scale examples, focusing on a key event or place, which are used to explore the key concepts and apply the skills learned from the course. These sections require students to learn lots of information, facts, and elements of narrative in order to present an assessment or judgement about a key theme, like natural disasters, climate and habitat, population, and so on. They are then tested using open-ended mini-essays requiring students to recall precise information and fit their facts to the question.

Part of what can be challenging is learning the material: students need a comprehensive understanding of each case study, with good recall of the different factors, outcomes, or other details. They also need to be judicious in their selection of evidence, as they only have limited time and space to write and will be marked on the organisation and fluency of their answer. Finally, they will need to ensure that their conclusions, judgements, or suggestions fit the key words of the question appropriately and are consistent throughout their answer.

Again, tutors can help by offering students the opportunity to answer practice questions and get detailed feedback. You can also use summary questions and listing exercises to encourage recall and use the specific case studies to revise the key concepts and vocabulary of the topic they're linked to.

2. **Struggling with extended answer questions**

    Because the format of the GCSE is mostly short answer and multiple-choice questions, many students find the extended answer questions difficult to adapt to. This can result in them not writing enough or not including the most relevant details.

    Model answer exercises are most helpful here, especially when combined with a WWW/EBI-style feedback opportunity so students can discuss what they think each model did well and what could be improved. Students can then extract sentence starters or paragraph structures they like to use in their own answers. Once they have had the chance to practise planning answers, you can offer past paper questions as homework.

How to tutor: A-level Science

LESSON TECHNIQUES

Starters

Basic lesson techniques

- Matching exercises (p. 84)

- Sorting exercises (p. 85)

How to tutor

- Word searches (p. 85)

- Crosswords (p. 85)

- Mind maps (p. 86)

- Quickfire questions (p. 87)

- Homework review (p. 87)

Plus

Memory game

This plenary helps encourage students to commit key content to memory, with a mix of visual and word-based clues. To create this game, you'll need to write a dozen or more key words, images, diagrams, or formulae on a slide, give the student 30 seconds to memorise it, and then ask them to write out as many as they can remember.

For bonus points, you can ask the student to give you a definition of the word or an example of the device. For an extra difficult twist, you could choose all of the items from a specific topic and ask the student which topic they think they were related to.

Explanations/demonstrations

Basic lesson techniques

- Slideshows (p. 87)

- YouTube videos (p. 89)

- Model answers (p. 89)

- Live modelling (p. 91)

- Worksheets (p. 93)

Plus

Big picture, small picture

One of the problems students sometimes identify in Science is that they will know some terminology or recognise some concepts but don't understand how those concepts fit together or what to do with the symbols or words they've learned.

To tackle this, I recommend 'zooming out' first – moving back out to general concepts and explanations, talking through their basic understanding of the key ideas first – before 'zooming in' on the specific elements that they will need to know for that topic.

This can be done using another of the methods for this section, such as a slideshow, but it can also be done more organically using a mind map or set of exam-style questions, allowing students to make links between the relevant content for themselves.

Alternatively, you can find worksheets that make a similar progression through the content, using questions of increasing complexity.

Main activities

Basic lesson techniques

- Past papers (p. 93)

- Worksheets (p. 95)

- Annotation (p. 94)

- Question-guessing (p. 95)

Plus

Tables

Using tables as a demonstration technique can help show students how to distil large amounts of information down to the key points, isolating key processes, events, and ideas. Using it as a main activity can help students to commit the information to memory and organise it usefully for further study.

It is up to you whether you put the information into the table yourself before you discuss it with the student or whether you work through paragraphs or lists of information together with the student, deciding what to put into each box together.

The first column in the table should have a heading which helps students group the most important information, like 'Topic', 'Experiment', 'Event', and so on. They can then list all of the elements under that heading, before adding a second column with 'Details', 'Outcomes', 'Terms', and so on. The boxes can be filled in with bullet points or phrases rather than full sentences.

Once students have created their table, they can then colour-code it, highlight key points, and download a copy to keep for revision or further study.

Protein structures in A-Level Biology

Level	Nature	Purpose
Primary	Sequence of amino acids in polypeptide chains	Dictates the protein's structure
Secondary	Hydrogen bonds between carboxyls and amino groups	

Plenaries

Basic lesson techniques

- Mind maps (p. 96)

- Lists (p. 96)

- WWW/EBI (p. 97)

- RAG (p. 97)

- Summary questions (p. 97)

- Quiz questions (p. 98)

- Quick exam question (p. 98)

Plus

'Spot the mistake'

'Spot the mistake' is a good plenary for more confident students, because it encourages them to look critically at the material and methods in front of them. It works especially well with the Maths-based topics in Chemistry and Physics or multi-step questions, because they have to practise reading the question carefully in order to see the mistake.

To create this plenary, you write out the workings and answer to an example question, but make a deliberate error in the process. This may be a simple miscalculation, like a wrong multiplication in the first step, or a bigger mistake, like drawing the wrong shape or a point on a graph in the wrong place. The more confident the student, the more subtle the error should be. The student then needs to read the question carefully, find the mistake, and correct the workings.

If the student is doing well or you have more time, you can always do a series of these exercises of increasing difficulty. You can also give a particularly tricky one to a group of students to see if they can work together to find the mistake.

Headlines

Breaking down key information into bite-sized chunks can make recalling it in the future easier. This plenary asks students to create 'headlines', like the short phrases that top newspaper articles, to capture the most significant information they learned that lesson. You can ask for two to five, depending on how much content you covered in the lesson. They can also draw a picture or diagram to accompany their headlines, if they want.

If needed, you can then return to the 'headlines' they wrote in a future lesson and ask them to create a mind map of that topic as a starter.

Homework

Basic lesson techniques

- Worksheets (p. 98)

- Past papers (p. 99)

Plus

Experiments

One of the main elements of Science lessons that is difficult to recreate or discuss in online lessons are the experiments, but students do still need to understand the equipment, methodologies, and results of common experiments.

If students want to learn more about the experiments they're learning about, or want a more interactive visual tool, you can recommend them an online experiment simulator. There are several that have been specifically tailored to the UK's KS3, GCSE, and A-level syllabi. These sites allow students to play with and explore the concepts they're learning about while learning the vocabulary and methods they will need to answer the relevant exam questions.

You can show students where to find these tools and even set them a worksheet or set of exam-style questions to complete on that experiment or topic.

Planning an A-level Science lesson

A sample A-level Science lesson might look like this:

Date	Starter	Explanation/demonstration	Main activity	Plenary	Homework
18/09	Summary questions: Five recall questions on the topic from the previous lesson	Slideshow: 1. Discuss key areas of content for this unit – focusing on key calculations and formulae 2. Summary questions on the slides at the end of each section	Past paper: 1. Using a compilation paper, work through a series of calculation questions 2. At the end of questions the student finds especially difficult, discuss what they struggle with and make notes on what to revise further	RAG: mark RAG on the different styles of question covered to know which to go over again in future	Worksheet: set of calculation questions, some single step and some multi-step, 30 minutes

A full 10-week timetable of lesson plans that can be adapted or used for any of your students can be found in the 'Lesson plans' chapter of this book.

Common issues

The most common issues I've come across when tutoring A-level Science are:

1. **Remembering and differentiating key concepts**

   Each of the Science A-levels requires students to become closely familiar with a range of complex concepts. This is made especially difficult by the fact that many concepts are simplified at GCSE level and then have to essentially be re-taught at an appropriate level of complexity at A-level, which can make the step up to A-level seem even bigger for some. Thus, one of the challenges that students report is finding it difficult to memorise, recall, and differentiate between the key concepts.

   In some instances, it's because the content itself contains lots of similar ideas. In Chemistry, for example, students are required to learn the methodology and use of a number of different chemical tests. These tests have a number of similarities in their equipment and method but very different outcomes and indicators, making them confusing upon recall.

   Other times, it's because the language and terminology that students are required to learn can appear similar but have wildly different meanings.

In Biology, there are lots of technical terms that must be memorised, many of which come from the same root words but are used very differently in a scientific context.

Finally, it can be because of the variety of ways that the concepts might be presented. In Physics, students can face very Maths-heavy explanations of concepts, confusing diagrams, and numerous ways of representing questions from key topics – all of which can mean that students feel that they understand a concept one minute but are confused by an alternative demonstration of it the next.

Tutors will need to discuss with students if they share any of these concerns, making sure that they are properly addressed during lessons. You can offer online resources, slideshows, and demonstrations to ensure that they understand topics, as well as consistently introducing practice questions to expose them to the range of ways questions can be phrased or formatted. You can also offer spelling tests and quizzes for complex terminology.

2. **Difficulty with topics and skills from other subjects that are used in the Sciences**

A common issue among students in all three Science A-levels is that they all require students to have a combination of skills from other subjects: predominantly Maths skills with the use of formulae and graphs, but also fluency and confidence with descriptions of scientific concepts, diagrams, and models. If the student already finds a particular skill difficult in Maths or English, they are going to find it ever harder to apply in a new context.

With some students, this can be a literacy issue, in that some students struggle with reading comprehension and complex vocabulary, which can trip them up when trying to access Science resources.

Tutors can offer pop quizzes or spelling tests to ensure that students are confident about their key vocabulary, as well as using techniques like basic reading comprehension and worksheets to give students a framework for developing their understanding of the more complicated topics.

Alternatively, it may be a numeracy issue. All three Sciences require at least some Maths skills, especially Chemistry and Physics: reading graphs, using formulae, calculating moles or gravity. Students who are already finding Maths difficult tend to find that their confusion translates into the Sciences, so tutors who notice this concern with their students should focus on these elements and offer to cover the basic Maths topics that underlie them if needed.

If you have significant concerns about a student's numeracy, you can speak to their parent or teacher about the student accessing dedicated Maths tutoring as well to support their exam performance.

TOP TIP

Content memorisation can be a real struggle at this level, so do use lesson time to model revision techniques and incorporate recall exercises, even if the student finds them very difficult to start with. Your regular lessons will help build good habits for them to benefit from later.

QUESTION

How will you tackle the cross-subject elements (i.e. calculations, extended writing) in these subjects?

Chapter 17

Personal statement mentoring

Personal statements are short personal essays that accompany students' university applications, giving details about their interests, suitability for that university and course, and reasons for applying. This statement, alongside exam results, academic awards, extracurricular activities, entrance exams, and interviews, represents a student's application to a course and institution. In the UK, the vast majority of students apply to university through a service called the Universities and Colleges Admissions Service (UCAS), which has a 4000-character and 47-line limit and provides guidance on style and content on their website (www.ucas.com/undergraduate/applying-university/how-write-ucas-undergraduate-personal-statement).

Students can struggle with writing their personal statements for lots of reasons: some students aren't given very much guidance from their teachers or sixth-form tutors, some students aren't confident about what they want to apply for or why, and some students just don't know where to start! Your role as a tutor is to offer advice about your experience at university, provide some guidance about what and how to write, and mark their draft to make sure it is coherent and well written.

Personal statement mentoring is usually an add-on service requested by A-level students, so most students only ask for between 1 and 3 hours working directly with a tutor, with some also requesting paid marking time.

You will notice later in the chapter that there is some specific advice for different degree applications, as well as advice for supporting students making Oxbridge applications. This is not to say that all tutors can mentor all personal statements – you should only offer guidance on applications that you yourself made or are very familiar with. These degree-specific sections are there to support tutors who do the most common degrees in the UK, who may get a lot of requests and want to make sure they've covered all of the essential information.

Starting with a new personal statement student

The first thing to do with a new personal statement mentee is to find out *what* they are applying to study and *where* they're applying to study it. You should also find out the details of *how* they are applying – whether they have just finished their A-levels or if they're a mature student, if they're applying to one university or five, whether they're applying through UCAS, and so on. Ideally, personal statements should be tailored to the specifics of their application as much as possible.

They should also be tailored to the university if the student is only applying to one university or if they are applying to one of the Oxbridge universities. If the student is only applying to one university, you can make the statement more specific and add in information about the institution, its facilities, and its staff.

If the student is applying to Oxbridge, there's an additional step: the Oxbridge-only personal statement. Oxford and Cambridge want to be confident that applicants have considered the unique style of university life that they offer, so they want to see why applicants think shorter terms, more intensive workloads, and collegiate life are for them. To help students to do so, they offer the opportunity to write a second, shorter personal statement as part of their application paperwork which will only be sent to the Admissions tutor at the Oxbridge college you apply to. This second personal statement is optional, but as I explain in the following, I would strongly encourage all applicants to include it.

Assessing their current work

Most students look for personal statement mentoring once they have started their application and realised that they are finding it difficult, so they usually already have a draft or two of the statement.

That said, some students may not have started yet because they don't know what to do or know that they are going to find it difficult. In these situations, tutors have to take extra care not to end up doing the bulk of the work for the student, since a personal statement written by someone other than the student won't accurately reflect them and may set them up to do poorly at interview or in other areas of their application.

What I recommend is to ask students to, at an absolute minimum, have written a plan of what they want the personal statement to contain and a first draft (essentially the plan written out in full sentences). You can help them to come up with the plan – making suggestions about what to include and possibly the order to put their ideas in – but they should write the entirety of the first draft themselves. This ensures that the main body of the statement has been written by the student and that they are personally responsible for what goes what in the first instance: even if it then undergoes heavy editing, it has originated from them. I usually tell students to ignore the character count in the first instance – you can edit back down to it afterwards – but I do suggest that they stick to around 500 words.

I like to start by reading through the first draft together in the first lesson, discussing any questions or obvious issues, and then give them a chance to go away and make changes before I mark it properly for the first time.

A useful checklist for reviewing their first draft could look something like this:

- How does it read the first time? Is it clear what they want to study and why from the opening paragraph?

- Does it read fluidly and confidently? Are there any issues with its structure/order of paragraphs?

- How many examples of extracurricular commitments can you find, and are they sufficiently evidenced?

- How many books/films/documentaries/shows/lectures and other key names or titles can you see? Have they reflected on why they were useful and what they learned?

- Have they named and explained any achievements/prizes/work experience? Have they reflected on what they learned in that time?

- Any obvious spelling mistakes, punctuation issues, or grammatical errors?

Lesson techniques

With some students, a quick read-through and a bit of feedback on their first draft may be all they need from you. With others, you may find that they need significantly more help. In that case, it can be useful to know the extent to which you can offer help and what the student will need.

Here I'm going to give some general advice about personal statement mentoring, and in the following you will find specific advice about the most common degree applications and Oxbridge personal statements. I haven't included most of the sections you'll find in other chapters, because personal statement mentoring lessons tend to be less structured and more discussion based, but there are some useful activities you can use to fill out your lesson plan.

Main activities

Generic advice

Most interesting anecdote

There isn't a 'one size fits all' method for personal statements, but most good advice would suggest that your opening paragraph should explain what you want to study and why in the most concise method possible. I would add that students' personal statements should open with their most interesting anecdote as a way to stand out from the crowd. Humour and originality can be a good tool, but as their tutor, you will need to help the student strike an appropriate balance between amusing and insincere.

'Focus of the essay'

Ultimately, the question that universities want you to answer is: *why you?* What makes you a good candidate for their course, and how can you prove it? This can be a good prompt for students who don't know where to start and prefer writing to an essay question rather than an open-ended task. The two-step question can also help students who are struggling to put enough evidence into their statement by creating a Why-How paragraph structure that they can plan around.

There are a number of ways to tackle this 'focus' on *why you* with the student: put in the middle of a mind-map, make a list, discuss the options, re-draft, and so on. Whatever method you use, you should always ensure that the key elements from the student's plan – their achievements, experience, and ambitions – are clear in the statement and are explained and evidenced well.

Spelling, punctuation, and grammar

Competition for university places has never been fiercer, especially since many have chosen to re-enter education in light of the pandemic. This means that simple mistakes can make a big difference in an application. Tutors who are being paid for additional marking time will be able to catch any small errors or inconsistencies, but if there are significant mistakes, this may be indicative of a bigger issue. It can be tempting to just wait until your student hands in a draft and correct all of the mistakes then, but if the student is willing to pay for time with you and you sense that they won't understand all of your corrections, then it may be worth spending some lesson time going over key SPAG errors. This is just as important in STEM subjects as it is in essay-based subjects, especially if the student is applying to a top university.

Basic issues I have seen include misuse of commas, run-on sentences, and poor paragraphing, so a quick recap of those basic skills can help students to improve their own editing skills.

Specific advice

Oxbridge personal statement

The bulk of the advice in this section refers to the main UCAS personal statement, which will be sent to every university the student applies to, including Oxford or Cambridge if they are applying there.

However, it is worth bearing in mind that both Cambridge and Oxford offer applicants the opportunity to write an additional, Oxbridge-specific personal statement as part of the application paperwork, and I would strongly recommend that you suggest to your students that they do this. This secondary personal statement is included as part of the Supplementary Application Questionnaire (SAQ) and is 1200 characters, giving students the opportunity to add any Oxford- or Cambridge-specific details to their personal statement. This additional statement should focus on why that Oxbridge experience would be a good fit for them, how the Oxbridge course differs from other offerings in the subject, and what they will bring to the table as a member of the university.

When it comes to supporting students to write personal statements for Oxbridge applications, there are some key things to remember:

1. **Make sure they've done their research**

   Oxbridge applicants should know everything they can about the course they're applying to, the syllabus and staff in that department, the college they want to apply to, and the extracurricular activities they want to try; in short, they need to do as much research as possible. College admissions tutors want to see that you have taken the time to learn about what the college offers and why it's the university for you.

   There is a huge amount of information available online both through the universities' official channels and from the personal accounts of current and former students, through blogs, YouTube channels, articles, books, and other resources. Most importantly, the student has you – a current or former Oxbridge student yourself! You should try to give impartial and informed guidance, pointing to official sources or giving anecdotal evidence wherever possible.

2. **Help them to demonstrate their interest in unique and personal ways**

   Oxbridge want more than just clever and hardworking – they want interesting and innovative, too, and it starts with the application process. The student will need to stand out from the crowd, but there should also be a warning here about going too far the other way. I've heard plenty of urban legends about Oxbridge personal statements: from that one Maths applicant who supposedly wrote their entire essay about spending their free time studying Rubik's Cubes or someone who apparently wrote their entire life story as a narrative essay. The point isn't to be unusual for the sake of being unusual – your student needs to stand out because they represent themselves well and write a compelling essay, not because their essay was bizarre. This will require you as a tutor to have a reasonable judgement about what is engaging and what is gimmicky.

Encourage the student to look outside of their A-level syllabus and to draw interesting conclusions based on their reading. They should try to demonstrate a genuine curiosity in their subject, alongside a commitment to the necessary academic skills. The key word there is 'demonstrate' – admissions tutors want to see that the student can show what they have learned and why it made them think or feel that way rather than just telling them.

Ultimately, the focus for the student should be on making the *content* of the personal statement as impressive and representative as possible. That said, in your marking, you can also point out any places where their writing style could be refined: avoiding starting consecutive sentences with 'I', for example, or catching repeated words or common buzzwords like 'keen', 'passion', and 'enjoy'.

3. **Encourage them to only include things they are totally committed to**

This final tip can be really significant in the Oxbridge application process, because Oxbridge are the most famous of an increasing handful of universities that conduct interviews. The personal statement plays a varying role in applications depending on the subject the student is applying for, but for some it can form the backbone of the personal interview. Therefore, students should only ever write about topics, books, or ideas that they know well and are genuinely interested in; otherwise they run the risk of being caught out in the interview.

Business/Management

1. **Help them find practical examples of their business experience**

Personal statements should always emphasise a student's suitability for a course, but this can be difficult if the course they're applying for isn't something they've been able to study directly at school.

Some students just need help finding a way to phrase their experiences in a suitable manner for their essay. However, if they're struggling to find any relevant examples at all, there are lots of options. There are a number of resources you can recommend to students. They can investigate Massive Open Online Courses (MOOCs) and free online courses offered by the Open University, Harvard University, and others, or look for documentaries and films related to the business world. Students can make reference to activities they enjoy outside of school or to jobs they have held.

If they don't have time to add anything new, students can demonstrate key skills that they have developed through less directly relevant means, such as sport or volunteering. Those activities look good in a personal statement in general, especially if the student has been doing them consistently for a long time, and can also be used to show leadership, resilience, commitment, and so on – all of which can be linked to business acumen.

2. **Dig into their reading**

Personal statements shouldn't be jam-packed with book titles, but extracurricular reading is an excellent way to demonstrate interest.

Many students will have already done reading they can reference as part of their A-level course or simply out of their own interest, so finding a compelling way to write about it is key. I suggest that students link their favourite elements of their reading to their practical experience or try show some reflection of what they learned from the writer. Just saying that they've read something isn't enough: students need to evidence their aptitude for a business course.

If they aren't sure where to start, you can recommend that they try a reading list. There are several business leaders, like Bill Gates, who publish summer reading lists with their personal recommendations, or they can look to publications like *Forbes* or the *Financial Times*, who publish yearly lists of bestsellers. Finally, students can also find the reading lists for BA and MBA courses on university websites, which can help them find degree-level authors and academic experts to quote or point to.

3. **Demonstrate knowledge, but avoid unnecessary jargon**

Students want to show the admissions tutors that they know their stuff, but they should try to avoid throwing in lots of complicated terminology just for the sake of it. They run the risk of using a term incorrectly or spelling something wrong, as well seeming to only have a shallow knowledge of the concepts.

Instead of telling their readers what they know, students should focus on demonstrating their knowledge through anecdotes or reflections, applying any key terms in an authentic and organic way. As their proofreader, you should be able to help students decide how much terminology is enough and whether they have used it appropriately.

Law

1. Encourage them to show, not tell

All students should try to 'show' their skills and experience rather than 'telling' because it makes for better-quality writing, but this is especially important when applying to a Law degree course.

This doesn't necessarily mean all students need direct work experience in the legal field – not everyone will have this opportunity – but it does mean that students might need to think creatively about their experiences to demonstrate the relevant skills.

Captain of the football team? Good leadership, communication, and teamwork. Enjoy debating? Confident public speaker, effective communicator, and excellent at research. Done lots of group projects in class? Hardworking and able to co-ordinate with others.

Alternatively, students can own their weaknesses or lack of experience and use them to say why they want to study that particular course. They can then link to the positive aspects of learning and advancing their skills at university.

2. Make sure they understand law as a concept, not just Law as a subject

This limitation can arise from the way that Law is taught at A-level, in that it tends to compartmentalise the subject for the sake of such a short course, and admissions tutors want to see that applicants have investigated their legal interest further than the boundaries of that syllabus.

Students should also try avoid focusing solely on the areas of law perceived to be most exciting – like criminal law – since most students will write about those elements, and they're just a small part of any complex legal system. All university degrees require students to learn about a broad cross-section of the law before they can specialise, so applicants need to show that they are engaging with the concept of the law as a whole, not just the bits they find most interesting.

3. **Aim for concise and engaging prose**

Law is not only a heavily essay-based subject, but it is a subject where the intricacies of vocabulary and grammar can bear huge significance. Therefore, there should be a greater emphasis on the style and quality of the student's writing. Applicants should write in an appropriately formal manner, but not academically – it's a personal essay, not an actual essay.

Psychology/Sociology

1. **Remind them to avoid overly emotional motives for study**

A common theme in Psychology/Sociology personal statements is that the student was inspired to study it further by a family member or friend who has a condition like autism, dementia, or schizophrenia. If this is genuinely the case for the student, then they should absolutely write about it – but they also need to demonstrate how it prompted further research into the subject, what they want to do after their degree, and what they are curious about in other areas of the course that aren't directly related to that motive.

If the student is extrapolating from an experience that didn't have such a significant impact for the sake of the personal statement, it may be a good idea to encourage them to explore a less common motive to study.

2. **Help them to pick examples that evidence their passion**

Students don't usually get the chance to study Psychology/Sociology in school, and it can be difficult for them to get work experience in these areas due to their clinical nature, so students need to find compelling evidence for their interest in these subjects.

The best way to do this is often through reading, resources, and opportunities through local institutions. This can include MOOCs and online lectures; free lectures, classes, and talks at universities or colleges; memoirs, biographies, and case studies; and even interviews with family or staff who work in the profession. In addition, working with children is often more accessible for students than working with adults, so any work experience they have in this area – mentoring, volunteering, caring for younger siblings – can demonstrate their interest in child psychology, caring and supporting work, and person-centred work.

3. Explore and explain their critical thinking

Depending on the university, Psychology can be a Science-based course or a Humanities-based course, so students will need to research which type of course they are applying for and adapt their personal statement appropriately.

If your student is applying for a predominantly Science-based course, it can help to explore the critical thinking and research skills required by demonstrating reflections and conclusions from their reading or experiences: criticisms of the field, interesting experiments, or new data.

If they are applying for a Humanities-based course, they may want to focus on the more literary, social science, or theoretical aspects of the subject and draw their conclusions from those areas: limitations of a particular treatment or school of thought, trends over time, and so on.

Students should try to avoid outright dismissing or deriding anything, just in case the admissions tutor feels very differently, but at the same time a strong opinion, backed by evidence, is a good demonstration of the relevant skills.

Medicine/Nursing

1. Ensure they have reflected on their work experiences

Medicine/Nursing are hugely competitive degree subjects, so students can be confident that everyone applying for these courses will have lots of work experience. The key to standing out is to show what you have learned from the experience, not just pointing out that you've done it.

As their tutor, you should encourage students to always include links between their experiences or aspirations and their evidence, in the form of reading or reflection. You can even model some sentence starters for them: 'Inspired by my experience, I . . .' or 'Having learned more about this condition, I . . .'

Students should also be encouraged to show other positive qualities using their work experience examples: working in the same place for more than six months shows commitment, multiple experiences show perseverance, and complementing any experience with relevant reading shows research skills and an interest in professional development.

2. **Help them to identify the qualities they think medical professionals should have and demonstrate that they have them**

Given that most people's interactions with medical professionals usually occur when something has gone wrong, it is crucial that said professionals be reassuring, respectful, and receptive. Your student will undoubtedly have their own adjectives to add to that list, and you should encourage them to think carefully about what they consider the most important qualities for doctors and nurses to have.

Once they've thought about their ideals, they should then try to demonstrate in their statement that they are a good candidate with those qualities, using thoughtful examples and reflections.

The examples don't necessarily need to be drawn from work experience: students can think about doctors and nurses from TV, films, theatre, and fiction as well as any real-life staff they have interacted with. The key aspect is the reflection: what does this character or person do or not do, and why would I want to be similar or different?

3. **Explore their understanding of the realities of both medical study and practice**

As a current or former medical student yourself, you are best placed to explain to students what studying Medicine or Nursing is like. Discussing students' hopes and fears can help you to get a sense of their understanding of the process, which will in turn help you to course-correct their personal statement. After all, Medicine is a gruelling course, requiring many additional years of study compared to other degrees. Students need to show admissions tutors that they understand the reality of what they are signing up for and are committed to their study, with an ambition to either go into medical research or into the field.

It is at this point that students can also start to think about how to show themselves as well-rounded individuals, because admissions tutors are not expecting you to do nothing but study for the next 5 to 7 years. Students can demonstrate their understanding of study–life or work–life balance by detailing what else they like to do, like sports or music, and there's no harm in showing how it will help to make them a better student and, later, professional. As their tutor, you can explain to them how you manage that balance and help them to include relevant details in their statement.

Planning a personal statement mentoring lesson

The lesson planning for a subject like personal statement mentoring can be more fluid than in other subjects, as you don't need as many exercises planned and the lessons are likely to be directed as much by the student as by you. You don't necessarily need elements like starters and plenaries, and you may even find that an unstructured lesson can allow the student to highlight the areas where they need the most help.

Nonetheless, it can be worth planning out a rough idea of how you're going to spend the hour.

This can take the form of a bullet-point list, a mind map, or even a table, like the following sample.

Table 17.1 A sample personal statement lesson

Date	Explanation/demonstration	Main activity
14/07	Read through edits from previous marking session together, discussing any significant issues – Quick demonstration of how to use commas in lists	Discuss possible edits – Re-write example 3 to make reflections on work experience clearer – Re-write the concluding section to link to body of the statement more coherently

Common issues

The main issues I've come across when mentoring personal statements are:

1. **Students being uncomfortable writing about themselves**

   Consistently, one of the biggest problems students seem to face when writing their personal statements is that they are really uncomfortable writing about themselves and their activities and achievements! Whether it's out of modesty or simply that they're embarrassed, helping students to find comfortable ways to talk themselves up in their statements has been a big part of the personal statement mentoring work that I've done. At the end of the day, applicants mustn't shy away from talking about themselves: admissions tutors are going to read a lot of personal statements, so applicants need to stand out, and the best way to do that is to show off their unique set of skills and experiences – in an articulate, thoughtful, and concise way.

2. **Inconsistent SPAG**

Spelling, punctuation, and grammar can be a sticking point for lots of students – especially those in STEM or other non-essay subjects who have now had a couple of years without compulsory English lessons each week. SPAG is important in every application, no matter what subject they're applying for. You may not have time to explain to your student all of the different ways that commas should be used, but at a minimum, you should ensure that you mark SPAG consistently and collaborate with the student if any significant edits are needed during your lessons or feedback. Students should always be encouraged to proofread as they go and to ask you as well as trusted friends, family members, or teachers to read it before it is submitted.

3. **Poor structure**

One of the biggest challenges that students seem to face with personal statements is that they aren't really essays in the form that they're used to – there's no title or question to answer, there isn't an 'introduction' and 'conclusion' in the traditional sense, and the whole thing is only roughly 500 words. Thus, students can sometimes struggle to work out what order to put the information they need to include. As I explain in the next bullet point, there isn't a magic formula for the structure of a personal statement, but there are some useful rules:

- Grab the reader's attention in the opening line

- State what you want to study and why in the first paragraph

- If you can, tell a bit of a story – what sparked your interest in this subject, what did you do about it, and how would this course help you on that journey?

- Give plenty of evidence of your interest and skills in the body of the statement

- Conclude with some key details about the university you've chosen and why you want to study there in particular

4. **Students using a template or other non-original draft**

Having just identified that many students struggle with personal statement structure, it should come as no surprise that many try to solve this by using a template or preprepared format that they have found online. Not only is using a template a sure-fire way for a student to blend into the masses of applications, and potentially be flagged for plagiarism, it also seriously weakens their chances of being able to represent their achievements and skills accurately and advantageously. If, when you read a student's first draft, you sense that they have simply copied and pasted their extracurricular activities into an existing format, you can try searching a section of their essay on Google to see if it returns any matches, or just ask them if they used a template. If the answer is yes, encourage them to write one from scratch and offer some of the strategies outlined previously to help them.

5. **Limited evidence of their interest outside of their subject**

A more general issue I've come across that tutors should watch out for is when students a struggling to demonstrate their interest in the subject they want to study beyond what they already cover in their course. All universities want applicants who are keen to learn, demonstrated by having read, watched, volunteered, or otherwise engaged with their subject beyond the compulsory elements or topics of their A-level courses. This doesn't necessarily mean students should be spending every waking moment on their subject – and many students may be facing this issue because they have to work, care for others, or look after themselves – but it does mean that, as their tutor, you might need to help them to get creative and find ways to relate their experiences to their subject. If they do a lot of sport, they can point to their leadership or teamwork skills; if they want to include more books, you can make recommendations based on your university reading lists; if they like watching TV, you can show them some documentaries or YouTube channels that might give them some new subject information. Whatever you do, do not let them lie or overly exaggerate. The student may be asked about what they've written on their statement as part of their application, and they should never be in a position where they can't fully explain the ideas they wrote about.

TOP TIP

As tempting as it can be to swoop in and save a draft that a student is obviously finding hard to improve, always try to give it back to the student to fix (even if you end up giving a lot of advice!). They will be much better served in the future having done it themselves.

QUESTION

What do you think is the most helpful feedback to give on a first draft of a personal statement?

Chapter 18

Higher education applications

Applying to university can be one of the most daunting experiences in a student's life. There is huge pressure on students to achieve their goals, and it can be easy for tutors to feel that they aren't able to help as much as they want to.

Undergraduates and recent graduates are often best placed to support university applicants, ahead of parents and even teachers, because they have such recent experience of the system. Your role as a tutor is to support your students through their application, answer any questions, and help them excel in their entrance exams and interviews.

What you will quickly notice is that this chapter, like the previous one, is structured slightly differently to most of the others in this book, for several reasons.

Largely, this is because university entrance exams in the UK are not nationally standardised: each university and college has a different system, and there are many variations of exam and interview. Thus, it would be almost impossible to write a chapter covering every possible application scenario your students might face. Instead, you will take the knowledge and skills you already have and turn that into a highly specialised tutoring ability.

Another reason that this chapter is a bit different is that you don't need so many lesson techniques with students of this age. Most university applicants will only want a few weeks of lessons with you rather than months or years, and the majority of the lessons will be taken up with practising, planning, and completing papers and discussing their answers rather than on learning specific content.

The rest of this chapter is a guide to supporting a university applicant through the various stages of their application, focusing on the two main obstacles they will face:

- **An entrance or aptitude exam** – these can vary significantly, from pre-interview exams at the student's school to a timed exam as part of the interview day or

DOI: 10.4324/9781003211648-22

week. Some Oxbridge colleges do both! The format of these exams can vary as well – from essays and written papers to multiple-choice questions and online quizzes.

- **One or more interviews** – most universities only interview for the most competitive courses, like Medicine and Veterinary Medicine, but Oxbridge both interview almost all applicants, and several London universities are now asking for interviews in Humanities and Science subjects. Cambridge usually only asks for two interviews, but Oxford applicants could end up staying for a week or more and face an interview every day, as Cambridge offers students to the college pool after interview rather than before. At both, there is usually one interview that focuses on your personality and suitability for Oxbridge life and another interview that specifically focuses on your subject ability and critical thinking.

In this chapter, I am going to cover the most common entrance exams, as well as the interviews made famous by Oxbridge but increasingly used by UCL, KCL, and others.

Entrance exams

University entrance exams in the UK are not standardised, but there is usually a common style of assessment in each subject, along with an Oxbridge-specific version and at least one other version. Tutors who have successfully entered university courses are best placed to advise students on how to study for and take these exams, so you should be careful to only offer advice on the exams you have actually taken or you know well.

The most common entrance exams university applicants will face are:

- Law (LNAT and CLT)

- Maths (MAT, STEP, and TMUA)

- Medical courses (BMAT, HCAT, and UMAT)

- Thinking Skills Assessments (TSAs) for a number of Humanities courses. The TSAs are specific to Oxford, Cambridge, and UCL, though some other universities have their own version of what is essentially a critical thinking and problem-solving assessment.

In addition, it is worth noting that, while I won't cover them all here, almost every course at Oxford and Cambridge has some form of aptitude assessment: the

English Language Aptitude Test (ELAT) for English; the Natural Sciences Admissions Assessment (NSAA) and the Physics Aptitude Test (PAT) for Veterinary Medicine and the various Sciences; the Engineering Admissions Assessment (ENGAA) and PAT again for engineering; and many others, including History, Modern Foreign Languages, Classics, and Philosophy.

I mention this because the vast majority of students who will face entrance exams will be Oxbridge applicants, because they are used in almost every subject. They vary year to year, with some sample papers published on each department's website. Not only would it be impossible to give details about every exam – that would take a book of its own – but it also wouldn't be necessary: as a current or former Oxbridge student, you already know everything you need to about what the exams in your subject are like, and there are lots of resources online specifically designed to support you and your student.

Assessing their current work

You will need to assess applicants looking for support with entrance exams so you know what the main issues are and what you'll need to do to support them. By the time you reach university applications, the only really reliable way to know how a student is doing in any subject is to have them do a full exam-style paper. This can either be from a past paper taken from their exam board or university's website, or, if you are familiar with the paper they will be taking, you can design some of your own. I usually ask students to do a paper as preparation for our first lesson, which we then go through together, or if they are very busy, I will ask them to send me one they have already completed.

If the applicant you're working with hasn't got the time to do additional work for you, you can ask them to send you some of their ongoing A-level work – an essay they wrote for their English teacher, for example, or a recent paper or piece of classwork in Maths or Sciences – which will give you a sense of their ability. However, the entrance exams they will face are often fairly specific or idiosyncratic, looking for skills and understanding not necessarily covered by the A-level syllabi, so it is worth spending some of your early lesson time together looking at the paper and recognising its additional demands.

Exploring the exam

Once you have a sense of the student's ability, the next step is to ensure that they are confident about exactly what they will be expected to do in the entrance exam.

The main reason that student has sought a tutor, above all of the information available for free on the internet, is because you have taken the same exam they are preparing for. Therefore, discussing your experience of the exam – what your paper was like, how you approached it, what you learned from it – is the most important thing to discuss. I like to start with a discussion of what they think they are being expected to do and then use my knowledge of the exam to adjust or modify any misunderstanding.

They may already know plenty about the exam, but I have worked with several students who had very little idea of what to expect, and with those students, the best place to start is by going through exactly what they will be expected to do. There are several ways to do this, including the basic lesson techniques of looking through a past paper together (p. 99) or making a slideshow of the various skills, questions, and expectations of the paper (p. 87).

Whichever method you pick, you should always leave some time focus on the differences between A-level exam questions and entrance exam papers using the model answer technique (p. 89). Using this method, you can present an individual question/essay from each in isolation and ask the student to identify key differences between them. This works particularly well for exams where the format may seem familiar, like STEP or the ELAT, but is asking the student for more than is assessed by the equivalent A-level.

As you continue to tutor, you will also develop your own methods of introducing students to the exam formats, but when starting out, it can be useful to have at least one go-to method for your subject. These methods have been tried and tested with a variety of students, both STEM and Humanities, and are designed to help students to feel as confident as possible about approaching the exam.

Once they are happy with what they need to do, the only real way to prepare is to practise – over and over and over again. You can always return to your recap materials if it becomes clear that the student has misunderstood something, and you can practise individual questions together rather than setting whole papers to help isolate specific skills and content.

Using resources

Once the student knows exactly what the exam looks like, where to find resources, and what they need to know to prepare, your role as an entrance exam tutor can change. What will undoubtedly have become apparent in the last step is that students facing entrance exams need a lot of practice – which means that you, as their tutor, need a lot of papers to give them. This can be one of the biggest challenges as a tutor, especially as a new one, as you may not be familiar with where to find resources or how to make them yourself.

Fortunately, there are lots of options.

The first thing to remember is that the universities want the students' performance on the day to be an accurate reflection of their skills rather than of their ability to revise for a specific exam. Thus, they don't share a lot of exam materials online. However, they are required to offer students at least an understanding of what the papers will look like, so both Oxford and Cambridge share a limited number of past papers for all of their entrance exams each year. You should be able to find, at minimum, a sample test and possibly several previous years' papers. You can use these in lessons with students and set them as practice work if needed. However, because the number of 'official' past papers is so limited, most students will have found and either looked at or used them all before. In that case, tutors may find it necessary to look elsewhere.

The second thing to remember is that, where there are high-profile exams with limited official resources, there are resource banks. Many sites offer both paid and free access to new sample papers that have been written by subject experts, official papers with model answers, and whole folders of sample questions that you can pick and choose from. If you decide to pay for a subscription or bulk download, be sure to factor that cost into your hourly rate. I have included some recommendations of both free and paid resource banks at the end of this chapter.

The third thing to remember is that you have previously taken the exam, so you can use some of your planning time for the lessons to create your own resources. With Humanities subjects like English or History, you may find that you are able to create papers and resources of your own by writing essay questions and compiling extracts or sources from texts you have worked on at university. First-year degree-level materials are usually similar to what is used in the entrance exams – I actually studied one of the poems from my ELAT in my first year – so you can choose accessible topics and find materials online to write your own questions. In Maths or Science, you may not be able to write your own questions, but you can create compilation papers from questions from a variety of papers, textbooks, or question sheets from your university study.

Whatever you use, you need to make sure that it is helping your student, so I like to re-assess regularly – every one or two lessons – to see how they are improving. This can be mini-assessments, like a single question or essay plan, or a full paper that they have written outside of the lesson that we discuss together. Depending on how much time you have with the student, you may wish to do this more or less frequently.

Offering additional marking

Because of the nature of these exams, which focus almost entirely on skills rather than content, the best preparation most students can get is simply practice – with the added benefit of a tutor, who can provide detailed feedback on their papers or essays.

However, reading and marking that much work can take up a significant amount of time, so you will need to consider how much time is reasonable to include as part of your lesson preparation time and how much time you will actually need to give helpful feedback. As I explain in the earlier section on 'Homework and Paid Marking Time', if reading and marking the paper or essay will take you longer than half an hour, you should consider asking the student (or their parent) to book paid marking time. You can find more guidance about PMT in Section 1 of this book.

How to tutor: interview mentoring

Most commonly, students will request interview coaching from a tutor who is already supporting them with their A-levels, or, if you are a tutor who specifically supports Oxbridge applications, you may have new students come to you seeking interview coaching.

Oxford and Cambridge have perhaps the most infamous interviews, which has been their standard procedure in all subjects for decades, but they're becoming an increasingly common part of applications across the country: UCL, Bristol, Manchester, and even Warwick now interview applicants in some of their most competitive subjects.

This chapter will mostly be Oxbridge specific, since they are still the most common interviews by far, but all of the material should translate to at least some degree for any other university interview.

Discussing the specifics

There are two areas to cover here: information about the interviews themselves and information about the applicant. As a current or former university student yourself, you should have a good grasp of what your university's interview process is like and how to prepare for it.

Oxbridge interviews fall into two types: personal interviews and subject interviews. Cambridge usually only asks for one of each, but at Oxford, the student may have a personal interview at every college they are considered for.

Personal interviews are about getting to know the applicant as a person: what are their interests, why do they want to apply to Oxbridge, what makes them a good candidate for that subject? They might ask about elements of the student's personal statement or portfolio if something has stood out to them as interesting. Impressive qualities include confidence and integrity, so students will need to be happy answering questions spontaneously and thinking carefully before they speak.

Subject interviews are the more peculiar ones – the ones that usually make headlines with questions like 'tell me about a cactus'! There's a brilliant book full of these kinds of questions that you and your student might find useful, called *So You Want to Go to Oxbridge?: Tell Me About a Banana.*

These interviews are designed to boil down the key qualities that applicants need to have to excel in that subject: critical thinking, perseverance, subject knowledge, intuition, attention to detail, and so on. In Maths, they might put an 'impossible' equation in front of them and ask them how might go about solving it. In English, they might ask them to take an exam beforehand, then analyse a poem out loud while that exam paper is marked in front of them. In Medicine, they might ask them about the differences between professional roles or about the ethics of a difficult situation. In Law, the questions can vary a lot: from situational assessments to moral judgements. Whatever the questions, there aren't any 'wrong' answers – the interviewers are far more interested in how the applicant thinks than what they say.

Once you and the student have discussed what will be expected of them, you will then need to find out more about the student. As with all students, you will need to conduct some sort of assessment to find out what you need to work on together in the lessons.

I like to start by giving the student the opportunity to tell me what they think their strengths and weaknesses are and then performing a short mock interview with a mix of personal and subject questions to see how they respond. This is especially useful to do with students who are new to you, because you are a fairly strange person to them at that point, so there will be some of the nerves without any of the pressure.

Offering strategies

Once you have an idea of where the student is currently at, you can start to suggest opportunities to improve. The best thing you as a tutor can offer is your own experience: what worked for you, what didn't, and what you wish you'd known at the time. The more you can share about how your interviews went and what the student can expect, the better.

That said, you may find that you aren't sure exactly what to say or how to translate your experience into advice with your first student. As time goes on, you will develop a supportive dialogue with students, but it can be good to have strategies up your sleeve with your first few students.

Because the most common interviews are one or both of two distinct types, I have split the list of strategies in two to make the suggestions more specific.

Some good interview strategies for personal interviews include:

- **'Prepare some answers to common questions'** – Students should not be encouraged to 'script' their answers, because interviewers can spot those answers easily, but it is sensible to help them come up with some responses to the most common questions. This can include questions like 'Why do you want to study here?' or 'Why did you choose this subject'.

- **'Be honest'** – This simple piece of advice is obvious but very important. Students may be tempted to talk up their achievements or aspirations, which they absolutely should do in this situation, but never beyond the bounds of the actual truth. Interviews can last a fair amount of time and cover a wide range of questions, so students need to be consistent and cogent in their answers. If the interviewer asks them if they've read a certain book or heard of a certain professor, they need to answer honestly – it's okay to say no and the interviewers are not expecting them to know everything.

- **'Know your application inside out'** – Students who had a lot of help with their personal statement or who didn't think through their choice of college or subject are going to struggle at interview, because the interviewers can sometimes lean heavily on other parts of the student's application when asking questions. It can help to go through the rest of their application with them and make sure they know well all of the books, documentaries, and work experiences that they wrote down, just in case.

Some good interview strategies for subject interviews include:

- **'Don't hold back'** – One of the most common reasons that students seek additional support with interviews is a lack of confidence. The purpose of subject interviews is for the interviewers to gauge the student's interest and understanding, as well as their academic curiosity. At Oxbridge, subject interviews are designed to mimic supervisions – the main small group or 1:1 form of teaching – so students who don't manage well in the interviews may not seem like good candidates for the Oxbridge system. Tutors should offer students the opportunity for mock interviews to tackle this, setting similarly challenging tasks to help students manage their nerves and practise spontaneously asking questions and offering explanations, analysis, or solutions.

- **'Draw on your own knowledge'** – Students are not expected to have degree-level knowledge when they come to interview, but they should demonstrate at least an interest in the course and some additional learning outside of the A-level curriculum. This can be useful when students are facing more open-ended interview questions, in that it helps to expose students to more potential questions, and they should be encouraged to draw on their own knowledge to answer questions, even if they aren't right the first time.

- **'Think outside of the box'** – This may seem like standard interview advice, but it is also a skill that can be practised in lessons. Setting students tasks that will help them to practise exploring a topic they've not seen before; using unseen texts, sources, or questions; asking them to argue against an extract or position they've just learned about: lesson planning for applicants should offer them the opportunity to test out theories or explore lines of argument in a safe environment with support. There are lots of sample interview questions available online and in books and pamphlets, with lots of examples available in the Resources at the end of this book.

Common issues

The most common issues I've come across when mentoring interview applicants are:

1. **Lack of confidence**

    By far the most common issues I have seen among interview candidates are a lack of confidence and resilience. Oxbridge interviews are designed to mimic the supervision systems, which requires students to be brave enough to say what they think and flexible enough to receive feedback. That means that students need to be able to speak up, offer an opinion, and be confident to say 'I don't know' or 'I think it's this' – otherwise they won't stand out at interview and won't be able to show the interviewers how much they really know. Tutors need to give students opportunities for academic discussion,

2. **Not saying enough**

    There are any number of ways an interview could go: some will ask probing questions, and others will wait for the student offer something for them to work with. A professor pushing the student into an academic debate is probably their worst nightmare, but students are often even less prepared for the more relaxed interviewer, who waits for the student to give their view in the conversation. In these instances, students need to persist in offering their ideas. Tutors can help students to practise extending and building on their answers, using scripts and sentence starters to offer alternative viewpoints or consider the opportunities or constraints of a situation or argument. In a worst-case scenario, students need to be comfortable saying 'I don't know but I'd like to' to help them seem academically curious rather than unsure.

3. **Feeling too much pressure**

Whether its from themselves, their teachers, or their parents, students facing interviews can feel a huge amount of pressure to achieve in what is already a high-pressure environment. As their tutor, it can help to offer them a space to discuss any major concerns they have about their interviews and make sure that you are not adding to that pressure. Students can definitely over-prepare, so once you are happy that you and the student have done everything necessary, you can remind them to take breaks, sleep, and be forgiving of themselves if they don't get the result they are hoping for.

If they want to, you can also have a realistic conversation with them about what to do if they don't get in. There are lots of options – taking a year and reapplying, applying somewhere else, trying clearing – and for people who have their heart set on Oxbridge, it can be reassuring to realise that not getting in is not the end of the world.

TOP TIP

If you have enough time before the interview date, try to schedule a couple of short mock interviews for the student to prepare for. That way, the nerves and preparation will feel more familiar to them, and it will be less disconcerting for them on the day. You can then workshop any answers they give that you think they can improve in other lessons.

QUESTION

What questions will you include in your mock interviews?

Chapter 19

English as a Foreign Language

So, you've assessed your student's progress and you know what they need to work on – so how do you plan your first lesson?

First, you'll need to look online and in textbooks for resources and worksheets related to the student's subject and topics. Second, you'll need to learn some lesson techniques. These are the activities you'll use with students to help develop their skills and understanding.

You'll find a detailed list of basic lesson techniques in the 'Online tutoring basics' chapter (pages 7–26), which are all applicable to any age and subject. In the following, you'll find them listed in the relevant section alongside more specific exercises and techniques that I feel work best for EFL tutoring.

I've divided the techniques into the key parts of a lesson, as outlined in Chapter 7, so you can find lists of exercises to use with your students. Once you've learned some techniques, you can use the different categories to create quick and easy lesson plans. There's a sample lesson at the end of each subject section to show you how to do that.

A note on the types of EFL tutoring

By far the most common type of EFL tutoring is academic tutoring, with students aiming for an exam or English proficiency test. That said, there are some students, usually adult learners, who may seek EFL tutoring on a more casual basis, as explained in Chapter 5.

However, the vast majority of techniques that you use for academic tutoring can also be used for non-academic tutoring – you can just ignore the instructions about exam boards or mark schemes. You will find that all of the following techniques will work for either type of tutoring, with the caveat of ignoring the references to exams when needed.

DOI: 10.4324/9781003211648-23

LESSON TECHNIQUES

Starters

Basic lesson techniques

- Matching exercises (p. 84)

- Sorting exercises (p. 85)

- Word-searches (p. 85)

- Crosswords (p. 85)

- Mind maps (p. 86)

- Quickfire questions (p. 87)

- Homework review (p. 87)

Plus

'Speedy reads'

'Speedy reads' is my name for small extracts with reading comprehension tasks and short answer questions. 'Speedy reads' work well for students who are worried about reading comprehension, because you can do one every lesson, and as a starter, they help students to get into the right frame of mind to begin to learn. In addition, by using unseen texts, it helps expose students who are not keen readers to a wide variety of types and styles of texts.

To create a 'Speedy read', I take a short extract – no longer than a dozen lines – from an unseen text. Next, I write several identification questions – 'What is the main character's job?' and so on – and then, if the student is confident, a few inference questions – 'How does the main character feel about losing their job?'

You can also use these exercises as a springboard for discussing topic vocabulary or as a prompt for creative writing.

'Fill the gap'/'Finish the sentence'

'Fill the gap', or 'Finish the sentence' if the gap is always at the end, can be an interesting way to prompt students to recall key information. 'Fill the gap' can be used in lots of ways:

Some of the best ways to use a 'Fill the gap' or 'Finish the sentence' are:

- Removing the conjugated verbs from a piece of writing and only offering the root verb so students have to infer which person and tense to use

- Removing all of the technical terminology from an analytical paragraph so students have to remember the key terms

- Offering partial definitions for key words

- Removing the dialogue from a piece of fiction writing so students can write their own as a creative exercise

It is up to you, depending on the level of the student, whether to offer the answers alongside the puzzle – I generally don't unless a student is really struggling, as it is more effective for them to recall the answers themselves.

Punctuation exercises

To make these exercises, I take a short passage from an unseen text, or one I have written myself, and remove all of the punctuation, including full stops, capital letters, commas, apostrophes, and so on. If the student is struggling I will put all of the removed punctuation in a list at the end of the extract for them to use, but if not I will simply present the extract minus the punctuation and see how many mistakes they can spot. This can be a useful way to test how familiar a student is with the rules of punctuation, highlighting any that they don't spot or add incorrectly. Because of the sheer number of ambiguities that can exist in the English language, this is less a perfect text of proofreading accuracy and more a chance to see how your student thinks about punctuation and which elements they are most confident with.

having reached the living room darcy was suddenly struck by the silence in the house it was quiet too quiet she could just about hear the wind coming through a far away window but that was all i dont like it she muttered to herself and now ive come too far to turn back she continued through the house and up the creaky stairs

Add any punctuation you think is missing: capital letters, full stops, commas, hyphens, speech marks, dashes, semi-colons, apostrophes

Explanations/demonstrations

Basic lesson techniques

- Slideshows (p. 87)

- YouTube videos (p. 89)

- Model answers (p. 89)

- Live modelling (p. 91)

- Worksheets (p. 93)

Plus

Reading together

If you are working with a student who is being home-schooled, taking time out of school for an illness or other absence, or struggling to commit to reading an entire set text, reading together can be a great way to demonstrate active reading strategies and make the most of time spent reading for practising other skills.

Reading together can take several forms: you can work through short sections of a text lesson by lesson, read a long section of a text for a portion of a lesson, set reading and recall questions as homework, and decide whether you want students to read out loud or in their heads depending on their ability and confidence.

Reading together can take up a lot of lesson time, so it shouldn't be used too heavily, but for students who aren't familiar with their texts, it can be a really useful technique. Tutors should always be judicious in their selection of extracts to read together to make the most of this technique.

SWAT/key word analysis demonstration

Single Word Analysis Techniques (SWAT), sometimes called Keyword Analysis, is crucial to achieving high grades in EFL exams, but it can be difficult for some students to grasp and is not necessarily an intuitive technique. It requires students to understand not only the literal meaning but some of the cultural context of the language and its effect on the reader, which can be difficult to articulate in their second language. Most EFL exams with reading comprehension components usually have, at a minimum, at least one extended analytical answer, so students need to develop an academic vocabulary – language and structural features, grammatical elements, and so on – in the same way as their native-speaking counterparts.

The best way to do this is to model SWAT, using a range of extracts and examples to continually expose them to new texts and vocabulary. There are a number of ways I like to demonstrate SWAT, my favourite being the mind map demonstration: reading a short extract together; selecting a short quotation or phrase; and creating a map of connotations, links, and ideas to walk students through the process of isolating key words from within it.

This demonstration segues well into an activity where students can try the technique themselves using the same extract you've been working on together, with the opportunity to explore their ideas and ask questions.

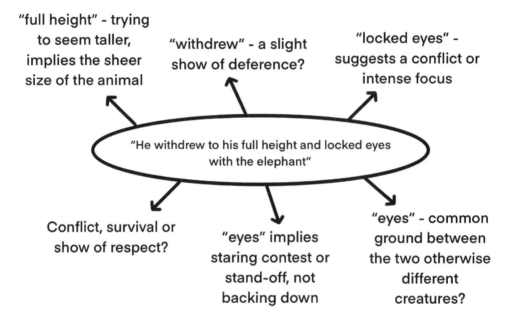

"full height" - trying to seem taller, implies the sheer size of the animal

"withdrew" - a slight show of deference?

"locked eyes" - suggests a conflict or intense focus

"He withdrew to his full height and locked eyes with the elephant"

Conflict, survival or show of respect?

"eyes" implies staring contest or stand-off, not backing down

"eyes" - common ground between the two otherwise different creatures?

Unseen material

Unseen material is one of the exam elements students can find very intimidating, so it should be used regularly. Some students may just want opportunities to write answers for these sections and have them marked, but others may want guidance on how to approach them.

Unseen prose extracts or poems can be introduced during another lesson activity, to explore a language analysis technique or plan an answer, but they can also be used on their own.

There are several activities that you can use to increase students' confidence when working with unseen material:

- **Read through the unseen material together, out loud for poems, and discuss structural ideas (rhyme/metre/paragraphing/pace, etc.)** – EFL students are often less confident at identifying these

- **Ask the student to identify and annotate language/structural features, either as pre-reading or in lesson, before discussing their ideas** – can be used to make answer plans

- Walk through model answers and discuss WWW/EBI before the student has a go themselves

- **Give the student 10 minutes to choose five features/quotes and present their argument against a given question** – discuss any issues or obvious missed ideas

Main activities

Basic lesson techniques

- Past papers (p. 93)

- Worksheets (p. 95)

- Annotation (p. 94)

- Question-guessing (p. 95)

Plus

Student presentation

This technique gives students the opportunity to collate the key information in their own words, then present it to you. This allows you to see their use of all four key skills – reading, writing, speaking/listening – as well as their confidence in presenting and using the relevant technology.

Once you have explained the topic of the lesson, you can ask students to read a passage/set of notes on the topic, discuss the key points together, and ask them if they need to recap any of the ideas. Once they are happy on the topic, you can then ask them to create a 2–5-minute presentation on the topic in the notes, to present to you at the end of the lesson.

Students can use the online whiteboard to draw, select images, and annotate, as well as writing a script for their presentation if they want to. Alternatively, you can allow the student to share their screen to create a slideshow using software like MS PowerPoint or Apple Keynote.

While they are working, you can write or find two to five questions on the topic to quiz them on at the end of their presentation. These can be more open ended with general English learners or exam-style for students with speaking and listening assessments. You can also try more formal questions for Business English students to help them practise for job interviews.

Once complete, students can download their presentations/scripts for revision or further study.

Reading

Reading together

If you are working with a student who is being homeschooled, taking time out of school for an illness or other absence, or struggling to commit to reading an entire set text, reading together can be a great way to demonstrate active reading strategies and make the most of time spent reading for practising other skills.

Reading together can take several forms: you can work through short sections of a text lesson by lesson, read a long section of a text for a portion of a lesson, set reading and recall questions as homework, and decide whether you want students to read out loud or in their heads depending on their ability and confidence.

Reading together can take up a lot of lesson time, so it shouldn't be used too heavily, but for students who aren't familiar with their texts, it can be a really useful technique. Tutors should always be judicious in their selection of extracts to read together to make the most of this technique.

Vocabulary fishing

This technique is an easy way to get a sense of the breadth of a student's vocabulary and organically identify areas to focus on.

A wide vocabulary is an EFL student's best friend, but it can be exhausting reading long lists of words and trying to commit them to memory. Instead, you can take extracts from both modern and older texts, especially classics, and read them together, discussing any unfamiliar vocabulary, idioms, and grammatical structures. Using this technique encourages students to read more actively, paying attention to details rather than just getting the gist, and it can help them to feel more confident with cadence and pronunciation if you ask them to read aloud.

Once you have highlighted all of the unfamiliar elements, you can then create targeted vocabulary lists to use for revision or spelling tests and isolate any grammatical structures for further study. Alternatively, you can use the vocabulary from the passage to create a mind map on that topic for them to go away and complete in their own time by researching related vocabulary.

Surface reading skills

Surface reading skills is an umbrella name for a number of reading skills, such as scanning, skimming, and predicting. To native speakers, these skills will be intuitive, but EFL students will need guidance on how to use them most effectively.

Skimming is used to get to grips with a large piece of text that you need a general understanding of. It is best practised with worksheets or structured texts like newspaper articles to start with, because you can give students specific instructions: for example, read the headline first, then the sub-heading, then the first paragraph, then the first and last sentences of paragraphs and key words in the main text. You can then use more difficult texts, like Victorian prose, with its long, comma-filled sentences, to show them how to identify key verbs and nouns as well as idioms.

Scanning, or scan-reading, by contrast, is used to extract answers from text, like those needed for answering reading comprehension questions, when the student already knows what to look for. Students can use the skimming skill to get a holistic sense of the text and then read it again to scan for the details, numbers, names, ideas, or key words from the question.

Finally, predicting is a skill required by some reading comprehension tasks, where the student must use their understanding of the text to infer or suggest what might happen next.

Proofreading

Proofreading is a required skill for some EFL exams and is a useful skill for General and Business English students.

It essentially involves reading a passage and either pointing out any mistakes or correcting them. These can be any kind of SPAG mistakes, as well as unnatural syntax or homophones.

You will need to cover as much SPAG content as you can before you start working on proofreading, and you can use the live modelling technique to demonstrate how you would approach the task. Once they're happy with what they need to do, you can set students independent tasks.

There are lots of practice materials created specifically for proofreading exams, so you can find extracts and passages with deliberate mistakes and guides on how to find them. You can also make your own, in the style of the punctuation exercise starters, or you can take a passage of existing text and add mistakes: swapping punctuation, removing capital letters, mixing up word order, and so on.

Writing

Writing formats

Once students are confident with the basics of grammar and syntax, you can introduce them to the different ways that written communication can be formatted.

For those studying for exams, they will likely already be familiar with short, long, and extended analytical answers and possibly essay formats. The persuasive tasks in the creative writing portion of exams are usually structured as a newspaper article, speech, or letter, so they may also be familiar with those. However, it is still useful to introduce them to other common modes of writing.

For general English learners, I recommend starting with an overview of the different types of texts – fiction, non-fiction, literary non-fiction, essays, and so on – before discussing with the student which they would like to focus on. As a guide, I would say the essentials are newspaper articles, emails and letters, essays, and instruction manuals/recipes.

For students learning Business English, you will need also to practise formats like letter headers, formal emails, transcripts, speeches, and social media posts, in case they need them at work.

Students should learn how to identify these formats, understand their purpose, and write their own versions accurately. You can find guides to all of these formats specifically tailored to EFL learners online.

Paragraphing practice

Unsurprisingly, this exercise simply involves the student practising writing paragraphs, in a variety of different settings. This can be as part of an exam-style answer, in response to a question you have designed, or as part of a worksheet or online resource.

It is always best to start with a discussion of how your student is used to writing paragraphs and what methods they have been taught. As I discuss during the assessment section, some students are taught to use an acronym like PEA or PEEL, while others use a more fluid format like 'What, How, Why?' Whatever the student has been taught, you should try to work with, as you are likely to confuse them if you try to use a different acronym. However, if the student is really struggling with the method they are taught in school and asks you for a different one, you can demonstrate a few to give them the chance to find one that works better for them.

'Layers of meaning'

As outlined previously in the Explanations/Demonstrations section, 'layers of meaning' is an analytical exercise which helps students to understand the different levels or layers of meaning that a quotation might contain.

This exercise is especially useful for EFL students, because it gives them space to understand the literal meaning, unpick any connotations or cultural associations, and construct extended answers for exam questions.

It is up to you whether to label or guide the layers of their analysis: with students who are struggling to unpick quotes, prompting them to think about identifying rhetorical devices, structural analysis, contextual information about the author or period, language and sounds, or other elements of analysis can help them to see how many ways there are to approach a quotation. With more confident students, I might leave them to see how many different layers they can think of on their own and then offer prompts once they run out of ideas.

You can offer students a worksheet or template with lines to write their ideas on, or you can simply draw lines onto the online whiteboard.

Photograph inspiration

One of the most common, and useful, exercises for EFL students who are struggling with creative writing is to use photo prompts – just like the ones they will see in some exam booklets. This can be photos of non-specific places (a random tall building, for example, rather than the Empire State Building), which can be used as the prompt for the setting of a story, or photos of individuals or small groups. The people in the pictures can be used as the inspiration for a story: who are they? What do/did they do? Where do they live? This exercise encourages students to flesh out their characters and settings while giving them a visual prompt to work from.

Photograph inspiration works especially well with old photos: I usually choose old black-and-white or sepia photographs to encourage them to use their historical knowledge and imagination.

You can also create vocabulary lists or themed grammar exercises around the subjects of photos.

Debate speech

Debate speech gives students the opportunity to practise their persuasive writing construction of arguments in a format that practises the key skills from the exam.

When working with confident students, you can offer them the option to write a speech about any topic they desire, but with most students, it can be useful to offer them something to argue against. This can be either something you have written or an example of a debate speech you have found online.

If you want to, you can offer students a template or script to help them write their speech, with sentence starters and other guidance, but with confident creative writers, you can leave them to write in whatever format they desire.

With these kinds of open-ended tasks, it can be useful to end the lesson by marking what they have written against the expectations of the exam mark scheme, so they can start to see how their own creative writing lines up with the grade boundaries they will be expected to meet.

Speaking/listening

Casual and formal conversations

One of the many advantages of online tutoring is that the student will be practising their speaking and listening just by being in the lesson, but it can also be worth devoting time to specifically practising conversation.

In particular, the nuances of English conversation often take time and practice to become familiar with. One sticking point for many students is formality: in some languages, like Japanese, the different levels of politeness and formality are baked into the grammar, but in English, it is usually more vaguely indicated by certain idioms or choices of language.

You can practise identifying and utilising these distinctions in a number of ways: using worksheets or slideshows, roleplaying and discussing vocabulary, or watching videos and discussing important phrases or language. You can also write partial scripts, with sentence starters or suggestions, to use them to mimic the different styles of conversation until the student is confident enough to ad-lib.

For adults or Business English students, it can be especially important to emphasise the different levels of formality required for customer service roles, inter-office communication with managers or co-workers, and interviews.

Some EFL exams have speaking assessments, though many have paused them during COVID, so if students have a time limit or set of topics that they must keep to, then you can use those parameters during your practice as well.

Phone conversations

In the days before the internet, EFL tutoring could be done entirely over the phone, with the tutor prompting topics for discussion. Nowadays, phone tutoring has been mostly replaced by the more holistic experience of video calling and online classrooms.

However, speaking on the phone is something that even native English speakers can find difficult, so if the student wants more practice at this you can try calling them or turning off both of your video feeds.

This technique will be especially useful for Business English learners, who may want to work in call centres or offices where confidence on the phone is a valuable asset. You may want to hold mock conversations, where you roleplay as a customer or co-worker, or to simply practise phone conversation conventions: typical greetings and good-byes, asking questions, and so on.

Common idioms

Idioms can trip even experienced listeners up, because they can use unusual combinations of sounds or words that are entirely unrelated to the intended meaning. However, they can be the key to sounding like a confident, fluent speaker and can be learned with a combination of vocabulary revision and regular use.

You can find long lists of common idioms online to use in specific activities, as well as phrases that may be useful to the student in lessons more generally: 'can I nip to the loo', 'can I grab a glass of water', 'I didn't get a chance to finish the homework', and so on.

Practising idioms can be incorporated into many of the previous techniques, but you can also ask students to practise them using flash cards and other revision techniques or to learn new ones from watching TV and films.

Plenaries

Basic lesson techniques

- Mind maps (p. 96)

- Lists (p. 96)

- WWW/EBI (p. 97)

- RAG (p. 97)

- Summary questions (p. 97)

- Quiz questions (p. 98)

- Quick exam question (p. 98)

Plus

Memory game

This plenary can be especially useful with students who have trouble committing key vocabulary to memory. To create this game, you'll need to write a dozen or more key words – word classes, language or structure devices, characters, plot points, and so on – on a slide, give the student 30 seconds to memorise it, and then ask them to write out as many words as they can remember.

For bonus points, you can ask the student to give you a definition of the word or an example of the device.

Dictionary definitions

For this plenary, the student will need to list any new vocabulary that they learned in the lesson, spell them correctly, and provide an accurate definition. This can be normal vocabulary but works especially well with technical terminology, like the names of language or structure devices.

If creative writing is a focus for the student, you can also ask them to provide an example of the word or device used in a sentence. Alternatively, you can create an example sentence and ask them to quickly analyse the effect of that word/device.

Headlines

Breaking down key information into bite-sized chunks can make recalling it in the future easier. This plenary asks students to create 'headlines', like the short phrases that top newspaper articles, to capture the most significant information they learned that lesson. You can ask for two to five, depending on how much content you covered in the lesson.

If needed, you can then return to the 'headlines' they wrote in a future lesson and ask them to create a mind map of that topic as a starter.

Homework

Basic lesson techniques

- Past papers (p. 98)

- Worksheets (p. 99)

Plus

Paragraph practice

Paragraph practice does what it says on the tin: it's an opportunity for students to practise their paragraph writing outside of the lesson time. I often find that with students I only see once a week, we just don't have enough time to write the paragraphs they need to practise, so setting just one or two to write at home can be a real help for them.

Conversation practice

You can ask students to try their conversational English with friends, family, and co-workers and give them topics to practise. If they don't have access to any English speakers, you can suggest sites like Discord (13+) or Tandem (14+), which offer opportunities to connect English learners with English native speakers, but ensure that you have parental permission to do so if the student is under 18.

Alternatively, students can try writing their own conversation prompts to use with you in a future lesson.

Planning an EFL lesson

I've written out a sample EFL lesson for the three most common types of lesson.

Table 19.1 A sample EFL qualifications lesson

Date	Starter	Explanation/ demonstration	Main activity	Plenary	Homework
07/11	Matching exercise: types of pronouns	Slideshow: 1. Discuss long answer analytical question from the exam paper – requirements, marks, key words of the question, and so on 2. Look at several examples to see common topics	Past paper: 1. Read and discuss an extract and question from a past paper 2. Link key words of the question to the extract and mind map initial ideas 3. Choose relevant quotations to use in answer 4. Plan answer	List: write down two to five things to remember when completing this style of question	Paragraph practice: write the full answer based on plan, 15–20 minutes

Table 19.2 A sample General English lesson

Date	Starter	Explanation/demonstration	Main activity	Plenary	Homework
07/11	Spelling test: five to ten words from the previous week	Slideshow: 1. Brief recap of simple past tenses 2. Introduce new topic – past perfect tense 3. Discuss how the tense is formed and any common irregular forms 4. Walk through some example sentences 5. Discuss any initial questions	Worksheet: 1. Use a set of basic 'Fill the gap' exercises to check understanding 2. Move to more difficult examples and extended sentences 3. Ask the student to complete the final set of questions independently	RAG: discuss how confident they feel about this new tense compared to previous past tenses learned	Worksheet: complete the worksheet from the lesson, 20 minutes

Table 19.3 A sample Business English lesson

Date	Starter	Explanation/ demonstration	Main activity	Plenary	Homework
07/11	Sorting exercise: casual and formal idioms	YouTube video: 1. Watch a short video of someone giving a business presentation and answering questions 2. Discuss the words and body language used 3. Agree on the topic of their presentation	Student presentation: 1. The student needs to write a 2–5-minute presentation on an agreed topic, creating a script and using some visual prompts 2. Once finished, they will need to answer some questions about their presentation	WWW/EBI: ask the student to self-evaluate, with at least 3 points for each	Vocabulary practice: set new vocabulary to learn for next lesson based on today's topic, five to ten words

Common issues

The most common issues I've come across when tutoring English as a Foreign Language are:

1. **Lack of vocabulary**

    For any student learning a new language, the best thing they can do, besides getting a general grounding in grammar, is to expand their vocabulary.

    This can be especially true of students studying for EFL qualifications, who may have learned the suggested vocabulary in the specification but not a lot more. If the exam paper or source uses a colloquial version of a word or a common but unfamiliar idiom, they may be at a disadvantage.

    Students learning English for a specific purpose, like Business English, will need specialist vocabulary, but they may also want a general grounding in conversational language for water-cooler talk.

    While simply memorising new words can be boring, there are many interesting ways to introduce more vocabulary into lessons: specific vocabulary-based exercises or worksheets, writing down new words learned every lesson to recap in starters/plenaries, spelling tests, spontaneous writing and speaking, and so on.

Whatever you do, you should encourage students to spend a little time every day – between 10 and 20 minutes – practising the vocabulary they have learned that week. Short, regular practice, on top of your lessons, will rapidly increase the pace of their vocabulary learning.

You should also encourage students to read widely in English to help expose them to new words, which they can then bring to lessons to practise.

2. Struggling with grammar

Besides vocabulary, grammar is a core part of language learning but can also be rather dull. Even students who are enthused about English will struggle with irregular tenses and inconsistent conjugations.

Whatever your student is finding difficult, you should be empathetic and offer a range of strategies. I like to use a timeline or diagram indicating the relative times and persons of different tenses to help students to visualise them, as well as creating memorable acronyms or rules to follow with tricky tenses. You can also help point them to the most common irregular tenses to memorise to cut down on the work they need to do.

You may find that you need to spend additional time on certain tenses and find creative ways to incorporate verb practice into lessons.

3. Struggling with creative writing

On the whole, I find that EFL students fall into two groups: ones who are already writing creatively in their own time and simply need their writing adapted to fit the exam, and ones who dislike writing creatively and prefer the analytical questions. The second group can be more of a challenge for tutors, as they may struggle to come up with their own ideas or refuse to write extended creative answers. I find that using prompted exercises, like those listed previously, can help them to focus on the key techniques of creative writing without having to invent too much themselves in the first instance. I also like to introduce the ideas from analytical writing – effect on the reader, language devices, and so on – into their planning stage, so they can use ideas that they are familiar with from their analytical writing in the creative writing questions.

TOP TIP

Don't be afraid to ask the student how they feel they are getting on and what they might like to look at in future lessons. Students can ask to update their aims and goals alongside your recommendations, which will make your lesson planning easier.

QUESTION

Do you have experience learning another language? What goals or progress markers did you find useful?

Chapter 20

Lesson plans

Details for all the basic lesson techniques can be found in Chapter 7.

DOI: 10.4324/9781003211648-24

KS2

Table 20.1 English

Week	1	2	3	4	5
Starter	Spelling test	Punctuation exercise	Spelling test	Word search	Spelling test
E/D	Slideshow or Worksheet (different types of punctuation)	Discussion (1st and 2nd chapters) + Reading together (3rd chapter together)	Slideshow or Worksheet (basic tenses)	Discussion (4th and 5th chapters) + Reading together (6th chapter together)	Mind map (recap of topics that will be in the mini-assessment)
Main Activity	Worksheet	Reading comprehension (using 3rd chapter)	Worksheet	Reading comprehension (using 6th chapter)	Mini-assessment
Plenary	Headlines (rules for using commas, semicolons, and colons)	RAG	'Give me five'	RAG	WWW/EBI
Homework	Worksheet	Reading (finish 4th and 5th chapters)	Worksheet	Reading (finish 6th and 7th chapters)	N/A

Week	6	7	8	9	10
Starter	Spelling test	Connect 4	Spelling test	Punctuation exercise	Spelling test
E/D	Worksheet (complex tenses)	Worksheet (complex tenses)	Reading together + Layers of meaning	Slideshow (types of non-fiction text)	Mind map (recap of topics that will be in the mini-assessment)
Main Activity	Worksheet	Worksheet	Layers of meaning	Prompted paragraphs	Mini-assessment
Plenary	WWW/EBI	WWW/EBI	Give me five	WWW/EBI	RAG
Home work	Worksheet	Worksheet	Layers of meaning	Paragraph practice	N/A

Table 20.2 Maths

Week	1	2	3	4	5
Starter	Discussion	Times tables test	Countdown	Times tables test	Matching exercise
E/D	Slideshow (compilation of questions)	Slideshow (topic marked 'Red')	Live modelling (topic marked 'Red')	Slideshow (topic marked 'Red')	Mind map (recap of topics that will be in the mini-assessment)
Main Activity	Live modelling (any simple topics from the compilation)	Worksheet	Slideshow (compilation of questions)	Murder mystery	Mini-assessment
Plenary	WWW/EBI	Instruction manual	Spot the mistake	Instruction manual	List (all topics they are happy with and any topics they want to cover again)
Home work	Worksheet	Worksheet	Worksheet	Worksheet	N/A

Week	6	7	8	9	10
Starter	Sorting exercise	Times tables test	Countdown	Times tables test	Quick activity starter
E/D	Slideshow (topic marked 'Red')	Slideshow (topic marked 'Red')	Slideshow (topic marked 'Red')	Live modelling (topic marked 'Red')	Mind map (recap of topics that will be in the mini-assessment)
Main Activity	Worksheet	Board game	Worksheet	Slideshow (compilation of questions)	Mini-assessment
Plenary	Instruction manual	WWW/EBI	Instruction manual	Spot the mistake	List (all topics they are happy with and any topics they want to cover again)
Home work	Worksheet	Worksheet	Worksheet	Worksheet	N/A

11+

Table 20.3 VR and NVR

Week	1	2	3	4	5
Starter	Spelling test	Spelling test	Spelling test	Spelling test	Spelling test
E/D	Slideshow (1–2 question styles)	Slideshow (1–2 question styles)	Slideshow (1–2 question styles)	Slideshow (1–2 question styles)	**Mind map** (recap of topics that will be in the mini-assessment)
Main Activity	Worksheet	Worksheet	Worksheet	Worksheet	Mini-assessment
Plenary	Instruction manual	RAG	RAG	RAG	RAG
Homework	Worksheet	Worksheet	Worksheet	Worksheet	N/A

Week	6	7	8	9	10
Starter	Spelling test	Spelling test	Spelling test	Spelling test	Spelling tests
E/D	Slideshow (1–2 question styles)	**Live modelling** (any areas of difficulty so far + revision strategies)	Slideshow (1–2 question styles)	Slideshow (1–2 question styles)	**Mind map** (recap of topics that will be in the mini-assessment)
Main Activity	Worksheet	Murder mystery	Worksheet	Worksheet	Mini-assessment
Plenary	RAG	WWW/EBI	Instruction manual	RAG	RAG
Homework	Worksheet	Worksheet	Worksheet	Worksheet	N/A

KS3

Table 20.4 English

Week	1	2	3	4	5
Starter	Discussion	Sorting exercise	Crossword	Empty boxes (non-fiction examples)	Punctuation exercise
E/D	Slideshow (types of non-fiction text)	Reading together (newspaper article close reading) + SWAT	Reading together (literary non-fiction close reading) + SWAT	Reading together (biography/travel writing close reading) + SWAT	Mind map (recap of topics that will be in the mini-assessment)
Main Activity	Worksheet (identifying features of different types of non-fiction texts)	Table of quotes	Table of quotes	Table of quotes	Mini-assessment
Plenary	Headlines (conventions of types of non-fiction texts)	WWW/EBI	WWW/EBI	RAG (non-fiction text types so far)	WWW/EBI
Home work	Paragraph practice (past paper question to write newspaper article/speech, etc.)	Paragraph practice (using table from lesson)	Paragraph practice (using table from lesson)	Paragraph practice (using table from lesson)	N/A

(Continued)

Table 20.4 (Conitnued)

Week	6	7	8	9	10
Starter	Matching exercise	Speedy reads	Word search	Sorting exercise	Punctuation exercise
E/D	**Slideshow** (fiction text types, spotting language and structural features, etc.) + **Empty box** activity if needed	**Reading comprehension** (fiction extract close reading) + **SWAT**	**Slideshow** (sociohistorical context for texts, how to use it in analysis of fiction texts, and example text; can be set text from school if needed)	**Reading comprehension** (fiction extract close reading; can be set text from school if needed) + **SWAT**	**Mind map** (recap of topics that will be in the mini-assessment)
Main Activity	**Worksheet**	**Paragraph practice**	**Table of quotes**	**Past paper** (compilation or isolated questions, with guidance)	**Mini-assessment**
Plenary	**RAG** (fiction text types so far)	**WWW/EBI**	**Headlines** (what to remember when including context)	**WWW/EBI**	**WWW/EBI**
Home work	**Worksheet**	**Paragraph practice**	**Paragraph practice**	**Past paper** (complete work from lesson)	N/A

Table 20.5 Maths

Week	1	2	3	4	5
Starter	Discussion	Times tables test	Countdown	Times tables test	Matching exercise
E/D	Slideshow (compilation of questions from all topics)	Slideshow (topic marked 'Red')	Live modelling (topic marked 'Red')	Slideshow (topic marked 'Red')	Mind map (recap of topics that will be in the mini-assessment)
Main Activity	Worksheet	Worksheet	Slideshow (compilation of questions)	Murder mystery	Mini-assessment
Plenary	WWW/EBI	Instruction manual	Spot the mistake	Instruction manual	List (all topics they are happy with and any topics they want to cover again)
Home work	Worksheet	Worksheet	Worksheet	Worksheet	N/A

Week	6	7	8	9	10
Starter	Sorting exercise	Times tables test	Countdown	Times tables test	Quick activity starter
E/D	Slideshow (topic marked 'Red')	Slideshow (topic marked 'Red')	Slideshow (topic marked 'Red')	Live modelling (topic marked 'Red')	Mind map (recap of topics that will be in the mini-assessment)
Main Activity	Worksheet	Board game	Worksheet	Slideshow (compilation of questions)	Mini-assessment
Plenary	Instruction manual	WWW/EBI	Instruction manual	Spot the mistake	List (all topics they are happy with and any topics they want to cover again)
Home work	Worksheet	Worksheet	Worksheet	Worksheet	N/A

Table 20.6 GCSE English Literature

Week	1	2	3	4	5
Starter	Discussion	Poetry starter	Punctuation starter	Poetry starter	Quickfire questions
E/D	Live modelling (short answer question – i.e. selecting key quotations)	Homework review + Model answers if needed	Live modelling (long answer question – i.e. how to plan part a) on an extract and part b) on whole text)	Slideshow (key quotations from set text) + Table of quotes if needed	Mini-assessment
Main Activity	Table of quotes	Paragraphing practice	Past paper	Layers of meaning or Mind map (for each key quote)	Past paper
Plenary	Paragraph practice (plan a paragraph based on discussion of two language features and effect)	Mind map (top tips for paragraph structure)	Paragraph practice (plan a paragraph from their favourite answer plan for part a))	RAG	WWW/EBI
Homework	Paragraph practice	Paragraph practice	Paragraph practice	Layers of meaning or Mind map (for an additional key quote)	Past paper (finish question from lesson if needed or try another)

Week	6	7	8	9	10
Starter	Poetry starter	'Speedy reads'	Poetry starter	'Fill the gap' (definitions of key terminology)	Poetry starter
E/D	Live modelling (short answer question – i.e. selecting key quotations)	Slideshow (key quotations from set text) or Table of quotes if needed	Slideshow (context for a set text)	Slideshow (key quotations from set text) + Table of quotes if needed	Mini-assessment
Main Activity	Table of quotes	Layers of meaning or Mind map (for each key quote)	Table of quotes (adding context notes to key quotes previously selected)	Layers of meaning or Mind map (for each key quote)	Past paper
Plenary	Paragraph practice (plan a paragraph based on discussion of two language features and effect)	RAG	Paragraph practice (plan a paragraph using new contextual knowledge)	RAG	WWW/EBI
Home work	Paragraph practice	Paragraph practice (building one Layers or Mind map into a paragraph)	Paragraph practice	Paragraph practice (building one Layers or Mind map into a paragraph)	Past paper (finish question from lesson if needed or try another)

Table 20.7 GCSE English Language

Week	1	2	3	4	5
Starter	**Mind map** (types of non-fiction they already know)	**Matching exercise** (word class)	**Finish the sentence** (non-fiction text conventions recap)	**Sorting exercise** (fiction/non-fiction text types)	**Discussion**
E/D	**Slideshow** (types of non-fiction text)	**Reading together** (newspaper article close reading) **+ SWAT**	**Reading together** (literary non-fiction extract) **+ SWAT**	**Live modelling** (short and longer answer questions)	**Mind map** (recap of topics that will be in the mini-assessment)
Main Activity	**Worksheet** (identifying features of different types of non-fiction texts)	**Table of quotes** (select features and comment on their effect)	**Table of quotes** (select features and comment on their effect)	**Past paper** (plan an answer and discuss quotes in detail, with **Mind map** if needed)	**Mini-assessment**
Plenary	**Headlines** (conventions of types of non-fiction texts)	**Memory game** (types of non-fiction texts)	**WWW/EBI**	**List** (personal rules for answering these questions)	**List** (all topics they are happy with and any topics they want to cover again)
Homework	**Paragraph practice** (past paper question to write newspaper article/ speech, etc.)	**Paragraph practice** (paragraph on one of features and effect from table)	**Paragraph practice** (paragraph on one of features and effect from table)	**Paragraph practice** (write out answer from plan)	N/A

Week	6	7	8	9	10
Starter	Matching exercise (structural features)	Speedy read (focus on structural features)	Quiz questions	Matching exercise (language features)	Discussion
E/D	Slideshow (extracts, demonstrating structural features) + Mind map if more detail is needed	Reading together (fiction extract close reading) + SWAT	Live modelling (extended answer creative writing questions)	Live modelling (extended answer questions)	Mind map (recap of topics that will be in the mini-assessment)
Main Activity	Worksheet (exploring and identifying structural features)	Table of quotes (select language and then structural features and comment on their effect)	Photograph inspiration or similar exam-board-relevant exercise	Past paper + Mind map if needed)	Mini-assessment
Plenary	Headlines (common structural features and their possible effects)	Quiz questions (structural features)	WWW/EBI	List (personal rules for answering these questions)	List (all topics they are happy with and any topics they want to cover again)
Homework	Paragraph practice (past paper question to comment on structural features in an extract)	Paragraph practice (paragraph on one of language and structural features and effect from table)	Paragraph practice	Paragraph practice (write out answer from plan)	N/A

Table 20.8 GCSE Maths

Week	1	2	3	4	5
Starter	Discussion	Homework review	Matching exercise	Quick activity starter	Quick activity starter
E/D	Slideshow (1 question from each area of the syllabus)	Slideshow (topic marked 'Red')	Slideshow (topic marked 'Red')	Live modelling (topic marked 'Red')	Mind map (recap of topics that will be in the mini-assessment)
Main Activity	Past paper (compilation paper)	Worksheet	Murder mystery	Slideshow (past paper questions)	Mini-assessment
Plenary	WWW/EBI	Instruction manual	Instruction manual	Spot the mistake	List (all topics they are happy with and any topics they want to cover again)
Home work	Worksheet	Worksheet	Worksheet	Worksheet	N/A

Week	6	7	8	9	10
Starter	Quick activity starter	Sorting exercise	Quick activity starter	Mind map	Quick activity starter
E/D	Slideshow (topic marked 'Red')	Slideshow (topic marked 'Red')	Slideshow (topic marked 'Red')	Live modelling	Mind map (recap of topics that will be in the mini-assessment)
Main Activity	Worksheet	Board game	Worksheet	Slideshow (compilation of topics covered so far)	Mini-assessment
Plenary	Instruction manual	WWW/EBI	Instruction manual	Spot the mistake	List (all topics they are happy with and any topics they want to cover again)
Home work	Past paper	Past paper	Past paper	Past paper	N/A

Other GCSEs

Table 20.9 History

Week	1	2	3	4	5
Starter	Discussion	Homework review	Matching exercise	Quick activity starter	Quick activity starter
E/D	Slideshow (1 question from each area of the syllabus)	Slideshow (topic marked 'Red')	Slideshow (topic marked 'Red')	Live modelling (short answer questions)	Mind map (recap of topics that will be in the mini-assessment)
Main Activity	Past paper (compilation paper)	Table	Worksheet	Slideshow (past paper questions)	Mini-assessment
Plenary	WWW/EBI	Instruction manual	Instruction manual	Spot the mistake	List (all topics they are happy with and any topics they want to cover again)
Homework	Worksheet	Worksheet	Worksheet	Worksheet	N/A

Week	6	7	8	9	10
Starter	Memory game	Sorting exercise	Quick activity starter	Mind map	Quick activity starter
E/D	Live modelling (source questions)	Slideshow (topic marked 'Red')	Slideshow (topic marked 'Red')	Live modelling (extended answer questions)	Mind map (recap of topics that will be in the mini-assessment)
Main Activity	Model answers	Table	Worksheet	Slideshow (compilation of topics covered so far)	Mini-assessment
Plenary	Instruction manual	WWW/EBI	Instruction manual	Spot the mistake	List (all topics they are happy with and any topics they want to cover again)
Homework	Past paper	Past paper	Past paper	Past paper	N/A

Table 20.10 Geography

Week	1	2	3	4	5
Starter	Discussion	Word search	Quickfire questions	Map starter	Flag quiz
E/D	Slideshow (question formats and styles)	Slideshow (topic marked 'Red') + Tables	Live modelling (short answer questions)	Slideshow (extended answer/case study question formats)	Mind map (recap of topics that will be in the mini-assessment)
Main Activity	Past paper (compilation paper)	Worksheet	Worksheet	Case study	Mini-assessment
Plenary	20 questions	WWW/EBI	RAG	5 Ws	List (all topics they are happy with and any topics they want to cover again)
Home work	Worksheet	Worksheet	Worksheet	Worksheet	N/A

Week	6	7	8	9	10
Starter	Crossword	Map starter	Flag quiz	Speedy read	Quickfire questions
E/D	Slideshow (topic marked 'Red')	Slideshow (topic marked 'Red') + Tables	Live modelling (longer answer questions)	Slideshow (extended answer/case study question formats)	Mind map (recap of topics that will be in the mini-assessment)
Main Activity	Flowchart	Worksheet	Worksheet	Case study	Mini-assessment
Plenary	WWW/EBI	WWW/EBI	RAG	5 Ws	List (all topics they are happy with and any topics they want to cover again)
Home work	Past paper	Past paper	Past paper	Past paper	N/A

Table 20.11 Science

Week	1	2	3	4	5
Starter	Discussion	Homework review	Matching exercise	Quick activity starter	Quick activity starter
E/D	Slideshow (1 question from each area of the syllabus)	Slideshow (topic marked 'Red')	Slideshow (topic marked 'Red')	Live modelling (topic marked 'Red')	Mind map (recap of topics that will be in the mini-assessment)
Main Activity	Past paper (compilation paper)	Table	Worksheet	Slideshow (past paper questions)	Mini-assessment
Plenary	WWW/EBI	Instruction manual	Instruction manual	Spot the mistake	List (all topics they are happy with and any topics they want to cover again)
Homework	Worksheet	Worksheet	Worksheet	Worksheet	N/A

Week	6	7	8	9	10
Starter	Memory game	Sorting exercise	Quick activity starter	Mind map	Quick activity starter
E/D	Slideshow (topic marked 'Red')	Slideshow (topic marked 'Red')	Slideshow (topic marked 'Red')	Live modelling	Mind map (recap of topics that will be in the mini-assessment)
Main Activity	Worksheet	Table	Worksheet	Slideshow (compilation of topics covered so far)	Mini-assessment
Plenary	Instruction manual	WWW/EBI	Instruction manual	Spot the mistake	List (all topics they are happy with and any topics they want to cover again)
Homework	Past paper	Past paper	Past paper	Past paper	N/A

A-level

Table 20.12 English Literature

Week	1	2	3	4	5
Starter	Discussion	5-minute recall (set text)	5-minute recall (set text)	Fill the gap (language features)	Quickfire questions
E/D	Plot review or Character review	Plot review or Character review	Plot review or Character review	Live modelling (language analysis)	Past paper (discussion of question) + Mind map + SWAT
Main Activity	Past paper (using exam questions as prompts to plan)	Past paper (using exam questions as prompts to plan)	Past paper (using exam questions as prompts to plan)	Past paper	Past paper (planning)
Plenary	RAG	RAG	RAG	Memory game (language features)	WWW/EBI
Homework	Paragraph practice or Essay planning	Paragraph practice or Essay planning	Paragraph practice or Essay planning	Paragraph practice	Paragraph practice (full essay, to be marked using PMT)

Week	6	7	8	9	10
Starter	Discussion + Homework review	Matching exercise (structural features)	5-minute recall (poetry anthology – key themes)	Quiz questions	Quickfire questions
E/D	Slideshow (introductions and conclusions)	Live modelling (essay structuring)	Live modelling (analysing and comparing poetry)	Live modelling (writing strategies, i.e. nominalisation, concision, incorporating context)	Past paper (discussion of question) + Mind map + SWAT
Main Activity	Past paper (using exam questions as prompts to write intros/concs)	Past paper	Past paper	Past paper	Past paper (planning)
Plenary	WWW/EBI	Mind map	Quiz questions	Paragraph practice	WWW/EBI
Homework	Paragraph practice	Paragraph practice or Essay planning	Paragraph practice	Paragraph practice	Paragraph practice (full essay, to be marked using PMT)

Table 20.13 Maths

Week	1	2	3	4	5
Starter	Discussion	Homework review	Matching exercise	Quick activity starter	Quick activity starter
E/D	Slideshow (1 question from each area of the syllabus)	Slideshow (topic marked 'Red')	Slideshow (topic marked 'Red')	Live modelling (topic marked 'Red')	Mind map (recap of topics that will be in the mini-assessment)
Main Activity	Past paper (compilation paper)	Past paper	Past paper	Slideshow (past paper questions)	Mini-assessment
Plenary	WWW/EBI	Instruction manual	Instruction manual	Spot the mistake	List (all topics they are happy with and any topics they want to cover again)
Home work	Past paper	Past paper	Past paper	Past paper	N/A

Week	6	7	8	9	10
Starter	Quick activity starter	Sorting exercise	Quick activity starter	Mind map	Quick activity starter
E/D	Slideshow (topic marked 'Red')	Slideshow (topic marked 'Red')	Slideshow (topic marked 'Red')	Live modelling	Mind map (recap of topics that will be in the mini-assessment)
Main Activity	Past paper	Past paper	Past paper	Slideshow (compilation of topics covered so far)	Mini-assessment
Plenary	Instruction manual	WWW/EBI	Instruction manual	Spot the mistake	List (all topics they are happy with and any topics they want to cover again)
Home work	Past paper	Past paper	Past paper	Past paper	N/A

Table 20.14 History

Week	1	2	3	4	5
Starter	Discussion	Homework review	Flowchart recall	Matching exercise	Quickfire questions
E/D	Slideshow (question formats and structures/ acronyms)	Slideshow	Live modelling (longer answer questions)	Slideshow	Mind map (recap of topics that will be in the mini-assessment)
Main Activity	Past paper (compilation of short answer questions)	Flowchart	Worksheet or Past paper	Flowchart	Mini-assessment
Plenary	WWW/EBI	Acrostic	Summary questions	WWW/EBI	WWW/EBI
Homework	Past paper	Past paper	Past paper	Past paper	N/A

Week	6	7	8	9	10
Starter	Timeline recall	Mind map	Timeline recall	Crossword	Quickfire questions
E/D	Live modelling (source questions)	Slideshow	Slideshow + Table if needed	Live modelling (extended answer questions)	Recap previous Flowcharts or Case studies
Main Activity	Past paper	Table	Past paper	Worksheet or Past paper	Mini-assessment on either
Plenary	RAG	Sequencing	WWW/EBI	Quick exam question	RAG
Homework	Past paper	Past paper	Past paper	Past paper	N/A

Table 20.15 Geography

Week	1	2	3	4	5
Starter	Discussion	Word search	Quickfire questions	Map starter	Flag quiz
E/D	Slideshow	Case study	Live modelling (longer answer questions)	Slideshow	Recap previous Flowcharts
Main Activity	Past paper (compilation of short answer questions)	Flowchart	Worksheet or Past paper	Flowchart	Mini-assessment
Plenary	20 questions	5 Ws	RAG	Quick exam question	WWW/EBI
Home work	Worksheet (short answer questions)	Worksheet (longer answer question)	Worksheet (longer answer questions)	Worksheet (mixed sheet of short and long answer questions)	N/A

Week	6	7	8	9	10
Starter	Crossword	Map starter	Flag quiz	Speedy read	Quickfire questions
E/D	Live modelling (questions based on graphs and charts)	Slideshow	Slideshow + Table if needed	Live modelling (extended answer questions or case study questions)	Recap previous Flowcharts or Case studies
Main Activity	Worksheet or Past paper	Table	Past paper	Worksheet or Past paper	Mini-assessment on either
Plenary	RAG		Summary questions	Quick exam question	RAG
Home work	Worksheet (graphs and charts questions)	Worksheet (longer answer questions)	Worksheet (mixed sheet of short and long answer questions)	Worksheet (mixed sheet of short and long answer questions)	N/A

Table 20.16 Science

Week	1	2	3	4	5
Starter	Discussion	Homework review	Matching exercise	Quick activity starter	Quick activity starter
E/D	Slideshow (1 question from each area of the syllabus)	Slideshow (topic marked 'Red')	Slideshow (topic marked 'Red')	Live modelling (topic marked 'Red')	Mind map (recap of topics that will be in the mini-assessment)
Main Activity	Past paper (compilation paper)	Worksheet or Table	Worksheet or Table	Slideshow (past paper questions)	Mini-assessment
Plenary	WWW/EBI	Instruction manual	Instruction manual	Spot the mistake	List (all topics they are happy with and any topics they want to cover again)
Homework	Past paper	Past paper	Past paper	Past paper	N/A

Week	6	7	8	9	10
Starter	Memory game	Sorting exercise	Quick activity starter	Mind map	Quick activity starter
E/D	Slideshow (topic marked 'Red')	Slideshow (topic marked 'Red')	Slideshow (topic marked 'Red')	Live modelling (longer answer questions)	Mind map (recap of topics that will be in the mini-assessment)
Main Activity	Past paper	Worksheet or Table	Worksheet or Table	Slideshow (compilation of exam questions on topics covered so far)	Mini-assessment
Plenary	WWW/EBI	Instruction manual	Instruction manual	Spot the mistake	List (all topics they are happy with and any topics they want to cover again)
Homework	Past paper	Past paper	Past paper	Past paper	N/A

Table 20.17 EFL/TEFL tutoring

Week	1	2	3	4	5
Starter	Matching exercise	Finish the sentence	Punctuation exercise	Word search	Finish the sentence
E/D	Slideshow (timeline of all tenses) + RAG	Reading together (first of three passages) + Slideshow on surface reading strategies if unfamiliar	Slideshow (set of 'Amber' tenses)	Live modelling (reading comprehension)	Mini-assessment (past or compilation paper or worksheet)
Main Activity	Worksheet (verbs marked 'Green')	Reading together (second passage) + Fill the gap as part of reading if needed	Worksheet	Worksheet	Marking + RAG
Plenary	Headlines (quick rules for all tenses marked 'Green')	Dictionary definitions	Headlines (quick rules for tenses from the lesson)	WWW/EBI	List (all topics they are happy with and any topics they want to cover again)
Homework	Worksheet (tenses)	Paragraph practice (final section from passage)	Worksheet (tenses)	Worksheet (third extract and set of questions)	N/A

Week	6	7	8	9	10
Starter	Speedy reads	Punctuation exercise	Finish the sentence	Quiz questions	Punctuation exercise
E/D	**Slideshow** (set of 'Amber' tenses)	**Worksheet** (proofreading) **+ Slideshow** on surface reading strategies if unfamiliar	**YouTube video** (idioms)	**Vocabulary fishing** (example letters/ emails/speeches, etc.)	**Mini-assessment** (past or compilation paper or worksheet)
Main Activity	**Worksheet** (tenses)	**Worksheet** (proofreading)	**Common idioms + Worksheet** or **Causal and formal conversation** if needed	**Writing formats** (letter/email/speech, etc.)	**Marking + RAG**
Plenary	**Headlines** (quick rules for tenses from the lesson)	**Memory game** (challenging words picked out of the proofreading exercises)	Quiz questions	WWW/EBI	**List** (all topics they are happy with and any topics they want to cover again)
Homework	**Worksheet** (tenses from the lesson)	**Worksheet** (proofreading)	**Worksheet** (more idioms to learn)	**Paragraph practice** (complete their writing)	N/A

Resources

Templates

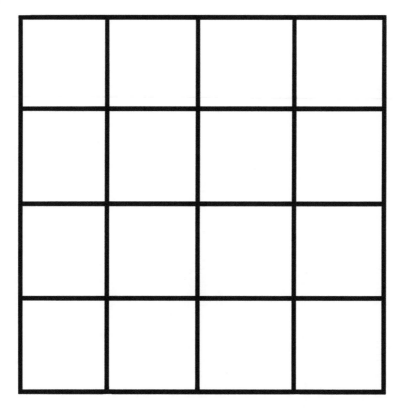

DOI: 10.4324/9781003211648-25

Device	Example	Effect

Topic:

Quote:

_____

Layer 1

_____

Layer 2

_____

Layer 3

_____

Layer 4

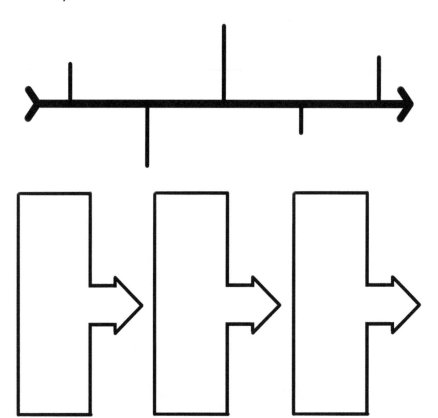

24 END	23	22	21	20 GO BACK 2 SPACES	19
9	8 GO BACK 3 SPACES	7	6	5 GO BACK 2 SPACES	18
10	1 START	2	3	4	17
11	12	13	14	15	16 GO FORWARD 3 SPACES

Lesson resources

Basic lesson techniques

personification

"as fast as the wind"

metaphor   alliteration   simile

"She laughed and laughed
and laughed"   "the door groaned"

"a sea of grass"

"the cold cat coughed"

"the wand fizzed and glowed
and crackled"   onomatopoeia

"the vase crashed onto
the floor"

repetition   triple

2D shapes	3D shapes

triangle

rectangle

cylinder

pyramid

circle

cuboid

cube

square   sphere   octagon

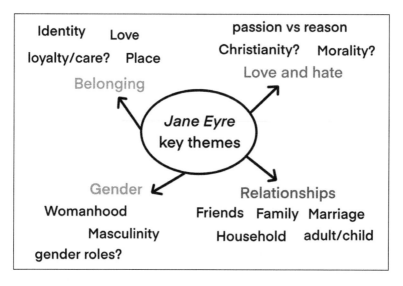

Identity   Love

passion vs reason

loyalty/care?   Place

Christianity?   Morality?

Belonging

Love and hate

Jane Eyre
key themes

Gender

Relationships

Womanhood

Friends   Family   Marriage

Masculinity

Household   adult/child

gender roles?

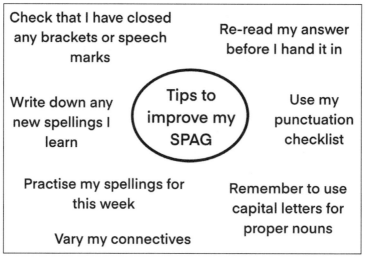

Check that I have closed any brackets or speech marks

Re-read my answer before I hand it in

Write down any new spellings I learn

Tips to improve my SPAG

Use my punctuation checklist

Practise my spellings for this week

Remember to use capital letters for proper nouns

Vary my connectives

Extra Basic exercises

Matching exercises

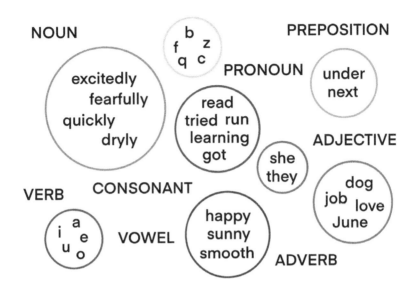

NOUN

excitedly
fearfully
quickly
dryly

b
f   z
q   c

PREPOSITION

PRONOUN

under
next

read
tried run
learning
got

ADJECTIVE

she
they

VERB   CONSONANT

dog
job   love
June

i   a
e
u   o

VOWEL

happy
sunny
smooth

ADVERB

"fish, chips, peas"

TIME PHRASES

"t-shirts, shorts, socks"

"ten minutes passed, for
what felt like an eternity"

"she was transported to her
childhood - suddenly, she was
small, vulnerable and alone"

TONE

FOCAL POINT

SYNDETIC LISTING

"as she looked out across
the landscape, her eye was
drawn to the circle of light in
the distance - home"

FLASHBACKS

"he looked as though
winning the lottery
wouldn't cheer him up"

SYNDETIC LISTING

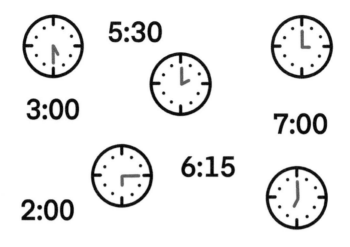

5:30

3:00

7:00

2:00

6:15

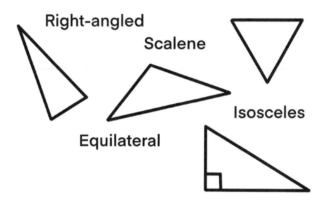

Right-angled

Scalene

Isosceles

Equilateral

Sorting exercises

ADJECTIVE	ADVERB
big	almost
	adorable
costly	now
	commonly
yearly	icy
	tremendously
very	

PASSIVE	ACTIVE

"I have done my homework."

"The flowers have been picked."

"The burglar was caught."

"Jack ate all of the cupcakes!"

"The post has to be delivered."

"Has my pen been stolen?"

"Tim was bitten by the hamster."

Mixed numbers	Improper fractions

$\frac{11}{5}$ $3\frac{3}{4}$ 14 $\frac{5}{3}$

$\frac{21}{3}$ $9\frac{2}{9}$ $11\frac{7}{8}$

$\frac{8}{4}$ 8 $\frac{24}{9}$ $\frac{45}{9}$

REGULAR	IRREGULAR

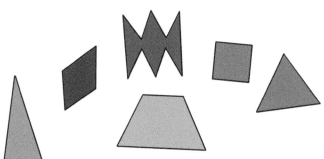

position	decide	quarter	various
island	circle	peculiar	early
trouble	refresh	especially	develop
begin	queue	narrator	achieve

jane gasped and ran toward the balcony she could see the fire growing in the next field it was bright and burning orange against the night sky how did it get so big so fast she wondered aloud

Add any punctuation you think is missing: capital letters, full stops, commas, speech marks, question marks

"The wind howled through the tall dark trees."

Layer 1 Language feature	Personification? Alliteration? Wind can't howl - but what can?
Layer 2 Sounds	'ow' sound Pain? Fear? Animal noises?
Layer 3 Themes/ associations	"tall dark trees" nighttime, creepy, lost in woods?

24 END $\frac{1}{3} - \frac{1}{6} = ?$	**23** $\frac{2}{5} + \frac{1}{4} = ?$	**22** $\frac{1}{4} \times \frac{1}{2} = ?$	**21** $5\frac{4}{5} = \frac{?}{5}$	**20** GO BACK 2 SPACES ←	**19** $12\frac{3}{4} = \frac{?}{4}$
9 $\frac{1}{6}$? $\frac{2}{5}$	**8** GO BACK 3 SPACES	**7** $\frac{3}{8} \times \frac{2}{3} = ?$	**6** $\frac{5}{7} + \frac{1}{7} = ?$	**5** GO BACK 2 SPACES ↑	**18** $\frac{1}{6}$? $\frac{2}{5}$
10 $2\frac{1}{7} = \frac{?}{7}$ ↓	**1** START $\frac{9}{2} = \frac{?}{4}$	**2** $\frac{7}{5} = \frac{?}{20}$	**3** $\frac{9}{2} = \frac{36}{?}$	**4** $\frac{1}{4} \times \frac{1}{2} = ?$ ↑	**17** $\frac{2}{3} - \frac{3}{7} = ?$
11 $\frac{1}{3} \times \frac{1}{6} = ?$	**12** $\frac{5}{7} + \frac{8}{21} = ?$	**13** $\frac{1}{8}$? $\frac{3}{4}$	**14** $2\frac{3}{4} = \frac{?}{4}$	**15** $8\frac{1}{5} = \frac{?}{5}$	**16** GO FORWARD 3 SPACES

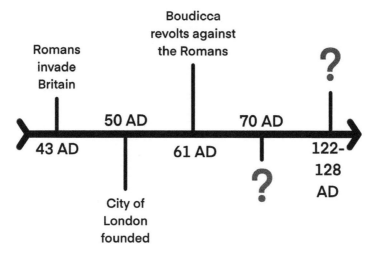

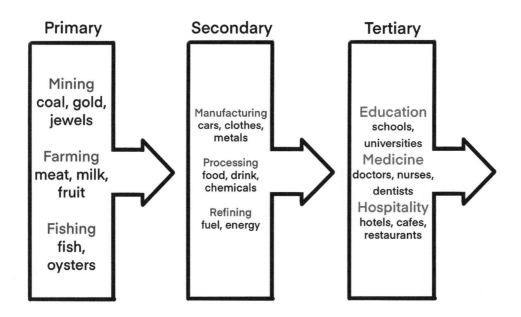

Device	Example	Effect
Simile	"My heart pounded like a bass drum"	Loud, strong and musical - like the rhythm of the heart
	"The tiny tortoise tiptoed away"	
	"The boy was a cheetah, dashing for the finish line"	Very fast, chasing, trying to survive?
Repetition	"They climbed and climbed but got no closer"	

having reached the living room darcy was suddenly struck by the silence in the house it was quiet too quiet she could just about hear the wind coming through a far away window but that was all i dont like it she muttered to herself and now ive come too far to turn back she continued through the house and up the creaky stairs

Add any punctuation you think is missing: capital letters, full stops, commas, hyphens, speech marks, dashes, semi-colons, apostrophes

"Deep in the heart of the forest, something was stirring."

Layer 1 Language feature	Personification? "heart of the forest" - centre? Origin/beginning? "heart" - alive? Ancient, angry, passion?
Layer 2 Sounds	Repeated 't' sound - hearT, foresT, sTirring Strong consonants contrasted with sibilant 's' - like wind through trees?
Layer 3 Themes/ associations	Trope of spooky ancient untouched forests with powerful inhabitants - Lord of the Rings etc Modern story, ideas about ecology and power?
Layer 4 Tense	Present 'ing' tense makes it feel current and happening - reminder of climate change?

Repetition of 'violent' - key theme

Foreshadowing the "violent end" of the play

Makes Juliet seem dead to reunite her with Romeo

"These violent delights have violent ends"
Friar Lawrence in *Romeo and Juliet*

Juxtaposition of 'delights' (life, love) with 'ends' (death, hate)?

"violent delights" - innuendo?

Love and violence are inherently connected? Anthropology?

24 END	23	22 Ratio of black to white?	21	20	19
What is the ratio of fingers to thumbs?	Simplify 16:20:24		Simplify 24:56:96	GO BACK 2 SPACES	3 hours : 30 mins = ?
9	8	7	6	5	18
4:5 = ?:10	GO BACK 3 SPACES	Simplify 20:120	Split £70 between Mr X and Mr Y by ratio 3:2	GO BACK 2 SPACES	Simplify 15:300
10	1 START	2	3	4	17
Write the ratio of dogs' tails to paws	Simplify 48:60	2 hours : 30 mins = ?	Write the ratio of heads to eyes	Simplify 36:96	Split 2.8kg of flour into 3 using ratio 4:3:7
11	12	13	14	15 Ratio of black to white?	16
2 hours : 20 mins = ?	Simplify 21:35	1:6 = ?:12	Simplify 28:16		GO FORWARD 3 SPACES

(Chapter 10.1 – *KS3 DLC*)

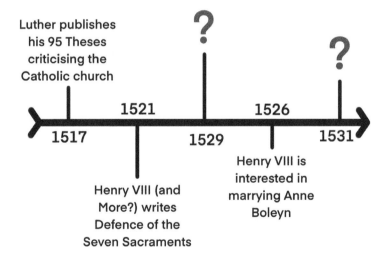

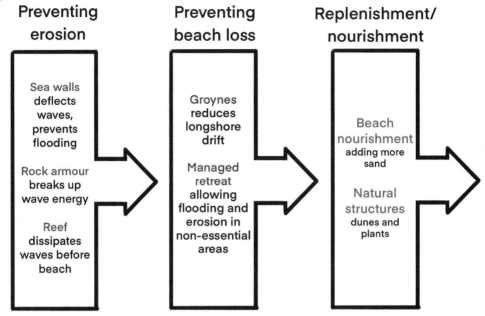

Chapter 11 – *GCSE English*

typical of them to leave steven said softly what does that mean clare replied sticking out her chin i just mean well they arent very thoughtful he replied tactfully clare knew he was right but didnt want to admit it where are you going now she asked steven got to his feet im off to the shops now but ill be back later

Add any punctuation you think is missing: capital letters, full stops, commas, speech marks, question marks

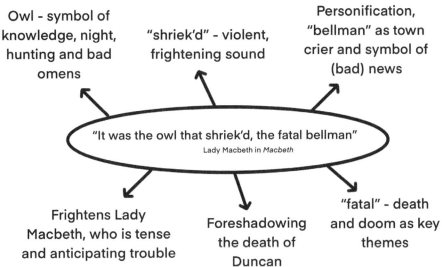

Owl - symbol of knowledge, night, hunting and bad omens

"shriek'd" - violent, frightening sound

Personification, "bellman" as town crier and symbol of (bad) news

"It was the owl that shriek'd, the fatal bellman"
Lady Macbeth in *Macbeth*

Frightens Lady Macbeth, who is tense and anticipating trouble

Foreshadowing the death of Duncan

"fatal" - death and doom as key themes

"You really are an automaton—a calculating-machine!"

Watson in *The Sign of Four*

Layer 1 Language feature	Metaphor - depersonalisation? "automaton" - self-operating, imitation of a person Logical, reasoning, cold - detached from humanity
Layer 2 Sounds	Lots of consonants - stiff and mechanical Exclamation mark indicates excited tone
Layer 3 Context	Rapid technological development and a fascination with human/machine relationship 'Fin de siècle' anxiety about tech
Layer 4 Punctuation	Dash creates pause - gasp for air or astonishment or grasping for right words

24 END Factorise ax+bx+cx	23 Solve $(x-1)^2 = 17$	22 Factorise $72ab+45a^2b$	21 Factorise $14x^2+21x^2$	20 GO BACK 2 SPACES ←	19 Solve $x^2 = 2 \times 8$
9 Solve $\frac{8}{x} = x-2$	8 GO BACK 3 SPACES	7 Solve $x^2 = x+2$	6 Factorise x^2-7	5 GO BACK 2 SPACES ↑	18 Factorise $12x^2y+18xy^2$
10 Factorise $4n+6mn^2$	1 START Factorise $15+25y$	2 Solve $\frac{3x}{5} + 3 = 7$	3 Solve $x^2-x=0$	4 Factorise x^2+6x+8	17 Solve $3(x^2+x) = 6$
11 Factorise x^2-x	12 Solve $x+2=3-x$	13 Solve $\frac{5x-11}{3} = x$	14 Factorise $27xy-18x^2$	15 Solve $\frac{3}{x} = 4$	16 GO FORWARD 3 SPACES

Chapter 13 – *Other GCSEs*

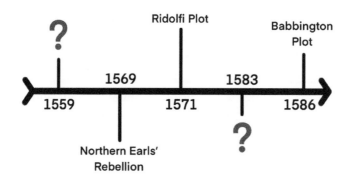

Case study event

Short-term impacts

Long-term impacts

Japan 2011
- 9.0 on Richter scale
- NE coast off Honshu
- 250 miles from Tokyo
- 20 miles deep

Existing risks
- Predominantly coastal regions are inhabited and used for farming and fishing
- 75% of Japan is mountains, so most live by coast
- Existing safety measures were thought safe

Earthquake
- 15,894 died and 6,152 injured
- 332,395 buildings and 2,126 roads destroyed
- Damaged 300 hospitals and destroyed 11

Tsunami
- Waves up to 40m
- Flooded Fukushima nuclear power plant
- 4.4mil houses lost electricity
- Destroyed 12m flood walls

After shocks
- 800 aftershocks of 4.5 magnitude or more
- Land subsided where coast was destroyed

Economy
- Most expensive natural disaster in history
- Approximate cost of $235 billion USD
- Destroyed many essential services

Physical
- Moved Earth's axis by 10-25cm
- Liquefaction destroyed 1000+ buildings
- Pacific Plate moved 20-40m west

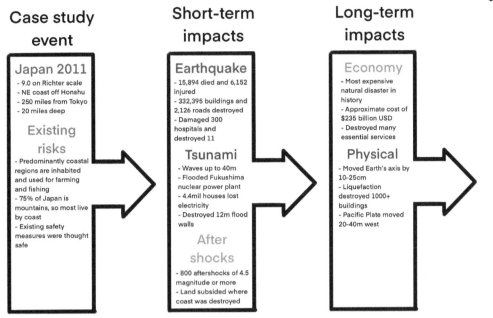

Chapter 14 – *A-level English*

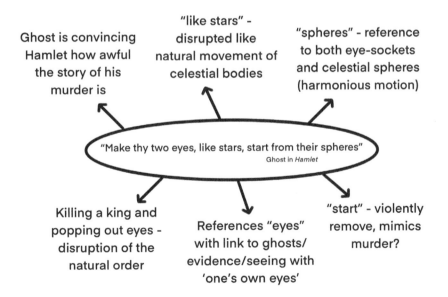

Ghost is convincing Hamlet how awful the story of his murder is

"like stars" - disrupted like natural movement of celestial bodies

"spheres" - reference to both eye-sockets and celestial spheres (harmonious motion)

"Make thy two eyes, like stars, start from their spheres"
Ghost in *Hamlet*

Killing a king and popping out eyes - disruption of the natural order

References "eyes" with link to ghosts/evidence/seeing with 'one's own eyes'

"start" - violently remove, mimics murder?

"In his blue gardens men and girls came and went like moths among the whispering and the champagne and the stars."

The Great Gatsby

Layer 1 Language features	Simile - "like moths" - gentle, flittering, patterned and nocturnal, attracted to light Triple - "whispering", "champagne", "stars"
Layer 2 Sounds	Soft sibilant sounds - "moTHS", "WHISPering" Soothing and calm, like a warm evening
Layer 3 Themes/ associations	"men and girls" - infantilises the women, indicates power imbalance and youth vs age Typical image of wealth
Layer 4 Tense	"came and went" - non-specific, implies repeated event over time Past tense - pattern now over?

Chapter 16 – *Other A-levels*

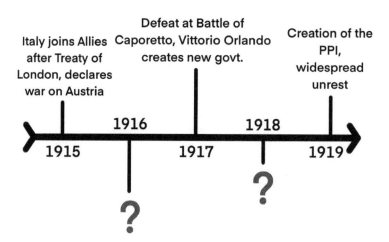

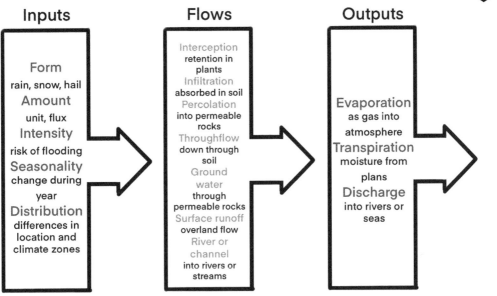

Chapter 19 – *EFL/TEFL tutoring*

stop i cant keep up shouted jemima
panting loudly and leaning on a tree for
support the rest of her hiking team had
already reached the top of the hill jemima
was worried that they would begin to
disappear over the other side i dont know
where i am she grumbled she was not
very good at reading maps

Add any punctuation you think is missing: capital letters,
full stops, commas, colons, speech marks, exclamation
marks, semi-colons, apostrophes

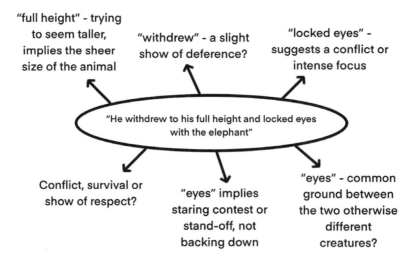

"full height" - trying to seem taller, implies the sheer size of the animal

"withdrew" - a slight show of deference?

"locked eyes" - suggests a conflict or intense focus

"He withdrew to his full height and locked eyes with the elephant"

Conflict, survival or show of respect?

"eyes" implies staring contest or stand-off, not backing down

"eyes" - common ground between the two otherwise different creatures?

Scaffolds

READING COMPREHENSION

Context/summary:

Extract:

Questions:

1.
2.
3.
4.
5.
6.

ARTICLE SCAFFOLD

Newspaper articles, in print or online, tell us what's happening around the world. They are used in exams as sample texts and sometimes in creative writing. You need to understand what they are made up of in order to write one.

Use the article structure below and the prompts in the box to fill in the article, making sure to cover all 5 Ws so your reader has all of the details.

What do you include?

WHAT	*PHOTOS*
WHO	*QUOTES*
WHERE	*FACTS*
WHY	*NUMBERS*
HOW	*STORIES*

Header:

Headline:

Sub-heading:

Paragraph 1

TIP: You need all 5 Ws in this paragraph, as a quick summary!

Paragraph 2

TIP: Use this paragraph to go into more detail - quotes from witnesses, details from research etc.

Paragraph 3

TIP: You can introduce an opposing view or long-term view here!

Conclusion

TIP: Use this paragraph to look forwards - what will happen next?

ESSAY SCAFFOLD

Essays are a common form of exam answer and an important style of non-fiction writing. Essays are usually written to answer a question, but you may also be asked to 'discuss' a statement or 'respond' to an idea.

Use the essay structure below and the paragraph structure here to fill in the boxes, ensuring that you use at least one piece of evidence per paragraph. If possible, try to include an 'alternative interpretaton' too!

Paragraph structure:

1. Topic sentence
What's your paragraph about? What's your point?
2. Evidence
What quotes/technical terms are you going to discuss?
3. Explanation
Unpack your ideas in detail
4. Mini-conclusion
Sum up your ideas and link to the question

Introduction

TIP: Remember to include the words of the question/title!

Paragraph 1

Paragraph 2

Paragraph 3

Conclusion

TIP: Try not to summarise your answer - instead, reach a judgement or evaluation!

FACT-FILE SCAFFOLD

A fact-file is a short summary of the key information about a person, place or event. They are most commonly used for people, especially historical figures.

For a fact-file about a person, you should try to include the following information:

When were they born?

What are 3 key facts about their life?

When did they die?

What are their achievements?

Draw a picture:

TIP: Remember to write in full sentences!

TIP: Remember to include dates, times and names!

TIP: Remember, your paragraphs should be easy to skim-read and understand!

REVIEW SCAFFOLD

You can review anything - a book, a film, a TV show, a play or even a lesson! Reviews are really useful because they inform us about the content of the work and give us your opinion about it.

You just have to remember to include some key information, by answering the questions in the boxes below.

What happened in the book/play/film?

In the beginning...

In the middle...

At the end...

What did you like about it?

My favourite character/scene was...

I particularly enjoyed...because...

I liked the section where...because...

How could it be improved?

To make it better, I would add...

I think it would have been more interesting if they had explored...

It could be improved by...

Age-appropriate reading lists

https://schoolreadinglist.co.uk/
www.scholastic.com/parents/books-and-reading/books-and-reading-guides/recommended-childrens-books-by-age.html
www.booktrust.org.uk/books-and-reading/bookfinder/

Content resources

ALL

www.gov.uk/government/collections/national-curriculum
www.gov.uk/government/publications/national-curriculum-in-england-mathematics-programmes-of-study
www.gov.uk/government/publications/national-curriculum-in-england-english-programmes-of-study/national-curriculum-in-england-english-programmes-of-study
www.bbc.co.uk/bitesize

KS2

www.gov.uk/government/publications/key-stage-2-english-reading-test-framework
www.gov.uk/government/publications/key-stage-2-mathematics-test-framework
https://home.oxfordowl.co.uk/at-school/primary-school-assessment-tests/
https://primaryenglished.co.uk/blog/rip-assessment-focuses-hello-content-domains

11+

www.elevenplusexams.co.uk/
www.bond11plus.co.uk/news/219-free-resources-sample

GCSE/A-level

www.aqa.org.uk/qualifications
https://qualifications.pearson.com/en/home.html
www.ocr.org.uk/qualifications/
www.eduqas.co.uk/qualifications/

Lesson technique resources

Note: These are just a few of the many hundreds of thousands of resources, materials, and websites you can find in just a quick Google search. Use these as a starting point to build a bank of resources that suits you!

All

https://revisionworld.com/
www.physicsandmathstutor.com/ (has papers in all subjects)
https://mathsmadeeasy.co.uk/ (also has English resources)
www.pastpapersz.com/

English

http://shakespeare.mit.edu/index.html
www.bardweb.net/
www.poetryfoundation.org/
http://rhetoric.byu.edu/Figures/Figures-Groupings.htm
https://academic-englishuk.com/writing/
https://blogasenglish.wordpress.com/

Maths

www.math-aids.com/
www.maths-starters.co.uk/
http://bland.in/
https://corbettmaths.com/
https://brilliant.org/

History

https://schoolhistory.co.uk/
www.keystagehistory.co.uk/

Geography

www.geography.org.uk/teaching-resources
www.rgs.org/schools/teaching-resources/

Science

https://phet.colorado.edu/en/simulations/browse
https://coresciences.co.uk/
https://flashyscience.com/

EFL

www.ef.co.uk/english-resources/
EnglishForEveryone.org
www.ego4u.com/
www.eslprintables.com/
www.grammarbank.com/
www.esl-galaxy.com/
www.eslpdf.com/
www.e-grammar.org/
https://en.islcollective.com/
ManyThings.org – www.manythings.org/

Index

Note: Page numbers in **bold** refers to tables on the corresponding page.

admissions 259, 260, 263–76
adult 9, 10, 20, 57–8, 66, 74, 76, 267, 284, 294
agency 12–16, 20–1, 23, 26, 28, 59, 100
A-level 6, 9, 10, 12, 13, 14, 19, 24, 54, 64, 260, 265–6, 272, 276, 279, 282; English 4, 38, 42, 54, 208–25; History and Geography 56, 73, 236–51; Maths 55, 71, 226–35; Science 57, 73, 95, 205, 251–8
algebra 44, 48–9, 56, 70–1, 121, 154, 184–5
anthology 51, 55, 140, **155**, **159**, 161, 167, 213, 219
AQA 10, **155**, **175**, 206, **209**, **210**, **226**

Biology 53, 57, 74, **254**, 257; *see also* Sciences

Cambridge 45, 260, 263, 275, 278–9
Chemistry 53, 57, 74, 94, **203**, 206, 254, 256–7; *see also* Sciences
classroom 7, 31, 83; online 5, 12, 23, 24, 27, 28, 30, 32, 89, 93, 294; software 17–19, 29
COVID-19 5, 9, 121, 153, 158, 176, 184, 208, 227, 234

curriculum 9, 41, 45, 47, 60, 69, 130, 154, 228, 282
CV 26

degree 13, 14, 16, 259, 261, 265, 266, 267, 268, 278, 279
dyslexia 84

Edexcel 10, **156–8**, **175**, **211**, **226**
Eduqas 10, **156–9**, **176**, **212**, 227
Engineering 276
English 4–5, 9–11, 15, 34, 63–5, 82, 88–91, 94, 257, 271; assessment method 66; EFL 58–61, 74–5, 284–99; KS2/11+ 41–2, 45–6, 71–2, 102–12, 123, 128, 130–1, **302**; KS3 47, 132–46, **305**; KS4/ GCSE 49–51, 95, 155–74, **308**, **310**; KS5/A-level 38, 54–5, 208–25, **316**; resources 338, 341, 349–51; university applications 276, 278, 280
extracurricular 4, 22, 42, 259, 261, 263, 265, 272

feedback 30; for students 9, 35, 37, 38, 51, 55, **80**, 87, 91, 97, 114, 120, 145, 152, **170**, 172, 200, **222**, **232**, 251, 261, 271, 273, 279; for tutors 13, 84 fiction 43, 46, 105, 130, 137, **157–8**, 160, 269, 286, 292

GCSE 10, 24, 48, 63, 64, 69, 71, 83, 90, 91; English 47, 50, 95, 137, 139, 144, 155–74, 218, 223, **308**, **310**, **338**; History and Geography 52, 72, 73, 186–200, 243, 251, **313**, **340**; iGCSE 59, 65; Maths 46, 48, 49, 51, 130, 175–85, 234, **312**, **340**; Science 53, 74, 201–7, 255
Geography 5, 34, 88, 89, 94; assessment method 64–6, 73, 77; KS2 41–2, 102; KS3 132; KS4/GCSE 47, 50, 52, 186, 193–206, **314**; KS5/A-level 54, 56, 236, 244–51, **320**; resources 351
geometry 44, 49, 70

handwriting 31, 34, 36
History 5, 41–2, 47, 50, 63–5, 82, 88–91, 94; assessment method 66, 72, 78; KS2 102; KS3 132, 247; KS4/GCSE 52, 53, 186–7, 192–3, 199, 206, **313**; KS5/A-level 54, 56–7, 236–7, 242–4, **319**; resources 350; university applications 276, 278
home-schooled 72–4, 99, 105, 135, 162, 287, 290
humanities 90, 91, 95, 98, 99, 268, 275, 277, 278

idiom **140**, 290, 291, 294, 295, **298**, **323**
iGCSE 59, 65
in-person 3, 5, 7, 8, 15, 19–22, 58, 59
interview 16, 37, 231, 259, 260, 264, 267, 274, 275, 279, 280, 281–9, 294

keyword 139, 162, 167, 214, 219, 287
KS2 4, 5, 9, 12, 41, 63, 80, 83, 92, 102; 11+ 71, 123; assessment 66, 70, 75, 76; curriculum 130; English 42, 47, 102–14, 302, 332; Geography 73; History 72, 334; Maths 43, 114–22; Science 74
KS3 4, 5, 9, 46, 63, 80, 108, 132, 205; assessment 66; curriculum 69; English 47, 132, 140–6, 305, 335, 337; Geography 73; History 72, 196; Maths 48, 69, 71, 149–54; Science 74
KS4 49, 66, 71; see also GCSE
KS5 54; see also A-level

language(s) 15–16, 34, 42–3, 50, 75, 91, 106–8, 110, 130, **140**, 142, 145, 161, 163–4, 166, 172, 294; A-level English Language 54, 64; analysis 46, 68; English as a Foreign/Second 9, 12, 57–61, 63, 284–300; English Language Aptitude test 276; features/devices 55, 59, 85, 92, 94, 114, 133, 135, 143, **144**, 146, 162, 169, 215, 217–18, 220, 221, **222**, 224, 256, **308**, **309**, **316**; GCSE English Language 4, 50–1, 64, 137–8, 155, **157**, 159, **171**, 173–4, **310–11**; KS3 English **306**; Modern Foreign 276
literacy 42, 47, 66, 68, 206, 257; see also English
literature 4; A-level English Literature 54–5, 208–25, **316**; GCSE English Literature 50–51, 64, 95, 144, 155–74, 308

marketplace 12, 14, 16–17, 19–21, 23
Maths 4, 9, 11, 31, 34, 38, 63–4, 66, 88–90, 92–5, 193, 203, 206, 254, 257–8; assessment method 69–72, 77, 82; KS2/11+ 41–3, 102, 114–22, 123–31, **303**; KS3 46–7, 132, 146–54, **307**; KS4/GCSE 48–50, 51–2, 175–85, **312**; KS5/A-level 54, 55–6, 226–35, **318**; resources 340, 349–50; university applications 275–80; virtual maths tools 18, 29
mentoring: interview 279, 282; personal statement 259–73

non-fiction 43, 46, 96, 130, **157–8**, 173, 292, **302**, **305**, **310**
NSPCC 21–3
numeracy 43, 206, 257, 258; see also Maths

OCR 10, **156**, **158**, **159**, **175**, **211**, **227**, 349
Ofqual 52, 53, 57

Oxbridge 259–61, 263–4, 275–6, 279–83
Oxford 260, 263, 275, 278, 279

parents 11–15, 17–18, 21–6, 33, 36–8, 41–6,
    51, 58, 61, 75–8, 94, 99–100, 106, 112–13,
    121, 130–1, 153, 157, 184, 234, 274, 283
Philosophy 276
Physics 53, 57, 74, 203, 206, 228, 230, 235,
    254, 257, 276, 350; *see also* Sciences
poetry 47, 135, 162, 174, 209–12;
    anthology 51, 55, 155–6; poem 135–6,
    143, 145; resources 350; starter 161,
    308–9, 317; unseen 155–6, 158–9, **209**
policy 23
postgraduate 5, 58
private 8, 10–11, 15, 28, 30, 50
proofreading 92, 161, 286, 291, **323**

referencing 92
revision 4, 35, 95, 165, 167; 11+ 304;
    A-level 216, 219, 221, **232**, 239, 240,
    242, 247, 248, 253, 258; EFL 290, 295;
    GCSE 189, 190, **192**, 196, 197, 203, 207;
    KS2 **112**; KS3 140

safeguarding 18, 20–3, 26
Sciences 4–5, 31, 34, 38, 64, 82, 88–90,
    92, 94–5; assessment method 66, 73–4,
77; KS2/11+ 41–2, 102; KS3 47, 132;
    KS4/GCSE 50, 53, 186, 187, 201–7, **315**;
    KS5/A-level 54, 57, 236, 251–8, **321**;
    resources 351; university applications
    268, 275–6, 278; *see also* Biology;
    Chemistry; Physics
Shakespeare **209–12**, 216, **220**
sixth-form 50, 259
software 12, 16–19, 27–32; graphic
    design 109, 142; mind map 86;
    slideshow 289

trigonometry 71

UCAS 259, 260, 263
undergraduate 3–4, 8, 13, 24, 223, 274
university 4, 10, 14, 25, 54; applications
    52, 56, 59, 228, 230, 231, 235, 274–9;
    entrance exams 46, 232; personal
    statements 259–72; tutors as students
    30, 80

Year: 3 42–3, 70, 72–4; 4 42–3, 70, 72–4;
    5 42–4, 46, 70, 72–4, 130; 6 42–4, 46,
    72–4, 130; 7 72–4, 83, 136, 154; 8 72–4;
    9 69, 74, 83; 10 4, 72–4, 153; 11 4, 83,
    198; 12 66, 73, 74, 77; 13 66, 76
year groups 46, 94